D0556879

REENGINEERING THE LIBRARY

ALA Editions purchases fund advocacy,
awareness, and accreditation programs
for library professionals worldwide.

AN ALCTS MONOGRAPH

REENGINEERING THE LIBRARY

Issues in Electronic Resources Management

Edited by
GEORGE STACHOKAS

ALA
Editions
CHICAGO | 2018

GEORGE STACHOKAS is the electronic resources librarian at Auburn University in Alabama. Previously, he served as head of resource services and special assistant to the dean for project management at Purdue University, electronic resources librarian at Indiana State University, and chair of the Resource Advisory Committee of the Academic Libraries of Indiana consortium. His research interests include electronic resources management, organizational change in libraries, and collection development. Stachokas holds an MLIS degree from the University of Illinois at Urbana-Champaign, an MA in history from Indiana State University, and a BS in economics from Purdue University—West Lafayette.

© 2018 by the American Library Association

Extensive effort has gone into ensuring the reliability of the information
in this book; however, the publisher makes no warranty, express or implied,
with respect to the material contained herein.

ISBNs
978-0-8389-1621-6 (paper)
978-0-8389-1748-0 (PDF)
978-0-8389-1747-3 (ePub)
978-0-8389-1749-7 (Kindle)

Library of Congress Cataloging-in-Publication Data

Names: Stachokas, George, editor.
Title: Reengineering the library : issues in electronic resources management / edited by George
    Stachokas.
Description: Chicago : ALA Editions, an imprint of the American Library Association, 2018. | Series:
    An ALCTS monograph | Includes bibliographical references and index.
Identifiers: LCCN 2018008549 | ISBN 9780838916216 (pbk. : alk. paper) | ISBN 9780838917473
    (epub) | ISBN 9780838917480 (pdf) | ISBN 9780838917497 (kindle)
Subjects: LCSH: Libraries—Special collections—Electronic information resources. | Electronic
    information resources—Management. | Libraries—Reorganization.
Classification: LCC Z692.C65 R44 2018 | DDC 025.17/4—dc23 LC record available at
    https://lccn.loc.gov/2018008549

Cover image © kentoh.

Text composition by Dianne M. Rooney in the Adobe Caslon Pro and Archer typefaces.

♾ This paper meets the requirements of ANSI/NISO Z39.48–1992 (Permanence of Paper).

Printed in the United States of America

22 21 20 19 18   5 4 3 2 1

CONTENTS

ACKNOWLEDGMENTS

First of all, I would like to thank all of the contributing authors. I hope that our readers will benefit as much as I have from their collective insight. Jennifer Bazeley read and edited my own chapter, which is much appreciated. Nadine Ellero also reviewed my chapter and has offered many helpful suggestions throughout this process. Scott Olszowiec created some of the figures used in this book. I appreciate the work of Susan Elaine Thomas and the ALCTS Monographs Editorial Board in reviewing the book proposal and facilitating its publication. Brooke Morris has provided guidance and assistance regarding every aspect of the logistics of this project. Finally, I thank Patrick Hogan, copy editor Paul Mendelson, and other staff at ALA Editions for making sure that this book will be published and in its best possible form.

INTRODUCTION

George Stachokas

Many of the assumptions that underlay electronic resources management in academic libraries were developed in the late 1990s and early 2000s, but much has changed during the past ten years. Collections are primarily electronic now in terms of both overall spending and usage. The previously solitary electronic resources librarian has now been joined by other personnel in reorganized technical services departments and units who increasingly share more complex and diverse types of work related to managing electronic resources.

Reengineering the Library: Issues in Electronic Resources Management is organized into fifteen chapters that address some of the most important changes impacting contemporary academic libraries. This book addresses licensing, cost containment strategies, the management of knowledge bases and metadata for electronic resources, the implementation of Webscale Discovery services, freely available electronic resources, troubleshooting and technical support, analytics and assessment, the transition to library service platforms, communication between public and technical services, the ongoing reorganization of technical services units, changes in professional roles, as well as efforts to define the scope of electronic resources management within the wider context of professional librarianship. All of the contributing authors were invited by the editor to write chapters because of their expertise and experience in different aspects of electronic resources management.

Lori Duggan, head of electronic resources acquisitions at Indiana University, discusses changes in licensing, including text and data mining rights, provisions for users with disabilities and issues in working with international vendors. Monica Moore, electronic resources librarian at the University of Notre Dame, reflects on the role of the electronic resources librarian within and beyond the electronic resources life cycle, including how to help ensure that other library personnel have a good understanding of electronic resources, business models, and online platforms. Richard Guajardo, director of resource discovery systems at the University of Houston, draws on his experience in managing knowledge bases and electronic resources metadata to discuss case studies, concepts and best practices at his own institution and beyond.

Regina Koury, assistant university librarian at Idaho State University, writes about the implementation of the EDS Webscale Discovery service. Jennifer Richard, academic librarian, Leanna Jantzi, head of the Fraser Library at Simon Fraser University, and Sandra Wong, electronic resources librarian, provide cases studies of the implementation of Primo and Summon respectively at Acadia University and Simon Fraser University. L. Angie Ohler, director of collection services at the University of Maryland, challenges librarians to take full advantage of the ongoing transition from ERM systems to library service platforms by changing our mindset and pursuing knowledge creation, not just the improved discovery and delivery of information. My own chapter recounts the struggle to pay for electronic resources during the Great Recession, controversies surrounding the big deal, and cost containment strategies. Jennifer Bazeley discusses how to improve communication between technical and public services by using one of the most ubiquitous tools in libraries: the LibGuide.

Sarah W. Sutton, assistant professor in the School of Library and Information Management at Emporia State University, writes about the *Core Competencies for Electronic Resources Librarianship* which her own scholarship and leadership did much to develop. Christine Dulaney, director of technical services at American University Library, and Kari Schmidt, technical services manager at Montgomery College, write about how the Competencies were used to help reorganize technical services at American University, including one department with centralized workflows at the Bender Library and another with distributed workflows at the Pence Law Library. Judith Emde, assistant dean for content and access services, and Angela Rathmel, head of acquisitions and resource sharing, discuss the merger of acquisitions and resource sharing units at the University of Kansas, including how to engage with all personnel in order to ensure a positive transition for both individual staff members and the library as a whole.

Chris Bulock, collection coordinator for electronic resources management at California State University Northridge, considers the opportunities and challenges of managing a growing number of Open Access and freely available electronic resources. Sunshine Carter, electronic resources librarian and manager of the E-Resource Management Unit, and Stacie A. Traill, metadata analyst, discuss how they have improved troubleshooting for electronic resources at the University of Minnesota by expanding the circle of qualified staff through expanded training, assessment, and a commitment to perpetual improvement. Oliver Pesch, chief product strategist for EBSCO Information Services, addresses the Standardized Usage Statistics Harvesting Initiative (SUSHI) and how it can be used to help automate the process of gathering some COUNTER usage statistics. Geoffrey Timms, librarian for marine resources at the College of Charleston, provides a thorough and systemic consideration of analytics and assessment of electronic resources.

Libraries are reengineering in terms of their professional skills, organizational structures, collections, systems, tools and assessment in order to provide users with a greater number and more types of electronic resources, but also to improve overall information services. Taken together, the words of these authors should help the reader to develop a better understanding of the ongoing changes in contemporary academic libraries.

1

Trends and Developments in Licensing Electronic Resources

Lori Duggan

O ne of the most important and complex areas in managing the electronic resources life cycle is licensing. The license dictates the terms of use and other legal parameters for electronic content. In addition to outlining traditional authorized uses for electronic resources, new and innovative license terms are emerging in response to developing trends in research and publishing. Information professionals are also taking into consideration the varying needs of users when negotiating license agreements. This chapter examines current trends and emerging developments in electronic resources licensing, noting both core concepts as well as new considerations for licensing professionals to take into account when engaging in licensing with content providers.

CORE CONCEPTS IN ELECTRONIC RESOURCES LICENSING

In examining new developments in the landscape of electronic resource licensing, it is helpful to take into account existing concepts that have been key elements in licensing throughout the years. One of the basic concepts underpinning electronic resources licensing is the distinction between copyright and contract law, the latter of which can vary depending on the country of origin of the content. "US copyright law, for example, famously guarantees the right of 'fair use,' outlining high-level generalities about what criteria we should use for determining whether a given use is fair. Licenses are transaction-specific, and in the US contracts are governed at the state level."[1] The terms of a license agreement can serve to restrict or embrace allowances recognized under copyright law, and it is the responsibility of information professionals to negotiate terms of agreement that are as nonrestrictive as possible in order to ensure ease of use and enhance the research experience for users of electronic content.

The anatomy of an electronic resource license agreement can encompass several aspects, including the general terms of use, information on the rights holder for the content, and warranties regarding the content. Authorized uses such as searching, downloading, and printing reasonable portions of the content for noncommercial use are typical allowances granted by a license agreement. Additional uses such as interlibrary loan and scholarly sharing allow for broader use of the content, and are areas in which librarians may wish to expand or refine the language of an agreement. The content provider will often outline the performance obligations their content will adhere to, as well as any specific restrictions on the use of the content. Common restrictions include downloading excessive amounts of the content, making the resource available electronically to unauthorized users, and using the content for noneducational or commercial purposes. The license may outline specifics on communication and cure periods for breaches that may occur, or any remedies that can be enacted in the event of a license breach. Information regarding the business transaction, such as the pricing and duration of the subscription agreement, may also be included in the license agreement, or may be outlined in a separate order form or appendix in tandem with the license portion of the agreement.

In addition to general terms outlining acceptable use and the parameters of the subscription or purchase, information professionals pay particular attention to terms articulating the legal venue and potential financial obligations outlined by the agreement for the licensing institution. Two terms that are commonly identified and negotiated by licensing officers are governing law and jurisdiction, and indemnification. Librarians typically are unable to accept terms specifying that the governing law and venue will reside outside of the home state of their institution. Similarly, institutions may be unable to accept or will be limited in their acceptance of indemnity clauses, which outline the financial and legal obligations of the institution in the event of legal action by a third party.[2] Other terms, such as language stipulating that the licensee will ensure that authorized users will adhere to the terms of use, can be softened by inserting language indicating that the licensee will use "reasonable efforts" to ensure compliance. Finally, it is advisable to insert any special accommodations or particulars regarding the procurement of the content into the license agreement in the form of an additional clause, addendum, or appendix. As experienced professionals know, any provision agreed upon above and beyond the license or official purchase agreement, such as a cap in price inflation or locking in pricing for subsequent subscription years, is best housed in the official agreement rather than in a string of e-mail correspondence or a verbal conversation.

License terms vary widely from publisher to publisher, and likewise local contract and purchasing parameters vary between institutions. Information professionals should inquire with their institution's purchasing and legal entities in order to identify the contract and licensing guidelines that are specific to their institution. Documenting local guidelines in the form of a model license or licensing checklist is a useful exercise for library licensing officers, and can serve as a working guide for license negotiations with content providers.[3] The Liblicense Model License is also a useful reference for locating commonly used terms and language for specific licensing situations.[4] Many institutions and content providers rely on the Shared Electronic Resource Understanding (SERU) developed by the National Information Standards Organization (NISO) as an alternative to traditional licensing activities.[5] Many institutions also rely on library consortia to represent their institutional interests and negotiate agreements on their behalf.

DEVELOPMENTS IN ELECTRONIC RESOURCES LICENSING

One of the major challenges associated with managing and licensing electronic resources is the need to balance consistency with innovation, taking into account new concepts and developments within the field while maintaining a core set of activities and services. While the focus of electronic resource license negotiations has traditionally been to protect the interests of the institution while ensuring terms that support and facilitate the capabilities of researchers, new and important considerations have been emerging in license negotiation. New methods of performing research necessitate new approaches to licensing electronic content. Similarly, ensuring equal access to electronic resources by users with varying needs warrants attention by information professionals. There are a wide variety of emerging areas in electronic resources licensing that present new and unique challenges in the development and negotiation of licensing provisions with content providers.

Text and Data Mining

Text and data mining have come to the fore in recent years as a new challenge for managers of library electronic resources. This form of research involves extracting information through the textual analysis of large data sets of information in a machine-readable format. Researchers derive meaningful conclusions and concepts based on the data that can be "mined" within these large sets of texts.[6] This method of research can lead to innovative and unique discoveries, allowing researchers to visualize information in new ways. "Text mining can be a highly useful tool in the beginnings of research exploration, allowing the textual data to suggest themes and concepts to the researcher during analysis."[7] While this research method is well supported through various open access means, such as PubMed Central or the Public Library of Science, there is an increasing desire on the part of scholars to mine the content of licensed library resources.[8] To this end, electronic resource licensing professionals may find themselves in the position of acting as an intermediary between researchers and content providers in an effort to accommodate text and data mining requests.

While publishers and content providers have been slow to accept text and data mining of their content, some have acknowledged the growing demand for this form of research by granting subscribing institutions and their authorized users the right to engage in text mining activities. Several of these providers have done so by means of an additional license agreement or an addendum to an existing agreement granting the right to engage in text mining of their resources according to specific parameters. Other providers may evaluate text and data mining requests on a case-by-case basis, and may accommodate the request by executing an additional agreement with the licensing institution or by establishing a separate agreement directly with the researcher. Such accommodations may or may not incur an additional fee for the content in question.

While this type of research has gained momentum over the years, there are still publishers and content providers that are unable to accommodate text and data mining requests. This refusal may be due to a variety of reasons on the publisher's part. For instance, a publisher may be restricted by copyright concerns or be bound by other limitations imposed by the rights holders of the content. Content providers may also be held back by technical constraints in terms of the format of the content, or they may simply be slow to accommodate requests due to a general lack of understanding of this form of research.[9] While these failed transactions can be frustrating for all involved, they serve a purpose in initiating a dialogue between subscribing institutions seeking to facilitate and enable research, and providers who are struggling to accept and ultimately support text and data mining as a legitimate and legal use of their content.

Including text mining language in agreements when licensing new resources is advantageous in facilitating text and data mining for researchers, and requests for inserting such language advances the conversation on text mining between subscribing institutions and content providers. The Liblicense Model License agreement contains the following suggested language on text and data mining which can serve as a guide when working with content providers to include such terms in a license agreement:

> Text and Data Mining. Authorized Users may use the Licensed Materials to perform and engage in text and/or data mining activities for academic research, scholarship, and other educational purposes, utilize and share the results of text and/or data mining in their scholarly work, and make the results available for use by others, so long as the purpose is not to create a product for use by third parties that would substitute for the Licensed Materials. Licensor will cooperate with Licensee and Authorized Users as reasonably necessary in making the Licensed Materials available in a manner and form most useful to the Authorized User. If Licensee or Authorized Users request the Licensor to deliver or otherwise prepare copies of the Licensed Materials for text and data mining purposes, any fees charged by Licensor shall be solely for preparing and delivering such copies on a time and materials basis.[10]

When working with a content provider to insert text and data mining language into a license, it is advisable to avoid any language that stipulates open-ended penalties or fees for potential license violations by authorized users engaged in text mining activities. It is preferable to strike any such language from the license, and in lieu of that, insert language into the agreement that limits any such fees to a reasonable amount.

Accessibility

Ensuring equal access to electronic resources for all users is another consideration that is coming to the fore in licensing. Public institutions are obligated to ensure that web resources are accessible to people with disabilities under the Americans with Disabilities Acts (ADA) and the Rehabilitation Act of 1973.[11] This yields a distinct challenge for information professionals acquiring electronic resources, since content providers are under no such obligation to make their products accessible. "While both Section 504 of the Rehabilitation Act of 1973 and the American with Disabilities Act (ADA) of 1998 (amended in 2008) mandate that programs and services must be accessible (Waddell,

2006, 2007), neither law contains specific technical guidelines with regard to e-resources."[12] While the design of vended electronic resources is not within the control of information professionals, it is possible to fill in the gap between electronic content and accessibility with specific licensing terms.

One term that can be inserted into a license agreement to address accessibility is the support of assistive technology as outlined by the Web Accessibility Initiative's Web Content Accessibility Guidelines. This initiative provides technical specifications that ensure equal access to Internet resources by individuals with disabilities.[13] Another term addressing accessibility is the stipulation that the licensor will complete and adhere to the Voluntary Product Accessibility Template. This form allows a content provider to assess whether or not their content complies with ADA criteria.[14] The Liblicense Model License agreement contains the following suggested language on accessibility which can serve as a guide when working with content providers to include such terms in a license agreement:

> Disabilities Compliance. Licensor shall comply with the Americans with Disabilities Act (ADA), by supporting assistive software or devices such as large print interfaces, text-to-speech output, voice-activated input, refreshable braille displays, and alternate keyboard or pointer interfaces, in a manner consistent with the Web Accessibility Initiative Web Content Accessibility Guidelines. Licensor shall provide to Licensee a current completed Voluntary Product Accessibility Template (VPAT) to demonstrate compliance with the federal Section 508 standards. If the product does not comply, the Licensee has the right to adapt the Licensed Materials in order to comply with federal and state law.[15]

As with text mining, there is no uniform path of acceptance on the part of content providers when it comes to accessibility. While many content providers recognize the importance of complying with accessibility standards in order to ensure equal access for users with disabilities, others may not view this as a high priority of concern in the development of their content. International vendors in particular may not be familiar with the standards and criteria involved in developing accessible content. The HathiTrust Digital Library has taken a strong stance on accessibility, providing an interface that accommodates accessibility needs and additional access services for users with disabilities.[16] While acceptance of license terms delineating accessibility may not be universal by content providers, it is a critical element of consideration for information professionals working to acquire electronic resources. Addressing accessibility in license negotiations advances the dialogue between institutions and content providers in the important area of equal access for patrons with disabilities.

Open Access

In addition to emerging user needs, there are emerging situations to consider when negotiating terms for electronic resources. One such area is open access (OA) publishing. An important area of scholarly communication, open access publishing has been growing in practice over the past several years. The open-access publishing movement offers new possibilities for access to unrestricted scholarship across user communities, including those in developing nations who would otherwise not have access to such content. Researchers and institutions of higher education are addressing this movement in various ways, with many institutions implementing open access policies and instituting repositories of unrestricted scholarly research, resulting in varying levels of success and adoption by researchers.[17]

While open access to scholarly output and research is both encouraging and desirable, this emerging situation is not without its challenges for information professionals tasked with licensing and acquiring electronic resources. "OA provision does not mean that access is provided with absolutely no costs associated with it. There are business models in use with OA publishing and they are as varied as the business models of our for-fee based content."[18] In addition to traditional subscription models, many publishers of scholarly journals offer an option for publishing articles on an open access basis at the expense of the author or the institution of the author, if applicable, through a fee or "article processing charge."[19] While many publishers engaging in this "hybrid" publishing model are transparent about the pricing principles driving both types of models, information professionals engaged in monitoring and assessing subscription costs have become wary of publishers receiving revenue for both publishing models without offsetting the price for content subscribers.[20]

The Liblicense Model License addresses concerns about costs associated with open-access publishing models by outlining terms requiring licensors to provide information on the number of open access works published, and to engage in dialogue regarding the revenue associated with open access publishing:

> Open Access Option. In the event that Licensor offers an open access option to its authors, Licensor will report to Licensee [annually] the number of works (such as articles) published under the open access

option by all authors, and the number and list of the works by title with full citation by authors at Licensee's institution.

Licensor will enter into good faith discussions with Licensee concerning mechanisms by which the open access publication fees received by Licensor can offset the fees paid by Licensee and other subscribers of Licensed Materials, with a goal of reducing such fees in proportion to the revenue received through such open access publication fees.[21]

As with text and data mining and accessibility, open access is an area in which there is no standardized path of adoption or attention. License negotiations and ongoing discussions are critical in furthering the dialogue between institutions, information professionals, and content providers in furthering open and unrestricted access to scholarly information for all users.

Digital Preservation

The preservation of content to which institutions have perpetual rights is a growing concern among information professionals. The dynamic nature of licensed digital content further complicates the already complex issue of preservation and perpetual access.[22] Many institutions are now addressing long-term preservation concerns for digital content by developing digital preservation strategy and policy documents. Such documents will outline specific actions to be taken on the part of various stakeholders in order to ensure the long-term preservation of owned or subscribed content. In terms of content that has been licensed through an external content provider, the policy may mandate that preservation language be inserted into purchase agreements. For instance, the Dartmouth College Library's Digital Preservation policy describes preservation strategies for licensed electronic content such as the participation in such archiving and preservation programs as LOCKSS, Portico, and HathiTrust, and stipulates that "the Library will negotiate such preservation agreements when developing subscription and license contracts with publishers and vendors."[23]

A policy mandating the negotiation of preservation rights for licensed electronic resources puts the responsibility on the licensing officer to fulfill this obligation in order to ensure perpetual access and preservation terms. Many publishers are already addressing the issue of preservation by archiving their output within services such as LOCKSS, CLOCKSS, or Portico. While many publishers do provide allowances for preservation or include perpetual access terms in their licenses, there is not one discrete path for articulating such terms. Furthermore, content providers may opt to remain silent on the issue of perpetual access or preservation, with no articulated stance on the availability of content over the long term.[24] The Liblicense Model License terms offer clearly articulated language that can serve as a guide for initiating the conversation of preservation via the use of external archiving programs with publishers:

> Third Party Archiving Services. Licensor and Licensee acknowledge that either party may engage the services of third-party trusted archives and/ or participate in collaborative archiving endeavors to exercise Licensee's rights under this section of the Agreement. Licensor agrees to cooperate with such archiving entities and/or initiatives as reasonably necessary to make the Licensed Materials available for archiving purposes. Licensee may perpetually use a third-party trusted system or collaborative archive to access or store the Licensed Materials, so long as Licensee's use is under the same terms as this Agreement.
>
> In the event the Licensor discontinues or changes the terms of its participation in a third-party archiving service, the Licensor shall notify the Licensee in advance, and shall in good faith seek to establish alternative arrangements for trusted archiving and perpetual access to the Licensed Materials.[25]

The Liblicense Model License also provides suggested language which outlines provisions by which a publisher will provide an archival copy or allow the licensee to create an archival copy of purchased content for preservation purposes. While less ideal, a provision of this nature will ensure archival access of some kind in lieu of preservation by a third-party service:

> Archival Copy. Licensor shall provide to Licensee upon request, or Licensee may create, one (1) copy of the entire set of Licensed Materials to be maintained as an archival copy. The archival copy from the Licensor shall be provided without any DRM in a mutually agreeable medium suitable to the content, and any fees for provision of copies will be on a time and materials basis only.[26]

International Content Providers

There are considerations that information professionals working within the United States should take into account when working with international content providers. While not necessarily a new or emerging issue in licensing, this represents an area of licensing that is not often addressed. Regardless, there are situations that information professionals may encounter when engaging in licensing with international vendors in which they should contact their office of general counsel or institutional purchasing department for further consultation. For instance, individuals working to initiate an electronic resource acquisition should contact an official purchasing unit within their institution if a content provider originates in a country upon which the United States has imposed comprehensive sanctions. As of 2016, the United States was engaged in comprehensive sanctions programs with six countries or regions: Cuba, Iran, Sudan, North Korea, Syria, and Crimea.[27] It is always advisable to notify the appropriate purchasing or legal unit within an institution when encountering content providers, sales representatives, or publishers originating from these sanctioned regions.

Another situation that US-based information professionals should be aware of when licensing with international vendors is boycott provisions. Any language that requires the licensee to agree not to do business with a certain country or group based on race, religion, gender, national origin, or nationality should be reported to the official purchasing or legal department of the licensee's institution, since language of this nature is in violation of US anti-boycott laws.[28] While the chances of encountering such language in an electronic resource license agreement are quite low, it is important for information professionals engaged in licensing activities to understand and identify such situations in order to ensure compliance with US laws. Finally, librarians should be aware of the differences that exist among international vendors in the area of copyright, since copyright provisions will vary depending on the origin of the content.[29] Contract and purchasing regulations will vary by institution, and information professionals should consult with their institution's legal or purchasing entities in order to determine what considerations should be taken into account when licensing with international content providers.

SUMMARY

Electronic resources licensing is a complex and evolving area of the electronic resources life cycle. The agreement set forth for an electronic resource will determine not only the parameters of use, but the inherent usefulness of the resource itself. In addition to core licensing concepts outlining the general terms of use and sale, there are trends in electronic resource licensing that have emerged in response to the changing landscape of research. Growing practices such as text and data mining and open access publishing require new ways of thinking when negotiating license agreements with content providers. Considerations such as accessibility, digital preservation, and international law should be taken into account by information professionals when reviewing and discussing agreements with publishers. In the dynamic field of electronic resources management, licensing professionals are addressing new and innovative developments in licensing that move access, usability, and scholarly communication forward.

NOTES

1. Ann Shumelda Okerson, "Reflections on Library Licensing," *Information Standards Quarterly* 26, no. 4 (winter 2014): 2–11.
2. Becky Albitz, *Licensing and Managing Electronic Resources* (Oxford: Chandos, 2008), 24.
3. Ryan O. Weir, *Managing Electronic Resources: A LITA Guide* (Chicago: American Library Association, 2012), 61.
4. "Liblicense: Licensing Digital Content, Model Licenses," Center for Research Libraries, http://liblicense.crl.edu/licensing-information/model-license/.
5. "SERU: Shared Electronic Resource Understanding," NISO (National Information Standards Organization), www.niso.org/workrooms/seru.
6. Leslie A. Williams et al., "Negotiating a Text Mining License for Faculty Researchers," *Information Technology & Libraries* 33, no. 3 (September 2014): 5–21.
7. Monica Maceli, "Introduction to Text Mining with R for Information Professionals," *Code4lib Journal* no. 33 (July 2016): 1.
8. Bernard F. Reilly, "Text-Mining and Libraries: Summary of a Conversation with Publishers," *Charleston Advisor* 14, no. 3 (January 2013): 59–60.
9. Ibid.
10. "Liblicense Model License Agreement with Commentary," Center for Research Libraries, http://liblicense.crl.edu/wp-content/uploads/2015/05/modellicensenew2014revmay2015.pdf.
11. David Klein et al., "Electronic Doors to Education: Study of High School Website Accessibility in Iowa," *Behavioral Sciences & the Law* 21, no. 1 (January 2003): 27–49.
12. Axel Schmetzke, "Collection Development, E-Resources, and Barrier-Free Access," *Advances in Librarianship* 40 (July 2015): 111–42.
13. "Web Design and Applications: Accessibility," World Wide Web Consortium (W3C), www.w3.0rg/standards/webdesign/accessibility.
14. "Voluntary Product Accessibility Template (VPAT)," U.S. Department of State Information Resource Management, Program for Accessible Computer/Communication Technology (IMPACT), www.state.gov/m/irm/impact/126343.htm.
15. "Liblicense Model License Agreement with Commentary."
16. "Accessibility," HathiTrust Digital Library, https://www.hathitrust.org/accessibility.
17. R. Serrano-Vicente, R. Melero, and E. Abadal, "Open Access Awareness and Perceptions in an Institutional Landscape," *Journal of Academic Librarianship* 42, no. 5 (September 2016): 595–603.
18. Jill Emery, "Mining for Gold: Identifying the Librarians' Toolkit for Managing Hybrid Open Access," *Insights* 26, no. 2 (July 1, 2013): 115–19.
19. Bo-Christer Bjork, "The Hybrid Model for Open Access Publication of Scholarly Articles: A Failed Experiment?" *Journal of the American Society for Information Science & Technology* 63, no. 8 (August 2012): 1496–1504.

20. Emery, "Mining for Gold."

21. "Liblicense Model License Agreement with Commentary."

22. Abby Smith, "The Digital Preservation Conundrum, Part 1," *Serials Librarian* 46, no. 1–2 (March 2004): 107–13.

23. "Dartmouth College Library Digital Preservation Policy," Dartmouth College Library, https://www.dartmouth.edu/~library/preservation/docs/dartmouth_digital _preservation_policy.pdf.

24. Chris Bulock, "Tracking Perpetual Access: A Survey of Librarian Practices," *Serials Review* 40, no. 2 (2014): 97–104.

25. "Liblicense Model License Agreement with Commentary."

26. Ibid.

27. "Sanctions Programs and Country Information," U.S. Department of the Treasury, https://www.treasury.gov/resource-center/sanctions/Programs/Pages/Programs.aspx.

28. "Office of Antiboycott Compliance (OAC)," Bureau of Industry and Security, U.S. Department of Commerce, https://www.bis.doc.gov/index.php/enforcement/oac.

29. John N. Gathegi, *The Digital Librarian's Legal Handbook* (New York: Neal-Schuman, 2012), 145.

"Oh, the Places You'll Go!"

Managing Electronic Resources across the Institution

Monica Moore

T his chapter highlights the interdepartmental nature of the electronic resource librarian (ERL) role in academic libraries by providing an overview of the development of this position and describing the type of work in which ERLs become involved. The e-resources life cycle referenced by the North America Serials Interest Group (NASIG) in its "Core Competencies for Electronic Resources Librarians" is used to frame the discussion and provide context. The emphasis is on the amount of coordination required to manage electronic resources, and how this coordination is really institutional and includes not only library units, but departments across campus as well as external entities such as vendors and publishers.

The author suggests that this coordination function is giving way to more of a collaboration among these entities, as the possibilities of digital content in both research and teaching continue to be explored. ERLs have a unique view of these possibilities because of their experience with acquiring and managing this content. While many of the life-cycle functions will remain static, the way they are done, and who does them, will evolve, leaving ERLs open to more collaboration and further involvement with other aspects of collection management such as evaluation, promotion of resources, and preservation.

WHAT DO ERLS DO ALL DAY?

You will come to a place where the streets are not marked.
Some windows are lighted. But mostly they're darked.[1]

Not surprisingly, the work of the ERL revolves around the management of electronic resources, also referred to as ERM. What makes ERM different from traditional collection management?

Print-based collection management comprises selection, acquisition, weeding, storage, preservation, policy development, promotion, evaluation, outreach, budgeting, liaison work, and soliciting funding.[2] The management of electronic resources shares many similarities with the management of print resources. However, the nature of this type of resource extends even those functions which it shares with print management, while adding several others that are unique to ERM. Electronic resources are information resources in digital format that are machine-readable, and are almost always delivered through some type of network. The format in which they are encoded and the tools used to interpret these formats all become part of the resource, in the sense that all of it has to be managed. A collection of digital content can be defined as not only the content itself, but the content plus the services and technology required to deliver, acquire, and support it.[3]

Even when ERM and traditional print collection management have functions in common, ERM tends to transform the way these functions are approached by introducing new technologies (and therefore new skills) and new, sometimes external, partnerships. ERM is often depicted using the e-resource life cycle, shown in figure 2.1.

At a high level, the functions described in this life-cycle figure seem to map well to traditional, print-based collection management functions. The "Acquire" bubble maps well to selection and acquisition; "Provide Access" could mean shelving, organizing, or circulation; and "Provide Support" could be construed to mean storage, preservation, and even budgeting and liaison work. But it does not take long for these comparisons to break down and diverge. As anyone who has worked with digital content knows, providing support is equated to technical support of the resource or its delivery mechanism; providing access usually means authentication and discovery through multiple library systems; and acquisition takes on a life of its own by extending the act of acquiring something into an ongoing, continual process of initial setup, updating, and migration as the digital product itself evolves, adds services, or is made available through different providers.

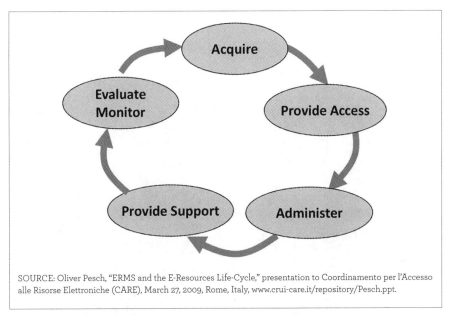

SOURCE: Oliver Pesch, "ERMS and the E-Resources Life-Cycle," presentation to Coordinamento per l'Accesso alle Risorse Elettroniche (CARE), March 27, 2009, Rome, Italy, www.crui-care.it/repository/Pesch.ppt.

Figure 2.1 | **Electronic resource life cycle as defined by Pesch**

In figure 2.2, Pesch extends these functional concepts to the actual ERM tasks and processes that are associated with them, and highlights which ones are new.

These processes as described above illustrate why ERM is so challenging. They require more equipment, a network, and support for that technical infrastructure, as well as applications that will handle authentication because the resources may be licensed to specific users, or the use of these resources may be restricted in some way that requires either a technical solution or a workflow adjustment on the part of library staff, which in turn may require the adoption of new skills to do all of these things. In addition to making them accessible, electronic resources can be discovered from more than one place, and all of these access points must be considered when activating access for the resource, and they must be constantly monitored as system upgrades happen and other access points are created for library patrons. All of these tasks and processes have the potential to distract the library from other collection management functions because they are so time-consuming and so dependent on shifting technology and an evolving publishing and provider landscape. Evaluation, both qualitative and quantitative, preservation, promotion and marketing, usability and instruction, and the overall relationship of the library collection to its community and its needs are things that often get short shrift.

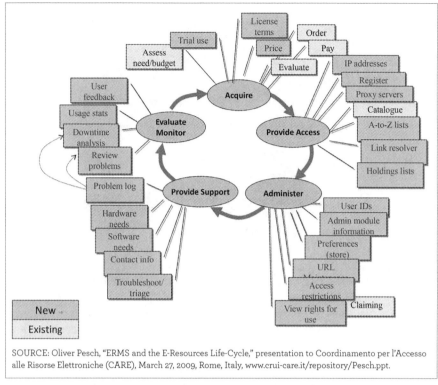

SOURCE: Oliver Pesch, "ERMS and the E-Resources Life-Cycle," presentation to Coordinamento per l'Accesso alle Risorse Elettroniche (CARE), March 27, 2009, Rome, Italy, www.crui-care.it/repository/Pesch.ppt.

Figure 2.2 | **Electronic resource life cycle with new processes**

These new requirements cut across traditional library divisions of labor, going beyond technical services to other library departments as well as departments and organizations of the larger institution of which the library is a part. Because of all the new processes needed for ERM, and also because of the effect of this type of information resource on the institution's goals and mission, the successful integration of electronic resources into a library's collection requires a great deal of coordination and communication across the institution.

LITERATURE REVIEW

The question of what needs to be done to integrate electronic resources successfully into library collections was formally addressed in fall 2002, when the Digital Library Federation and the National Information Standards Organization (NISO) began working on the Electronic Resource Management Initiative (ERMI).

Prior to this, libraries were struggling to adapt to the growing number of electronic resources being acquired, and upon realizing the limitations of their integrated library systems (ILS), they were cobbling together other ways to track and manage this new content type through a variety of methods, tools, and homegrown systems. A 2001 report by Jewell[4] researched and analyzed these early approaches to ERM, documenting the functions and data elements used by each institution and the systems used to track the information, as well as organizational responses to the selection, acquisition, licensing, discovery, preservation, and evaluation of these electronic resources. By 2004 the work of ERMI had resulted in a set of functional requirements, a data dictionary, and an entity-relationship diagram, as well as a report describing the initial problem and the remaining issues that would need to be addressed.[5]

The Jewell report and the ERMI standard captured the systems and organizational responses to the growing acquisition of electronic resources up to that time. One of the most common early organizational responses[6] was the recognition of the need for coordination to manage the growing amount of digital content being acquired.[7] This resulted in the creation of an "electronic resources coordinator" role within the library, which has evolved into the ERL position that is prevalent in most academic libraries today. While most ERLs are now found in technical service areas of the library, this role evolved out of a public services need for library staff to work with users and to train other library staff on the use of electronic content that was originally installed on library computers. While the creation of the role is a primary example of the library response to electronic information sources, its evolution within the library organizational structure reflects the increasing demands and complexity of ERM. How did a position that started at the reference desk morph into one that is associated with technical services or library systems?

Fisher[8] attempted to trace the roots of this position by examining position announcements over a seventeen-year period, all of which had job titles related to electronic information sources. Through analysis of the described duties and responsibilities in each ad, he found a strong connection to public services, especially reference/instruction services, and personal attributes such as communication, management, and interpersonal skills. The "electronic services librarian" as described by Wei He and Knee[9] detailed a position that was very much a part of the reference service of the library, at least initially. However, as the selection, acquisition, and ongoing management of these resources became more complicated, the position became more common in technical services departments, evolving more frequently from serials acquisitions positions, in spite of its roots in public services positions.[10] This shift was also observed by

Croneis and Henderson[11] in their content analysis of electronic and digital librarian positions from 1990 through 2000. For the first three years of their study, all of the positions were in public services; but starting in 1993, the positions appeared in nonpublic service areas such as technical services, systems, and digital projects.

As the role of the ERL became more established, it became more important to understand the skills needed to be successful in this role. Sutton[12] published an initial list of core competencies based on position requirements included in ERL ads from 2005 to 2009. A task force of NASIG took this list and developed it into NASIG's "Core Competencies for Electronic Resources Librarians," which was formally approved in July 2013. The "Core Competencies" describe the area of operations for ERLs. This area is quite broad, and includes the following categories: life cycle of the resource, technology, research and assessment, effective communication, supervising and management, trends and professional development, and personal qualities. These competencies have already shifted, as shown by Hartnett's study[13] in 2014 which extended the original work by Sutton to include more recent years of position descriptions. He found that some of the descriptors that were included in the original 2005–2009 study by Sutton were no longer trending, and suggested that the electronic resources librarian position was becoming more consolidated, with requirements such as cataloging, database design, website design, and reference duties becoming less critical.

The competencies for the ERL position may have evolved past a specific position in the library and could be considered more of a checklist of skills required of an organization for successful electronic resource management, and it is likely that some of them have become diffused among other library staff members. However, the ERL position still requires a variety of expertise and knowledge across a broad swathe of the organization. Albitz's[14] conclusion that ERLs are "Jacks-and-Jills of all trades" and that "electronic resource responsibilities might well include almost any library function" still rings true. The emphasis on such a broad set of competencies for this role in the library can lead to an expectation that ERM can be handled by one person in a library. This was one of two trends documented by Jewell,[15] in which one individual was "responsible for coordination or orchestration of electronic resource purchases." He also found, however, that these new electronic resource coordinator positions were problematic because of the "broad scope of possible responsibility." This led to the second trend he observed, which involved institutions developing ways to distribute tasks related to electronic resource management, through the creation of additional positions, such as "resource liaisons," "stewards," and "product sponsors."[16] In table 2 of this same report, which lists suggested practices for each area of ERM discussed in the report, he includes the necessity of a central coordinating entity as well as the "distribution of responsibilities for resource stewardship." It was clear even in the early days that while ERM may be overseen by one individual, it would require much coordination and communication to do it successfully. Subsequent articles in the literature[17] have borne this out.[18]

In addition to the organizational responses to the proliferation of electronic resources, libraries began to scrutinize their existing systems and procedures for handling this type of content. Local institutional solutions were implemented, and ranged from paper-based checklists to homegrown electronic resource management systems. With the advent of the ERMI standard, vendor-provided solutions became more prevalent, allowing more institutions to adopt these newer systems that were not only designed for basic collection maintenance, but aimed to expand their capabilities to allow for better collection development decisions.[19] In spite of recognizing the need for this functionality, ERMS implementation is still not ubiquitous.[20] While the perceived benefits are acknowledged, it still takes time and money to fully implement and maintain such a system, and even to investigate which one might be the best fit for a library's needs and workflow. In addition, successful integration of an ERMS is also tied to staffing and training, as well as local conditions.[21]

The impact of the ERMI standard and these new systems for ERM on the number of e-resource personnel hired and their job responsibilities was studied by Murdock[22] through an analysis of position descriptions from 2000 to 2008. The data gathered did not show a significant decrease in the number of personnel being sought for ERM, and the duties described were very similar to ads posted before the work of the ERMI, despite an increase in the implementation by these institutions, as mentioned in these same ads, of the existence of an ERMS. It is clear that electronic resource management continues to be something that requires a great deal of local customization and coordination for libraries to fully realize the benefits of adding this type of content to their collections.

A Day in the Life of the Life Cycle: ERM in Practice

"And when things start to happen, don't worry.

Don't stew. Just go right along.

You'll start happening too."[23]

The previous section gave an overview of what ERM entails, how it differs from traditional collection management, and confirmed the need for coordination among various departments and functions within the library. The e-resources life cycle that was described in figure 2.1 provided an abstraction of what happens when a library decides to subscribe to an electronic information source, while figure 2.2 offered more detail on some of the actual tasks and functions associated with each phase in this life cycle. In this next section, specific examples of projects are described to illustrate the type of cross-departmental and institutional collaboration that is required when working with electronic resources.

Many of the challenges with regard to ERM are related to the ongoing nature of this type of content. Even when a library has mastered a workflow across various departments in order to acquire an e-journal package, for example, there is always the possibility of a post-acquisition issue related to the package's continued technical or financial support: a publisher could transfer some of the titles in the e-journal package to another publisher, or the package could be hosted by another platform provider, or the publisher could decide to vend the content differently, repackaging it in a way that causes a change in how libraries renew and pay for it. Along with a platform change, providing ongoing access may involve the creation and deletion ("weeding") of the various access points for these resources, such as the implementation of a new discovery layer, or the inclusion of the e-journals in the package in a link resolver Knowledge base which will populate an A-Z list or be exported to Google Scholar, which involves administering access to them through updates to authentication procedures that are outside the library. New requests for unforeseen uses of existing resources may crop up; a new type of content may become available; and something that required payment may now become freely available. All of these things bring the ERL and other staff involved with ERM into contact with existing library departments as well as new campus partners.

Implementing New E-Book Acquisition Models

Like many academic libraries, Hesburgh Libraries at the University of Notre Dame has increased its acquisition of e-books, from single-title firm orders to the acquisition of e-book packages from scholarly presses. While there are still questions about the optimal way to handle some of the life cycle steps related to the purchase of this content, it is a fairly well-established workflow, at least in terms of activation of the e-book content in the library catalog and link resolver Knowledge base. However, the advent of different acquisition models, such as demand-drive acquisition (DDA) and evidence-based acquisition

(EBA), require more coordination with other library departments responsible for the discovery of these records and their subsequent maintenance once purchases are triggered or made specifically at the end of a set time period, as in the case of EBA.

In spring 2015 Hesburgh Libraries initiated an EBA pilot with a major publisher. It became clear from initial meetings that more involvement would be required for this new acquisition model, which placed more responsibility on library staff to monitor usage and make selection decisions at the end of a defined access period. As decisions were made with subject librarians about the best content to include in the pilot, technical decisions about record loads had to be discussed with other library staff. Because the library would be monitoring usage of content from the EBA title pool, it was important to start and end the pilot with enough time to allow for maximum discovery, and since discovery played such a key role with this model, additional thought went into understanding all of the access points for this content. All of these issues had to be worked out before the license could be drawn up and the order officially placed. Having a specific time to access the content was a catalyst for increased collaboration among the library departments which provide many of these discovery functions, since problems loading records often required follow-up meetings and calls with vendors to resolve issues and answer questions. Coordination was much more critical with this acquisition model because of the involvement of departments not usually involved in standard e-book acquisitions and the ongoing nature of this coordination.

As e-book records for the EBA title pool began to appear in the catalog in fall 2015, a new e-book DDA program was contemplated by Hesburgh Libraries. The availability of an increasing number of scholarly press e-books through an aggregator with a new DDA option prompted another foray into an alternative acquisition model for e-books. While similar in many ways to the EBA pilot just initiated, this additional order expanded the scope of this acquisition because of the existence of the EBA pilot as well as another existing DDA program from a different aggregator. It took weeks to develop a de-duplication strategy so that a DDA title pool could be determined, and additional meetings with subject librarians and acquisitions staff to understand the timing of existing record loads to library systems and the process for excluding publishers from the various title pools that were now in place. Like the EBA pilot, this new DDA program initiated more frequent meetings with many library stakeholders as well as external vendors.

The acquisition of e-book content using a variety of acquisition strategies is a particularly good example of the type of coordination that is required for

ERM. The change from a purchase model to a "just in time" model like the EBA pilot means that while the e-resource life-cycle steps may be the same, there is more urgency, more project management, and ongoing issues which in turn require more involvement with other library units, as well as expertise outside the library and with vendors. It is also a good example of an ongoing process that requires departments which would not normally be involved with an acquisition, at least beyond the initial stages, to communicate regularly through ERM staff and to understand ERM systems in more detail.

Increasing Discovery Options for Electronic Resources

Acquiring content has its own challenges, especially when the way it is vended changes, but the discovery of it is also becoming more complicated. Users are no longer using the library catalog as the primary access point for electronic resources.[24] Like many libraries responding to the need to provide a more Google-like searching experience for their users, Hesburgh Libraries implemented a discovery layer, OneSearch, using Primo Central Index from Ex Libris, in 2012. Since an undertaking like this involves both content stakeholders and end users from various disciplines at different stages of their academic career, it took a lot of protracted collaboration in the form of focus groups with end users, discussions about interface design and usability, and consultations with other librarians to determine resource-specific as well as subject coverage, as well as the most common use cases for library staff on the front lines of public service points. In the middle of this was a core team that included the two ERLs who had recently been hired and other library staff from other departments such as technical services, systems and information technology, and public services. The implementation of a discovery layer extends the Provide Access step of the e-resources life cycle in a way that involves ERLs in meetings with people and departments with whom they may never have worked regularly, over a period of time. It also requires the development of new skills, including coding, project management, and even web analytics, so that in addition to increased collaboration there is frequently a need to learn new things in order to either perform additional tasks related to the discovery of electronic resources, or to be able to communicate effectively with the people in other departments who have this expertise.

The question of content discoverability as part of ERM involves not only a discovery layer implemented "on top of" a traditional integrated library system (ILS). It involves other systems or applications that provide additional access and discovery points for electronic content, such as a LibGuide, a federated search, or a data feed from a link resolver Knowledge base to an external discovery interface such as PubMed or Google Scholar. Because the indexing for a library's subscribed electronic content may not necessarily be included in the library's discovery layer, ERLs will often find themselves involved in meetings with vendors, publishers, and even standards organizations such as the National Information Standards Organization which grapple with these issues.[25]

The examples of the e-book DDA and EBA programs given above, and the subsequent discovery issues that need to be considered with electronic resources, are still part of an initial acquisition workflow, even though there is some monitoring that happens after the order is placed. Increasingly, post-acquisition issues seem to push the boundaries of the life cycle. Vendor changes, platform changes, publisher mergers, and product enhancements and consolidations all have significant trickle-down effects on discovery, licensing, and even payment and invoicing for electronic resources. Even if something becomes open access, or freely available, it still entails work: orders must be closed out in the ILS, funds transferred, links changed, and so on. Much of the work of an ERL has to do with explaining what happens after a resource is acquired, through direct notifications from a vendor or from discussion list communications.

In addition to this post-acquisition monitoring, ERLs are also seeing more interest from campus stakeholders in unanticipated uses of electronic resources. Two examples of recent projects that illustrate this include an increased interest in seeking access for alumni, and the growing need for text mining rights for faculty members for licensed library resources.

Providing Access for Institutional Alumni

An interest in granting alumni access to licensed electronic resources has led to more communication and collaboration between library staff who manage electronic resources and other campus entities, whose uses of this content do not always align with the original intended uses of the content when it was licensed. License agreements for electronic resources include language that describes who will be authorized to access the content and what these authorized users can do with the content. Most agreements limit authorized users to currently enrolled students, faculty, and staff, so a request from an alumni or development office on campus frequently involves inspecting the agreement for the resource desired, followed by a series of communications between the publisher and library staff. While it may not always be the ERL who communicates with the publisher to seek these rights, it generally falls to her lot to implement this access if the rights can be secured, or if the agreement does in fact allow for alumni access.

In recent years, the Thomas Mahaffey Jr. Business Library at the University of Notre Dame has worked with various partners on campus to offer access for specific electronic resources to its alumni. This has required many meetings between library staff, business school staff, and the alumni office to determine the feasibility of doing this as well as the best way to handle it technically. Working with campus partners that do not always understand the nature of this type of content and how it is acquired and licensed can be challenging, adding another aspect or nuance to the Provide Access or Administer step of the life cycle; namely, one of communication and education regarding what the resource is and how it can and cannot be used. This work also disperses the post-acquisition role of the ERL somewhat to include the monitoring of these external relationships when things come up for renewal or are under evaluation by the original stakeholders. In addition, it highlights the question of support for electronic resources that are no longer hosted specifically by library access points, and how to calculate usage of them.

Seeking Text and Data Mining Rights for Electronic Resources

Another unanticipated use of previously acquired or licensed electronic resources is text and data mining. Text and data mining rights to support digital humanities research by campus faculty are another twist on rights and technical issues related to existing electronic resource content use. In the spring and fall of 2014, Hesburgh Libraries negotiated text mining rights for several licensed resources in support of a research project related to evolutionary biology. While it is possible, and increasingly more common, to ask for these rights for licensed content, libraries still need to understand how researchers intend to access the content, technically, and what they intend to do with data they get back as well as how they will include this information in any contemplated published research. The challenge of negotiating text mining rights lies in this interplay between how the data will be accessed from the licensed resources, where it will live, how long it will be kept, what type of analysis may be done on it, and if this analysis will be published or made available outside of any "black box" where the raw data being extracted from the licensed resource "lives." Answering these questions requires a lot of communication between researchers, information technology staff, the university's legal counsel, and the vendor and/or publishers, and it is also potentially a steep learning curve for the person managing all of this. This process may apply to more than one publisher or vendor, depending on the content needed to answer the research questions, and each solution may be slightly different and require a different type of oversight or monitoring.

The above examples were chosen because they illustrate the ripple effect of networked, licensed content in digital format not just on the library, but on the institution of which the library is a part. They show all the places an ERL must go in order to not only acquire and manage electronic resources, but to make them relevant to institutional users. These places include library technical services (cataloging, acquisitions); public services (instruction librarians, subject librarians); administrative departments related to budgeting, finance, and assessment; information technology departments or units; and university entities such as the alumni office, the development office, faculty departments, and scholarly communication offices. In each example, coordination was required, but increasingly, collaboration to achieve a shared goal became more important. These examples also describe the evolution from an acquisition mindset— *"acquire the resource and make it accessible"*—to one of discovery—*"make the resource and its related content discoverable"*—to the relevance of the resource— *"make it useful to researchers, students, and teaching faculty."* From the viewpoint of the ERL, is this mission creep, or an evolution of the ERL role, or an invitation to keep going to new places?

Beyond the Life Cycle

"You have brains in your head.
You have feet in your shoes.
You can steer yourself any direction you choose."[26]

Do ERLs, through coordination with colleagues within and outside the library, ever master electronic resource management? If ERM involved just the acquisition and maintenance of the electronic resource, then perhaps that would be possible, even with all of the changes that occur within the electronic resource landscape. However, the last step in the ERM life cycle is "Evaluate," and within that step is a world of nuance. It is this last step that is the most important, yet it is the most difficult one for most libraries. This is due not only to the amount of extra time and effort it takes to gather data for evaluation; it brings up questions about what evaluation means for electronic resources.

Evaluation

The most common form of evaluation for electronic resources, or at least the one that is the best understood, is the gathering of usage statistics which measure user activity such as searches, downloads, sessions, abstract views, and other clicks or choices made by the user on a platform or from an interface. The standard for measuring electronic resource usage is COUNTER,[27] which defines what is meant by searches, sessions, and downloads, and this has been extremely useful for libraries trying to compare usage across different products from different vendors, for similar content types. There are also vendor-specific measures, and other data points which can be gathered through the application of web analytics and from link resolver Knowledge bases, and other sources such as transaction logs. There is no shortage of data that can be gathered, and there are tools and best practices for gathering it, but it still requires analysis and interpretation. Because this process is in fact so time-consuming, it is critical that libraries understand what the data can and cannot tell them, and not confuse measuring with evaluation.[28]

ERLs usually become the focal point for understanding the various data collection methods and the analysis and interpretation of what the data means, and in which contexts. They are often involved with overall assessment efforts within the library, either through membership on a committee tasked with assessment, or by working closely with assessment librarians. ERLs are often called upon to gather usage statistics and to help define best practices for gathering and compiling those statistics, including the evaluation of electronic resource assessment systems,[29] and the mapping of system data to questions about how the collection is being used, such as the significance of a particular link resolver report.[30] This specialized knowledge, when combined with ERLs' understanding of electronic resources, contributes to an assessment culture[31] and to larger assessment projects within libraries, such as reporting out information to the Association of Research Libraries or the Association of College & Research Libraries. These examples all illustrate how much coordination with other departments is required, but assessment is an area where more coordination and collaboration are needed so that the data helps to elicit questions about the overall value of the collection to its user community. This could be initiated through the development of a more holistic framework for cumulative evaluation as suggested by Nicholson,[32] or by measuring the situational relevance of electronic resources to different user groups in various settings, as described by Pluye et al.[33]

Evaluation is a step that comes at the end of the life cycle, and it usually is done with a resource that is already acquired and up for renewal, but it could also be considered a first step in the life cycle. Scrutinizing the content contained in electronic resources for quality and that content's relationship to the larger pedagogical goals of the institution is important,[34] as is examining the potential overlap of that content with other sources the library has. ERLs can assist with all of this, in conjunction with other colleagues, and it would make the subsequent gathering of usage statistics more purposeful.

Preservation

When traditional, print-based collection management is described,[35] preservation is included. However, it seems to be missing from the ERM life cycle, although perhaps it could be folded into the Provide Access step. For how long is access expected to be provided when an electronic resource is acquired? And how explicit are libraries with this idea of preservation and long-term access for content that comes in different containers, is acquired through nontraditional acquisition models, and is hosted on platforms that can frequently change?

Usually these expectations are addressed in license agreements through the negotiation of perpetual access rights, but even when these rights are secured, the way in which this access is provided is not uniform and relies frequently on third-party entities outside the library, thus becoming another part of the scholarly information ecosystem which ERLs have to monitor. Tracking these rights is an additional burden that requires much time and coordination, as well as post-acquisition monitoring as content moves between publishers. It does not appear to be something that librarians are doing on a regular basis as part of their jobs, either because it is so time-consuming, or because there are no best practices for doing so, or perhaps it is not as important an issue as previously thought.[36] While there are techniques that librarians can develop and employ to make this task easier,[37] they do not cover content that may not be licensed or for which perpetual access rights have not been negotiated.

Signing license agreements for electronic content seems to be the only place where preservation is part of ERM, primarily through the Acquire and Provide Access steps. There is no reference to the digital preservation of the content itself, and no assumptions about this the way there might be with print objects, which a library knows it can store, conserve, or repair. Does the preservation of a collection comprised of mostly electronic resources mean the same thing as preservation of a print collection? It might be assumed that preservation is not part of ERM because content is more often leased, and the perpetual access rights, if negotiated correctly, are handled by a third party responsible for digital preservation of the content, through migration, refreshing, or some other means, and perhaps libraries have outsourced this function effectively and it only requires monitoring and tracking. Still, libraries do purchase some quantity of electronic content, and even if it is the case that digital preservation will be done by another party, libraries still need to have a workflow in place for tracking this, or at least specifically state through some kind of policy that preservation and ongoing access will not be required under specific circumstances that make sense locally.

A search through the literature does not turn up much on the role of preservation related to electronic resources in an acquisition context, other than articles that include perpetual access rights discussion. Most of the focus with regard to the preservation of electronic resources seems to be on the digital preservation of content produced by the local institution for storage in a repository, or for special collections which have been digitized. Neither of these areas addresses the retention and digital preservation of purchased electronic resources or subscribed electronic resources for which the library has post-cancellation access. One exception[38] stressed the need for libraries to become involved with e-journal preservation, while acknowledging that preservation does not figure greatly in the ERM life cycle or the "Core Competencies" from NASIG, and the responsibility for this work is not specifically tied to the ERL role within the library. In Regan's suggestions for increasing the quantity of e-journals preserved, she outlines several steps that usually involve the ERL in some way: license negotiation, renewals, title transfers, funding, and outreach and awareness.

Whether a library decides to more actively track and monitor the preservation of electronic resources, or to make a collection development decision that this is something that should *not* be pursued, the ERL is in a unique position to provide the necessary coordination and knowledge for all of the parties who would be involved in such a decision. Nadal,[39] in his article "The Human Element in Digital Preservation," addresses the need for human intervention to coordinate digital preservation activities, and it is reflective of the nature of ERM and its need for a coordinator. In addition, Nadal specifically points to the ERL as being crucial to the role of preservation within a collection:

> Because of their connections to the publishers and distributors of ER of every variety, they are the natural spokespersons in the library community for the implementation of good standards and practices. Through advocacy for standardized license terms that will require vendor/publishers to adopt standards-based best practices from publishers and preferential treatment in terms of spending to digital information suppliers who engage in practices that are favorable to libraries, ER

librarians can effect important change and, thus, limit the scope of preservation challenges to be faced in the future.

This may not be possible at this point in time because other areas of ERM are still so time-consuming; however, this may not always be the case. Improved ERMS workflows, next-generation integrated library systems, increased staff skills and training, and more familiarity and adaptation to electronic resources and their ways will free up more time for ERL involvement with this issue.

Promotion

Increasing users' awareness of the library's collection is part of collection management,[40] and it is another example of a collection management function which does not get as much attention with electronic resources management. It is implied in the Acquire step that the selection of a resource meets a specific or anticipated need of a library user, but this may not always be the case. The ERL usually is not involved with this kind of analysis and tailoring of a potential resource to the collection, unless he or she is also serving in a liaison or public services role or is charged with oversight of the collection as a whole. Yet because of their involvement with the e-resources life cycle, ERLs need to become more involved with selection, and not just because they understand the process of acquisition and its workflows. They are constantly observing the changing electronic resource provider landscape, and they see not just the pitfalls of various acquisition models and new types of resources: they see their potential. They are in a unique position to help with overall marketing and awareness of the library's collection through specific promotion efforts. These efforts could be the promotion of a resource to faculty or students through nontraditional access points, new collaborations, or new and nontraditional uses of a resource.

Many teaching faculty members use learning management systems (LMS) such as Moodle, Blackboard, or Sakai. An LMS represents an opportunity for librarians to engage with students in their virtual learning space or classroom. Tumbleson[41] described this as LMS-embedded librarianship, and its benefits include the ability to connect with students in order to help with their research process, and to direct them to library resources that would benefit them in their research. Tumbleson[42] cited the advantages of being able to counteract the trend of decreasing reference desk transactions by being present with students in their courses and connecting with them through LMS messages, conferencing, e-mails, and online instruction. From a promotion standpoint, this is also an opportunity for electronic resources to be accessed by students who may never go to the library's home page, but will most certainly log in to their classes through an LMS. At Miami University in 2014, three librarians embedded in LMS classes were able to reach 2,000 students.[43] This new access point for library resources should be leveraged. It could be something that ERLs are able to make part of an acquisitions workflow or through collaboration with librarians who have more direct contact with teaching faculty. In addition to providing electronic resource links for the LMS, ERLs could help to develop a way to track usage of these resources from the LMS or from other research starting points.

Another nontraditional place to engage with regard to electronic resources are university teaching and learning centers, which offer faculty development programs. Such centers are very common on university campuses.[44] At the University of Notre Dame, the Kaneb Center for Teaching and Learning offers workshops and programming to "encourage the adoption of practices that enhance learning."[45] Fostering a partnership with these teaching and learning centers for faculty is another opportunity for the promotion of electronic resources, especially those which lend themselves to classroom use, including streaming video, digitized primary source material, and other multimedia collections that the library has leased or purchased. One way to initiate such a partnership might be through hosting a vendor fair or vendor expo specifically aimed at faculty who participate in the faculty development programs offered at these centers, in order to highlight some of these resources. The concept of a vendor fair or vendor expo[46] has been explored by other academic libraries,[47] and could be customized to target faculty members who participate in faculty development programs that focus on integrating digital technologies into their teaching and classrooms.

As faculty continue to explore the use of text mining in their research and ERLs pursue the necessary rights to do this, the latter can point out other opportunities to use this same data or rights for other purposes. For example, in response to a need from a business professor, Hesburgh Libraries added a subscription to an API (application programming interface) offered by Lexis Nexis for current subscribers to their Lexis Nexis Academic product. While the resource was acquired to support the retrieval of the underlying data for a specific research question, the license also allowed for the building of a customized interface to query this same content.

In the year prior to this subscription, the electronic resource acquisition unit had received an e-mail from the president of the student body. He was scrutinizing the university's participation in the Collegiate Readership Program—which provides free print versions of the *New York Times* to students on campus—and wanted to know more about the library's access to online newspaper content. The decision was made to keep participating in the Collegiate Readership Program for various reasons, but one interesting finding from this interaction was the discovery of a student preference for a more browsable newspaper experience than what was currently available through the library.

The subsequent licensing a year later of the API for a resource that contains all of this same newspaper content, but allows for a customized presentation of it, is an example of an opportunity to connect two distinct uses cases to the same resource used in two different ways. The ERL is usually the common denominator in these types of scenarios, and this ability to see connections and possibilities for electronic resources or services is a contribution that the ERL can make to an organization. Digital humanities is another area where these connections of learners, researchers, and educators to relevant information in new formats are happening,[48] and new opportunities for ERLs are also emerging in other areas of digital scholarship and scholarly communications.[49]

CONCLUDING THOUGHTS

This chapter began with a theoretical explanation and description of the work involved with acquiring electronic resources, followed by some specific examples of ERL work and how it involves collaboration with other departments throughout the library and the institution. This collaboration is necessitated by the nature of digital content itself as well as by external factors related to how it is acquired and provisioned, but it is also due to an evolution of how this type of content is starting to be used by teaching faculty, students, and researchers. As people begin to see possibilities for this type of information container that did not exist before, the work of ERM, and thus the ERL, has begun to evolve from a workflow to a project, from coordination of an acquisition to collaboration in order to create something new.[50] Many of the questions that ERLs field related to electronic resources are unanticipated, and can become opportunities to connect the value of the library's collection to the research projects and initiatives of the institution.

The fact that so much coordination is needed allows ERLs a unique view of their library and institution. Functioning as they do at the crossroads for various technical and public service needs, and as the individuals seeing and working within and beyond the life cycle, they see how things should be from a process improvement standpoint, but also from a larger perspective; namely, what things could become.

NOTES

1. Dr. Seuss, *Oh, the Places You'll Go!* (London: HarperCollins Children's Books), 2016.
2. Peggy Johnson, *Fundamentals of Collection Development and Management* (Chicago: American Library Association, 2004), 3.
3. Ibid., 200.
4. Timothy D. Jewell, "Selection and Presentation of Commercially Available Electronic Resources: Issues and Practices," Digital Library Federation and Council on Library and Information Resources, 2001, https://old.diglib.org/pubs/dlf093/dlf093.pdf.
5. Timothy D. Jewell et al., "Electronic Resource Management: Report of the DLF ERM Initiative," Digital Library Federation, 2004, https://old.diglib.org/pubs/dlf102/.
6. Kristin H. Gerhard, "Coordination and Collaboration: A Model for Electronic Resources Management," *The Serials Librarian* 33, no. 3–4 (1998): 279–86, doi:10.1300/J123v33n03_06.
7. Richard P. Jasper, "Collaborative Roles in Managing Electronic Publications," *Library Collections, Acquisitions, & Technical Services* 26, no. 4 (2002): 355–61, doi:10.1080/14649055.2002.10765872.
8. William Fisher, "The Electronic Resources Librarian Position: A Public Services Phenomenon?" *Library Collections, Acquisitions, and Technical Services* 27, no. 1 (2003): 3–17, doi:10.1080/14649055.2003.10765892.
9. Peter Wei He and Michael Knee, "The Challenge of Electronic Services Librarianship," *Reference Services Review* 23, no. 4 (1995): 7–12, doi:10.1108/eb049260.
10. Andrew M. Cox and Sheila Corrall, "Evolving Academic Library Specialties," *Journal of the American Society for Information Science & Technology* 64, no. 8 (2013): 1526–42, doi:10.1002/asi.22847.
11. Karen S. Croneis and Pat Henderson, "Electronic and Digital Librarian Positions: A Content Analysis of Announcements from 1990 through 2000," *The Journal of Academic Librarianship* 28, no. 4 (2002): 232–37, doi:10.1016/S0099-1333(02)00287-2.
12. Sarah Sutton and Susan Davis, "Core Competencies for Electronic Resources Librarians," *The Serials Librarian* 60, no. 1–4 (2011): 147–52, doi:10.1080/0361526X.2011.556025.
13. Eric Hartnett, "NASIG's Core Competencies for Electronic Resources Librarians Revisited: An Analysis of Job Advertisement Trends, 2000–2012," *Journal of Academic Librarianship* 40, no. 3 (2014): 247–58, doi:10.1016/j.acalib.2014.03.013.
14. Rebecca S. Albitz, "Electronic Resource Librarians in Academic Libraries: A Position Announcement Analysis, 1996–2001," *portal: Libraries and the Academy* 2, no. 4 (2002): 589–600, doi:10.1353/pla.2002.0069.
15. Jewell, "Selection and Presentation of Commercially Available Electronic Resources," 15.
16. Ibid., 15.
17. Jodi Poe et al., "Sharing the Albatross of E-Resources Management Workflow," in *Electronic Resource Management in Libraries: Research and Practice* (Hershey, PA: IGI Global, 2008), 71.

18. Stephen C. Boss and Lawrence O. Schmidt, "Electronic Resources (ER) Management in the Academic Library," *Collection Management* 32, no. 1–2 (2007): 117–40, doi:10 .1300/J105v32n01_09.

19. Tamar Sadeh and Mark Ellingsen, "Electronic Resource Management Systems: The Need and the Realization," *New Library World* 106, no. 5 (2005): 208–18, doi:10.1108/03074800510595823.

20. Jill Emery and Graham Stone, "Introduction and Literature Review," *Library Technology Reports* 49, no. 2 (2013): 5, https://journals.ala.org/index.php/ltr/article/view/4732/5634.

21. Nat Gustafson-Sundell, "Think Locally: A Prudent Approach to Electronic Resource Management Systems," *Journal of Electronic Resources Librarianship* 23, no. 2 (2011): 126–41, doi:10.1080/1941126X.2011.576955.

22. Dawn Murdock, "Relevance of Electronic Resource Management Systems to Hiring Practices for Electronic Resources Personnel," *Library Collections, Acquisitions, and Technical Services* 34, no. 1 (2010): 25–42, doi:10.1016/j.lcats.2009.11.001.

23. Dr. Seuss, *Oh, the Places You'll Go!*

24. Sommer Browning, "The Discovery–Collection Librarian Connection: Cultivating Collaboration for Better Discovery," *Collection Management* 40, no. 4 (2015): 197–206, doi:10.1080/01462679.2015.1093985.

25. "Open Discovery Initiative," National Information Standards Organization, www.niso .org/workrooms/odi/.

26. Dr. Seuss, *Oh, the Places You'll Go!*

27. COUNTER, https://www.projectcounter.org/.

28. Scott Nicholson, "A Conceptual Framework for the Holistic Measurement and Cumulative Evaluation of Library Services," *Journal of Documentation* 60, no. 2 (2004): 164–82, doi:10.1108/00220410410522043.

29. Fei Xu, "Implementation of an Electronic Resource Assessment System in an Academic Library," *Program* 44, no. 4 (2010): 374–92, doi:10.1108/00330331011083257.

30. Tina E. Chrzastowski, Michael Norman, and Sarah Elizabeth Miller, "SFX Statistical Reports: A Primer for Collection Assessment Librarians," *Collection Management* 34, no. 4 (2009): 286–303, doi:10.1080/01462670903177912.

31. Mark Emmons and Megan Oakleaf, "The ACRL Standards for Proficiencies for Assessment Librarians and Coordinators: A New Document to Support and Strengthen Assessment Efforts in Academic Libraries," *The Journal of Academic Librarianship* 5, no. 42 (2016): 622–24, doi:10.1016/j.acalib.2016.07.006.

32. Nicholson, "A Conceptual Framework for the Holistic Measurement and Cumulative Evaluation of Library Services," 1.

33. Pierre Pluye et al., "Systematically Assessing the Situational Relevance of Electronic Knowledge Resources: A Mixed Methods Study," *Journal of the American Medical Informatics Association* 14, no. 5 (2007): 616–25, doi:10.1197/jamia.M2203.

34. William H. Walters, "Evaluating Online Resources for College and University Libraries: Assessing Value and Cost Based on Academic Needs," *Serials Review* 42, no. 1 (2016): 10–17, doi:10.1080/00987913.2015.1131519.

35. Johnson, *Fundamentals of Collection Development and Management*, 3.

36. Chris Bulock, "Tracking Perpetual Access: A Survey of Librarian Practices," *Serials Review* 40, no. 2 (2014): 97–104, doi:10.1080/00987913.2014.923369.

37. Chris Bulock, "Techniques for Tracking Perpetual Access," *The Serials Librarian* 68, no. 1–4 (2015): 290–98, doi:10.1080/0361526X.2015.1017711.

38. Shannon Regan, "Strategies for Expanding E-Journal Preservation," *The Serials Librarian* 70, no. 1–4 (2016): 89–99, doi:10.1080/0361526X.2016.1144159.

39. Jacob Nadal, "The Human Element in Digital Preservation," *Collection Management* 32, no. 3–4 (2008): 289–303, doi:10.1300/J105v32n03_04.

40. Johnson, *Fundamentals of Collection Development and Management*, 3.

41. Beth E. Tumbleson, "Collaborating in Research: Embedded Librarianship in the Learning Management System," *The Reference Librarian* 57, no. 3 (2016): 224–34, doi:10 .1080/02763877.2015.1134376.

42. Ibid., 229.

43. Ibid., 228.

44. Karron G. Lewis, "Pathways toward Improving Teaching and Learning in Higher Education: International Context and Background." *New Directions for Teaching and Learning,* no. 122 (2010): 13–23, doi:10.1002/t1.394.

45. Kaneb Center for Teaching and Learning, University of Notre Dame, http://kaneb .nd.edu/.

46. Lateka J. Grays and James Cory Tucker, "Vendor of the Month: A Marketing Collaboration," *Collaborative Librarianship* 5, no. 2 (2013): 7, http://digitalcommons .du.edu/collaborativelibrarianship/v015/iss2/7.

47. Lia Hemphill and Elena M. Soltau, "'Passport to Information Day' as a Promotion Tool," *The Charleston Advisor* 8, no. 4 (2007): 55–57, www.ingentaconnect.com/content/ charleston/chadv/2007/00000008/00000004/art00019.

48. Jane A. Burns, "Role of the Information Professional in the Development and Promotion of Digital Humanities Content for Research, Teaching, and Learning in the Modern Academic Library: An Irish Case Study," *New Review of Academic Librarianship* 22, no. 2–3 (2016): 238–48, doi:10.1080/13614533.2016.1191520.

49. Angela Dresselhaus, "Opportunities beyond Electronic Resource Management: An Extension of the Core Competencies for Electronic Resources Librarians to Digital Scholarship and Scholarly Communications," *The Serials Librarian* 68, no. 1–4 (2015): 361–69, doi:10.1080/0361526X.2015.1017716.

50. Michael Schrage, *Shared Minds: The New Technologies of Collaboration* (New York: Random House, 1990), 36.

Managing Knowledge Bases and Electronic Resources Metadata

Richard Guajardo

This chapter will focus on knowledge bases and metadata management for electronic resources. This will include a discussion of commercial and open environment knowledge bases, the development and rationale for community-managed knowledge bases, and the management of MARC records (machine-readable cataloging records) and non-MARC metadata for electronic resources.

A precursor to the knowledge base was the OpenURL link resolver. Later an A-to-Z list of electronic journals became an added feature of the link resolver. The knowledge base describes collections or holdings that a library has purchased or has subscribed to and which the library will be providing access to its users. The knowledge base contains unique identifiers such as ISBNs, ISSNs, author names, publisher names, titles, and variant titles. An important feature provided by a knowledge base is that titles can be grouped or sorted by the package that was acquired for the library. In this way, the knowledge base helps libraries track changes in a vendor's package or by the publisher. Knowledge bases contain numerous metadata elements such as the title, publisher, distributor, and the name of any organization involved in the creation of the resource. Knowledge bases typically contain an administrative interface that allows the library to configure the local settings. A knowledge base's functionality allows it to interact with discovery systems and the library services platforms (LSP). In more recent uses, knowledge base metadata are being leveraged to support additional functions for electronic course reserves.

Libraries have undertaken various projects to address issues that perplex and confound a library's ability to manage its electronic collections. OCLC's perspective on electronic resources management focuses on improved systems and on increased collaboration within the library community. Some OCLC member libraries have embraced this idea in how they manage their electronic collections and metadata. This includes moving away from workflows that are not sustainable by our library systems. More broadly, they advocate the need for community-managed knowledge bases, eliminating silos, and developing best practices for both publishers and librarians. Community-managed knowledge bases are available on some vendor platforms. A project called the Global Open Knowledgebase (GOKb) has created an open environment, community-managed platform of metadata for managing electronic journals and e-books. These community-managed knowledge bases seek to reduce duplication of effort for libraries.

The University of Houston has undertaken a number of metadata initiatives and has implemented a modular approach to its electronic resources management workflows and the systems it uses for these tasks. It has deployed its own intranet-based license repository, and utilizes a web-based project management and collaboration tool to track workflow between four departments charged with the responsibility for the electronic resources life cycle.

The importance of distinguishing between policy, procedures, and workflows for electronic resources management, as well as the maintenance of supporting documentation, is discussed in a description of best practices implemented at the University of California Irvine. Workflows may exist at more than one level and are designed to follow the intent of policy statements. Procedures provide a set of detailed steps needed to accomplish a specific task. Each workflow will require its own procedures. Depending on the resource type, procedures may follow a different set of steps.

The California State Polytechnic University worked with GOBI Library Services to create a set of MARC records for a demand-driven acquisitions (DDA) implementation of an ebrary collection. Significant efforts were made to avoid duplication from the library's existing holdings in the DDA record set. Local customization of the records was needed to facilitate management of the DDA and to avoid the interruption of existing workflows in the library.

The University of Chicago launched a project to participate in the Library of Congress's RDA Test and implement the new cataloging rules, Resource Description and Access (RDA), in most of the cataloging units. This included a retrofit of their data elements for the library catalog in order to accommodate RDA requirements. This project helps lay a foundation for additional uses of library metadata, including linked data initiatives.

The University of Illinois at Chicago implemented a project to improve the quality of vendor-supplied metadata for the Springer e-book collection sets. The project highlighted the shift from single-record editing of MARC records to a batch process of whole record replacement for the maintenance of the metadata. Their work included the use of an off-line tool for editing MARC records.

A related project at Iowa State University to train cataloging staff in creating non-MARC metadata for digital collections was of interest for its efforts to document and track metadata workflows. Their project describes the need to provide training geared to managing metadata for current use, but also for developing uses. Familiarity with markup languages, and an understanding of how MARC and non-MARC metadata are used in discovery platforms, were identified as potential learning outcomes.

A study by Boydston and Leysen reviewed the role of catalog librarians in Association of Research Libraries (ARL) libraries and provided more in-depth information about their increasing responsibilities for non-MARC metadata. These responsibilities include managing additional formats such as streaming media and data sets. Some respondents commented that there appeared to be a shift in responsibilities from metadata creation to metadata management.

North Carolina State University played a lead role in the implementation of the Global Open Knowledgebase. This is a community-managed knowledge base for electronic journals and e-books. It was designed to import data from other sources and allow routine maintenance. GOKb helps to reduce duplication of effort for vendors and libraries by providing an open environment for electronic resource management (ERM) metadata.

■ ■ ■

CASE STUDIES

THE UNIVERSITY OF HOUSTON

The University of Houston has for a number of years experimented with finding a better organizational fit for electronic resources management. Electronic Resources was at one time a separate department within the Public Services division. Later, it became a unit in several departments, first in collection management, next it moved to acquisitions, and then to cataloging. In 2011 it appeared that the electronic resources unit was headed to becoming a separate department again. However, our required skill set for the electronic resources librarian had grown to include an increasing technology and library systems related focus. The library tried to recruit a candidate for this position; however, they were not able to find a candidate to meet the new position requirements. As a result, some reorganization and repurposing of positions was implemented. The electronic resources unit merged into the ILS department to create a new department. The Resource Discovery Systems Department included the ILS, discovery system, and electronic resources functions. Over time, some of the unit's technology and troubleshooting duties were absorbed by other members of the department with similar responsibilities.

ERM Tools

The University of Houston has deployed a number of commercial systems and local tools to manage electronic resources. These products and services are focused on specific functional areas: Serials Solutions 360 Resource Manager, EBSCO Usage Consolidation, numerous spreadsheets, project management software (Basecamp), link resolvers, a local A-Z database listing, Innovative Interfaces' Sierra Integrated Library System, and our intranet-based electronic resources license repository (ERLR).

The Serials Solutions 360 Suite was our first major initiative for the management of electronic resources. We implemented Serials Solutions in the 2007/2008 academic year. Our early concerns were about the portability of the data we were about to begin creating. Populating Serials Solutions with our local data was a slow process to populate the data. In order to make Serials Solutions a routine part of the daily workflow, we needed to outline key functional tasks and determine which department would be in the best position to handle these responsibilities. A major portion of the work would need to be done by support staff. We began by flowcharting numerous tasks to eventually arrive at a general workflow that was tied to the functional areas supported in Serials Solutions

360 Resource Manager. Additional workflows would be needed for acquisitions and licensing. The end result was a color-coded document with flowcharts for various tasks. The color codes were used to represent a department or unit in the technical services area. Years later many portions of the workflow are still in use. Over time additional workflows have been created as new formats such as streaming media and data sets have been acquired.

Additional tools are included in our electronic resources workflow. About two years ago, the EBSCO Usage Consolidation product was acquired as a replacement for Serials Solutions 360 COUNTER. The EBSCO interface is favored by our public services librarians for its ability to create graphical representations of usage data. Recently, we expanded our use of the product to include more resources in our subscription. Spreadsheets continue to be used for various tasks. Collection development projects, cost comparisons, usage data, trials for new resources, and the tracking of new or changed resources are often spreadsheet-intensive activities.

We also rely on a project management service called Basecamp. It is a critical tool for both our Collection Management Committee (CMC) meetings and for our Electronic Resources Management Team (ERMT). Meeting agendas, minutes, and spreadsheets are uploaded to help keep everyone in the loop on the monthly activities. Basecamp is also useful for messaging group members for a quick decision and providing links for documentation about issues.

While we use the Serials Solutions A-Z list for e-journals, for databases we have developed a local A-Z database listing. It is populated from data fields in the OPAC MARC record. The list is refreshed overnight with a daily extract. For licensing data we created an intranet site, the ERLR, to provide access to PDF versions of our license agreements. Additional information on the ERLR will be included in the discussion on ERM metadata.

Over the years we have used several link resolvers: EBSCO, Serials Solutions, and SFX. Recently we selected a link resolver based on the discovery system we implemented. Our experience with a previous discovery system was that problems described as "discovery system issues" were in fact link resolver issues. One difference we discovered with SFX was that with individual resources it is able to handle volume-specific information rather than only the date.

It would not be surprising to question the number of platforms we are currently using. It was a process that did not happen overnight. The members of our CMC and ERMT have long been frustrated with the limitations and support for some of these products. Perhaps we have followed a mindset that our library is its own silo, rather than approaching electronic resources management as a challenge for all libraries. No single library can solve all of the problems of electronic resources on its own. Arriving at better solutions will require a collaborative effort that will depend heavily on the efforts of product working groups, professional associations, and technical standards task forces on a national and international level.

ER Functions Move to the Systems Division

About five years ago electronic resources management became a part of the Systems Division in our library at the University of Houston. The electronic resources unit was merged into the ILS Department to create a new Resource Discovery Systems (RDS) Department. This was the result of a desire to increase the technology requirements for electronic resources librarians. It had become very difficult to recruit for those positions. Consequently, the chemistry seemed right to include management of electronic resources, the integrated library system, and the discovery system in the same department. We found that some of the functions in place within RDS and other departments in the Systems Division could be applied to electronic resources. As an example, we subscribe to a service for monitoring system downtime on library-supported websites. We soon began adding new or problematic electronic resources platforms to the monitoring service. This allowed us to track platform outages and gather statistics on platform availability for use at the time of renewals, or as documentation to submit to the vendor for troubleshooting. Within the new department, it was easier to collaborate on website or intranet projects targeting electronic resources functions. After a couple of years, the responsibilities for the EZproxy server were moved into the RDS Department. By sending staff to EZproxy pre-conferences we were able to develop more in-depth expertise in EZproxy configuration.

Under the new department structure, communications about the electronic resources workflow became more important. This led us to the creation of the Electronic Resources Management Team. The team's membership includes key department heads and coordinators directly involved in the electronic resources workflow. The team is designed to function as the workflow component of the Collection Management Committee. In this way, decisions can be made about a workflow for a specific purchase. At this point, the licensing process can be started if it was not begun during the product trial period. The team also gathers information about the availability of MARC records and any additional metadata requirements. When records are not available from Serials Solutions and we must rely on a vendor-provided record set, an investigation of available customization options is begun. Questions about the distribution of the records will be discussed: is it a subscription that is updated monthly, are records available for deleted titles (to expedite maintenance of the collection set), are the records available on a website or FTP site, do we need a log-in to access the records for download, what is the anticipated time line for access by patrons, and does a faculty member need access ASAP? These and other related topics are discussed in meetings of the ERMT.

MARC Record Batch Loads

We have relied on several methods for management of the metadata for electronic resources. In the early days of vendor record sets we turned to the MarcEdit (http://marcedit.reeset.net) software developed by Terry Reese to customize the MARC records. With MarcEdit the library can customize records in a batch process in order to prepare them for upload into the local catalog. When editing of the records was completed, they generally did not require any additional modifications by staff or librarians within the local catalog. At the time, most record sets came "as is" without any customization.

MARC records supplied by Serials Solutions MARC 360 and Link 360 Ebooks provide some customization options. Their MARC records can be uploaded into the local catalog using the default load table in the Sierra ILS. It is important to add metadata for tracking record sets by the name of the collection or vendor. This makes it easier to discern record sets by the same vendor, but also for a different campus or library in our shared local catalog. Sometimes the bibliographic records consist of only brief descriptions with little or no authority control of name headings.

Some vendors provide records through a third party for any customization options that may be required. Occasionally there is an added cost to the library for the customization, but it is usually worth the effort in the long run. Records for newer formats such as streaming media and data sets may lack data fields such as record number or source of records, and do not allow routine batch loads without additional work by the library. I recall a time when it was said that if a vendor told you they offered "free MARC records" you ran the other way; it would surely mean that record loading was going to be a time-consuming project. Fortunately, times have changed for the better. It is now only the occasional new vendor on the market that requires an adjustment period to bring their MARC record sets up to customer expectations.

Streaming-media MARC record sets are still a work in progress. Vendors are not currently able to provide any library-specific data elects to help libraries streamline the batch load process. We have found that this is a key factor for us when making a decision about creating a new load table in the ILS to upload vendor records. It is time-consuming to create a new load table for every vendor. With additional load tables being created, we increase the risk of loading a MARC record file with the wrong load table. When this happens the entire record set must be deleted, and then be uploaded again with the correct load table.

Our best practices for adding electronic resource MARC records is to check for their availability in Serials Solutions 360. If not available there, then team members are on notice that providing access in the local catalog may take a longer time to implement than usual.

ERM Metadata

We have installed CORAL to investigate using it for trials of new materials being considered for the collection. It also provides a platform to investigate migrating ERM data from other platforms and perhaps some of our licensing data from our ERLR intranet site. Some recent releases of CORAL look very promising for ingesting data from other sources. We have also installed a sandbox server for CORAL in case we go into a production environment for trials on the main server. We want to further investigate the data input and output options of this ERM tool.

Another project we would like to move ahead with is to refresh our instance of SFX from Serials Solutions output files. Serials Solutions is our main link resolver. We will look at how feasible it is to support two link resolvers and to keep both in sync. We are concerned about any consequences for the user experience in Primo.

Electronic Resources License Repository

Initially, we used Serials Solutions to manage out licensing agreements. We found that the time required to input licensing data became more difficult to sustain, so instead we created an intranet site called the ERLR. A core set of data elements for the ERLR was determined based on feedback from members of the ERMT, and the interlibrary loan (ILL) staff. Data elements such as terms of use information, ILL privileges, Blackboard linking, and vendor cancellation policy were included in separate data fields. We are considering adding an option for text mining, and any additional limitations. The drawback to the ERLR is that we are only able to search by vendor rather than by the resource.

The data fields included in the ERLR database were based on the following questions from internal users:

- What are the title of the resource and the name of the provider?
- Is this resource a database, journal, or e-book?
- Does the vendor provide usage statistics on a regular basis? If so, are they COUNTER-compliant?
- According to the license agreement, who is authorized to access the licensed material (i.e., faculty, staff, students, walk-ins)?
- What is the number of concurrent users that the license allows for one resource, or when shared across one interface?
- Is this resource part of a consortium agreement?
- Is scholarly sharing allowed? Are the licensee (and other authorized users) permitted to share a portion of the licensed material, in print or electronic form, with a third party that is not an authorized user?
- Does the licensee have the right to share the licensed material via ILL in the form of printed copies or fax transmissions (print) and/or by way of secure electronic transmission?
- Do the licensee (and other authorized users) have the right to make and store print and/or electronic copies for purposes of course instruction?
- Do the licensee (and other authorized users) have the right to use licensed materials in print and/or electronic collections compiled by faculty for classroom purposes?
- Do the licensee (and other authorized users) have the right to store licensed materials on a web server-based software package for educational use that enables faculty and staff to post course materials on a secure network server?
- Does the licensee have the right to perpetual access to the licensed material after the license has terminated?
- Does the licensee have the right to terminate access to a licensed resource during a contract period?
- Are there any other restrictions of use stated in the license agreement that are not covered in the questions above?
- Does the institution or licensee have the right to archive an article that is pre-refereed?
- Does the institution or licensee have the right to archive an article that is post-refereed?
- Are there additional resources associated with the license?
- Are there any additional notes related to this resource?

The corresponding ERLR data elements include:

Title
Provider
Resource Type
Usage Statistics Available (if so, COUNTER-compliant?)
Authorized Users
Simultaneous Users
Consortium Agreement
Scholarly Sharing
Is ILL Allowed (in print, secure electronic, e-mail)?
Are Course Reserves Allowed (in print, electronic, e-reserves)?
Are Course Packs Allowed (in print, electronic)?
Can You Put Content on Blackboard?
Perpetual Access
Cancellation Policy
Other Restrictions
Preprint Allowed
Post-Print Allowed
Other Resources
Notes
Attachment: PDF Copy of License Agreement

THE UNIVERSITY OF CALIFORNIA IRVINE

Lisa Mackinder is head of electronic resources and serials acquisitions at the University of California Irvine (UCI). She advocates for workflow documentation as a key component of electronic resources management. Mackinder describes workflows as "overarching directives." These directives help guide the work ahead and provide a reference point for decisions that may need to be made along the way. The Techniques for Electronic Resource Management (TERMS)[1] "project is important in that it aims to gather and disseminate best practices for managing electronic resources through their lifecycle."[2] While workflow implementation may vary from library to library, TERMS provides a framework to better understand the electronic resources (ER) life cycle. The workflows are designed to help manage the ER life cycle. At UCI the ER life cycle consists of several workflows: new acquisitions, activation, cataloging, maintaining access, troubleshooting, and evaluation. (It may occur to the reader that licensing warrants a separate workflow, but including a negotiation in the workflow diagram might prove to be a challenging task.)[3]

Circumstances may suggest a need to drill deeper into the workflow, and create a separate workflow within a workflow. This can result in additional complexity, but there must be a way to create flexibility in our procedures. Our activation and cancellation procedures take "the type of resource into account, and lead staff down different roads, and into different systems, based on whether the 'task' is affecting the entire package, a single title, or a database." Usually, "procedures are often determined by the systems in place and can include precise system-based directions."[4]

Mackinder advocates the following principles in distinguishing between policy, procedures, and workflows:

- Policy decisions determine the form a workflow will take
- The workflow should outline the guidelines to be followed in the procedures that pertain to it
- Workflows should be system-agnostic and bridge the gap between policy and procedure[5]

The daily work is all about the details, and often there are many details in our procedures. Over time these workflows will change, but at a much slower rate than our daily procedures. The documentation of procedures and the maintenance of documentation are a continuous challenge. Procedures are where we include the step-by-step process for tasks we expect to complete. A number of factors influence the types of tasks that are appropriate with individual resources or resource types. Changes in technology, the publisher marketplace, and fluctuations in staffing are factors that are often beyond the control of the library manager, but they can result in a revision of procedures and documentation.

CALIFORNIA STATE POLYTECHNIC UNIVERSITY

Wendolyn C. Vermeer is the metadata librarian at California State Polytechnic University in Pomona, California. She describes a pilot project for demand-driven acquisitions (DDA) of electronic books. DDA is also referred to as patron-driven acquisitions (PDA).

A frequent model for DDA includes uploading a large collection of vendor-supplied MARC records into the library catalog. DDA titles are individually ordered and purchased when triggered by the library's preestablished patron usage threshold. There were several reasons for implementing a DDA project. Most importantly, Cal Poly Pomona's annual statistics indicated a decline in the circulation of print materials, while online usage statistics were growing exponentially.

Perhaps the diverse research needs of the library patrons provided one reason for the shift in usage from print to electronic resources. Yet another factor helping to escalate electronic resource usage was the library's recent implementation of a discovery system, which by its nature provides increased exposure for electronic content. There was initial apprehension that the project would siphon off or replace funding for bibliographer selection of electronic books. Instead, the rationale for the project was to help maximize the return on a declining pool of monographic collection development dollars.[6]

The library DDA team worked closely with YBP Library Services (YBP) to develop an acquisitions and cataloging workflow for the project. There were two reasons in particular why ebrary was chosen for the project. Library staff had indicated that the administrator interface for the DDA account within the ebrary platform was easy to learn and use. Secondly, a review of their MARC records determined "that enough quality metadata was provided in the ebrary-supplied vendor records for effective discoverability and recall by users."[7] The MARC record file for the DDA titles, available for patron browsing and selection, is called the discovery record set. Ebrary was able to customize these records for the library, including the 856 field (URL).

After the records were uploaded into the library catalog, a library-supplied code was added to each record. This would help the library exclude these titles from the new acquisitions statistics, and the monthly authority control headings report. It is usually not cost-effective to provide authority control maintenance for DDA records until a title has been triggered for purchase. Additional modifications of the records included suppressing the Library of Congress call number from public view in the library catalog. University of California Irvine decided to change the call number field from an 050 or 090 field to an 070 field. This step removes the indexing from the call number field but retains the call number in an unindexed field that will not display in the patron view of the library catalog. When a DDA purchase is triggered, by a patron, the library receives another full MARC record for the e-book, but with the addition of electronic invoicing, and with order record data included. The goal is to handle these DDA records as little as possible.

The duplication of titles in the DDA profile with the library's existing collection was something the project team wanted to avoid. The YBP implementation procedures included an option to address this problem. YBP requested a list of International Standard Book Numbers (ISBNs) from the library. The list would identify existing holdings and help reduce duplication. The library exported a file from the library catalog with the ISBN data. Extraneous and duplicate data in the ISBN field required a significant effort to reformat the data for upload to YBP. An elaborate cleanup routine for the ISBN data was devised that included using macros and other spreadsheet tools to expedite the file preparation. Despite this effort, some duplication of existing holdings was found later due to the multiple "silos" and knowledge bases that maintain the library's metadata (such as the ILS, YBP, OCLC, and other vendors). These systems are not always in sync and may require manual updating. Various methods used for detecting the duplication of DDA titles were cumbersome and time-consuming. Another problem was noticed after implementation of the project: a subject selector searching for a specific title received an error message indicating that the e-book was no longer available for DDA purchase. Upon further investigation by project staff, they "found that several hundred titles had seemingly dropped out of the DDA pool with no notification." After consultation with the vendor, it was determined that the best approach in the future was to delete all the discovery records and upload a complete and up-to-date MARC record set. "The DDA acquisitions workflow remains fluid and changeable." It has become apparent that the "mass management of records in a static local catalog" will remain a challenge.[8]

In a more hopeful development for the future, Vermeer mentions that the California State University Library system is moving ahead with implementation of Ex Libris's Alma, a next-generation library management system. It is possible that with Structured Query Language (SQL) queries, metadata that is not easily retrievable from the ILS will be more easily found in a library system like Alma.

THE UNIVERSITY OF CHICAGO

Christopher Cronin was director of metadata and cataloging services at the University of Chicago Library. He discussed their experiences leading to the adoption of the new cataloging code RDA at the library. The initial implementation of RDA began when the library was selected to participate in the U.S. National Libraries' RDA Test held from October to December 2010. They launched an enterprising plan to include all original catalogers in the RDA Test. They began by identifying key areas to address in their implementation plan. These included staffing, updating policies and procedures for RDA purposes, preparing the ILS for RDA metadata fields, integrating AACR2 and RDA records and their display in the library catalog, vendor-sourced authority control, contract cataloging procedures, and RDA implementation costs.[9]

RDA training for staff was preceded by an introduction to the Functional Requirements for Bibliographic Records (FRBR). "RDA is organized and structured around FRBR, and uses the same terminology."[10] It is recommended that organizations creating authority headings also include training on the Functional Requirements for Authority Data (FRAD). Looking back at their training, Cronin states that it would have been a good idea to spend additional time on FRBR before beginning the RDA training.

When preparing the ILS to receive RDA metadata, the library should consider the level of expertise it has available to implement the changes in MARC formats for bibliographic and authority records. Some ILS vendors provide local administrators with access to make the system RDA-ready, while others may rely on the library to submit a service request before beginning work on the changes. Some changes need to be made to the library catalog display for the General Material Designation (GMD), and 33X fields. Discussions in the library were held to help determine if the GMD and 33X would be displayed. While the GMD would not be included in original RDA cataloging, it could be present in existing records. While several options are available for handling the GMD, no change is required for existing AACR2 records.

A library's procedure for reviewing authority control headings and for managing vendor-supplied services might need to be adapted or modified. Name Authority Cooperative Program libraries should investigate new requirements for the coding of original RDA authority records. Some optional elements will also be up for consideration. Vendors may need more time to assess the needs of the marketplace before they are comfortable in moving ahead on various stages of RDA implementation. Copy catalogers will be alternating between RDA and AACR2 records, but they will need to learn to spot errors or omissions when revising records for copy cataloging.

The University of Chicago Library contributed over 2,500 bibliographic and authority records for the RDA Test. This was far more than was expected for the participants. Based on the results of this experience and what was learned during the RDA Test, a decision to continue with RDA cataloging for most of the library's original cataloging was made. Great care was taken to follow the Program for Cooperative Cataloging (PCC) requirements and adapt policies and procedures to incorporate RDA into their workflow. After the testing period, catalog librarians who were adding the 37X fields into authority records could begin to visualize what library data in the semantic web might look like. This provided a glimpse of how Uniform Resource Identifiers (URIs) would support linked data projects in the future. Cronin believes that "it is these URIs, these linked data—not the literals and display values that we currently encode—that represent our data future, our data imperative. The benefits of RDA cannot and will not be realized until we can create an infrastructure that supports this functionality, and we invest in the continuing education of catalogers who will need to make the transition."[11] Cronin, commenting on issues to be addressed after RDA is widely adopted, said: "Linked data, linked data, linked data. The international effort to move us out of MARC and into a next generation data infrastructure is key not just to the success of RDA, but more importantly to the enduring success and value of library-related data more generally. Our catalogs cannot continue to be silos of 'library-use-only' metadata if we are to survive and thrive in the larger data landscape."[12]

UNIVERSITY OF ILLINOIS AT CHICAGO

Batch processing of MARC records has become a significant production factor in the cataloging of electronic resources for our libraries. Kristin E. Martin, metadata librarian, and Kavita Mundle, assistant catalog librarian, both at the University of Illinois at Chicago (UIC), detail their experiences managing the Springer e-book collection sets. They also discuss the methods and tools used to improve the quality of vendor-supplied MARC records in their consortium environment.

They explain how, in 2006, the PCC issued guidelines for the cataloging of e-books that treat an e-book as if it were a reproduction of a print publication.[13] Each vendor's e-book would require its own MARC record with a corresponding 533 field reproduction note. Before long, these vendor-specific e-book reproduction records came to be regarded as an undesired duplication. In 2009 the PCC issued new e-book guidelines that would instead create a single generic record, which would be provider-neutral.[14] The PCC also issued a publication intended for vendors producing the cataloging for aggregator MARC records.[15] This publication encouraged vendors to follow the new guidelines and create provider-neutral records.

These significant developments signaled a shift from single-record editing to whole-record replacement as the standard method used for updating electronic resources metadata. MARC record sets in the library catalog were then more likely to be updated in a batch process. Serial Solutions 360 MARC and Ex Libris MARCit! are two MARC record services that are able to track changes in e-book and e-journal holdings for the library. Previously, updating individual records manually had been the norm in most libraries. Batch uploads and batch updates of MARC records in the library catalog became more common. ILS functionality for batch updates was limited, but some vendors offered an upgrade option. The ILS needed the ability to update individual fields when entire record replacements were not required. Some vendor systems refer to this functionality as rapid update and global update. While this was an improvement for the batch editing function, it was only available for specific fields and often required that batch updates use exact matching of metadata descriptors and formatting.

The project case study "describes how the UIC Library, working with the CIC CLI (hereafter CLI), evaluated and improved vendor-supplied MARC records for Springer e-books and then worked with the Consortium of Academic and Research Libraries of Illinois (CARLI) to load those records into the UIC Library catalog."[16] The Springer e-book collection was a purchase made by the Center for Library Initiatives through a partnership with the Committee of Institutional Cooperation, a consortium representing the Big Ten universities and the University of Chicago.

Their project to analyze MARC record sets was greatly facilitated by the use of the MarcEdit software. MarcEdit was used to extract and review metadata at the individual field level and for batch edits to prepare MARC record files for upload into the library catalog. The ability of MarcEdit to export MARC record fields to a tab-delimited file provided a critical tool for analyzing record quality. Problems with incorrect or missing URLs were found, as well as broken links due to platform issues that the vendor would need to resolve. Many records lacked recent authority control updates. Access points contained errors that would need to be manually corrected after records were uploaded. Providing access to individual volumes for multivolume sets was also problematic with the inconsistent numbering patterns found. Of significant concern were data irregularities with record number fields, vendor control number fields, and ISBN fields; these presented potential record overlay problems and would need to be addressed prior to uploading into the library catalog. A comment from one participant regarding vendor-supplied MARC records was that "the 'free' records ended up being quite expensive." Significant revision was required to update the metadata for accuracy and quality control purposes.[17]

This project served to create a shared sense of responsibility between the members of the consortium and the e-book vendor to provide reliable access to a large collection of licensed content. Their combined effort was a major step forward to streamline the introduction of the Springer content into the library catalog and to help prevent user frustration by faculty and student researchers.

IOWA STATE UNIVERSITY

Kelly J. Thompson, metadata management and cataloging librarian at Iowa State University, relates her experiences with an assignment to train catalogers to create non-MARC metadata for digital collections and institutional repository collections. While this project does not specifically pertain to electronic resources metadata, there are some lessons that can be learned from their experiences. Aside from the training exercise, some preliminary training was needed on using spreadsheets to format data, file management strategies, reviewing or creating documentation, and constructing workflows based on concepts familiar to the department or library. Documenting these procedures became an iterative process to include additional updates and ongoing refinements. Creating documentation that would help keep project team members on the same page was a goal that was often not reached on the first attempt.[18]

Thompson suggests some prerequisites for staff that would be useful prior to the non-MARC training. These include a background or knowledge in markup languages, familiarity with the library's discovery platforms, an understanding of how metadata can be created or managed independently of the individual MARC record, and a review and discussion about definitions for a project's vocabulary. Finding a workflow management procedure that works for your library is not always an easy task. Before long, the spreadsheet became the standard method for tracking workflows and project status. One of the project strategies used was to adapt the non-MARC metadata procedures to parallel the existing MARC record procedures. This proved to be a useful practice to help reduce the anxiety that most participants in the project were experiencing.

While the focus of this project was metadata creation for digital collections, it yielded some useful advice about staff training and the library project management process.

ARL Cataloger Librarian Roles

In 2014 Jeanne M. K. Boydston, emeritus associate professor, and Joan M. Leysen, e-resources cataloging coordinator, both at Iowa State University, conducted a study to review the current and future roles of ARL catalog librarians. When surveyed about the types of materials that were currently being cataloged, it was not surprising to learn from respondents that print resources were being cataloged by 100 percent of participants, followed next by electronic resources at 93.8 percent. In this study, electronic resources included websites, databases, electronic dissertations, and documents in Portable Document Format (PDF).

Additional types of material cataloged included media materials at 90.6 percent, electronic books at 83.9 percent, and electronic journals at 80.6 percent.[19]

Over half of the respondents mentioned that new types of materials had been added to their cataloging responsibilities in the previous two years. Streaming media, electronic books, and special collections formats were the most cited responses. There were several mentions of batch processing and editing of vendor-supplied MARC record sets, electronic theses and dissertations, PDF documents, government documents, and cartographic materials in print and electronic formats.[20]

The findings suggest that the cataloging of electronic resources and local or unique digital collections is taking on a greater focus. The addition of non-MARC metadata responsibilities has become more prevalent in libraries. Some catalogers view their role as shifting in focus from metadata creation to data management. A significant increase in vendor-supplied MARC records from multiple vendors and authority control services has also increased the amount of time catalogers are spending on the maintenance of batch processes.

Respondents indicated they had participated in training on numerous topics over the preceding two years, and particularly on emerging technologies, such as RDA/FRBR, library services platforms, discovery systems, linked data and the semantic web, XML and other markup languages, data curation, and relational database systems such as Oracle. Managing a larger number of resource types and a heavier volume of vendor-supplied MARC records are factors that may call for additional skill sets for catalog librarians.[21]

Individual respondents to the study mentioned that future cataloger librarians would need data management skills and should be able to work with MARC record batch files. Others have commented that "cataloger librarians should be able to work with interoperable systems, web-scale discovery tools, digital repositories and resources."[22] More specialized skill sets for markup languages, SQL, and Perl scripting were also listed in respondent comments for future cataloger librarian responsibilities. Boydston and Leysen also state the importance of training on the following topics: Virtual International Authority File (VIAF), Bibliographic Framework Initiative (BIBFRAME), semantic web, and linked data for cataloger librarians.

NORTH CAROLINA STATE UNIVERSITY

"The Global Open Knowledgebase (GOKb) is a project to develop and maintain a freely available repository of metadata that describes electronic journals and books using a community-managed approach."[23]

North Carolina State University (NCSU) was the lead partner of the GOKb project, which was funded chiefly by a grant from the Andrew W. Mellon Foundation. Additional partners since the start of the project in 2012 were Kuali Open Library Environment (OLE) and Jisc Collections. The early objectives were to create a data model, determine a set of data elements, expose the metadata with application programming interfaces (APIs), and develop functionality to support the import of metadata from other sources and routine maintenance.

"GOKb was initially conceived as a Knowledgebase to support e-resources management in Kuali OLE, an open source library management system."[24] It was also important for the GOKb project to develop a model for tracking e-resource changes over time. This includes title changes, publisher changes, and potentially platform changes.

While traditional models limit community management of the knowledge base to its customers, GOKb data are available in an open environment that has the potential to reduce the duplication of maintenance for individual vendor platforms.

The NCSU library was responsible for uploading and maintaining the GOKb data. A team was formed to test uploading one of Elsevier's e-journal packages. OpenRefine, an open-source data manipulation tool, was used to ingest the data into the knowledge base. Project partners were encouraged to target their activity to packages that would address local needs.

The GOKb project was tasked to develop workflows and the documentation for creating and maintaining contributed metadata. Project teams were interested in developing a workflow and documentation that could be used or adapted by other GOKb partners. NCSU was also investigating additional contributions to the project—beyond what most partners would expect to offer.

A second phase of the grant proposal was interested in publishing GOKb metadata as linked data. This would create the opportunity for GOKb to connect to other linked data sets published on the Web. GOKb's web application includes linked data targets such as the Virtual International Authority, the Library of Congress Linked Data Service, the International Standard Number Identifier, and others. "The data model uses many properties from existing linked data vocabularies, such as Simple Knowledge Organization

System (SKOS), RDF Schema, Friend of a Friend (FOAF), Dublin Core, and BIBFRAME."[25] Additional properties can be created when existing properties are not sufficient for describing data for GOKb.

PERSPECTIVES ON ELECTRONIC RESOURCES MANAGEMENT

Improved library systems are being developed to enhance electronic resources management and workflows. These new systems will go a long way to increase the quality of our metadata and services for our patrons.

In our present environment, the use of spreadsheets for e-resources is fairly common in libraries. Maria Collins is head of acquisitions and discovery at North Carolina State University in Raleigh; she proposes that electronic resources management "should be seen as a core function in libraries." These processes must be streamlined and made workflow-specific in order to help reduce costs and exceptions to workflows. "In addition, staff need to transition from production-oriented tasks to problem solving tasks" in their work with electronic resources. "Creating scalability in processes requires eliminating silos, creating community-supported knowledge bases, and identifying best practices among publishers and librarians." Libraries need to move away from workflows that are not sustainable by our library systems.[26]

Dawn Hale is head of technical services at Johns Hopkins University in Baltimore, Maryland. He says that in our current environment "stand-alone systems require efforts to populate and manage a separate knowledge base, which then needs to be synchronized with the integrated library system (ILS), link resolver, proxy server, and discovery layer(s). The fairly recent introduction of web-scale systems has eliminated some of these redundancies and integrated the knowledge base with other services such as acquisitions, cataloging, and discovery, resulting in many opportunities to streamline workflows. In addition, the interoperability of book jobbers and subscription agent systems with web-scale e-resource management integrates the selection" of library materials. Hale further states that libraries need to break "free of localized conventions" and utilize collective expertise at the network level in order to provide services that meet user needs.[27]

Andrew Pace is executive director of networked library services at OCLC in Dublin, Ohio. He describes OCLC's WorldShare Management Services (WMS) as an example of an electronic resource management system (ERMS) that focuses on six key functions: materials selection, acquisitions, description, discovery, access, and renewal. The WMS knowledge base supports community data management, which allows individual libraries and other content partners to contribute and edit content for use by other libraries.

CONCLUSION

For many years, libraries have endeavored to find solutions for improving electronic resources management and the underlying metadata that describes our collections. Each library's approach has been unique, influenced by organizational structures, available management tools, the level of staffing, and the strengths and talents of individuals participating in the electronic resources life cycle. Many important contributions are being made in the field of electronic resources management, but often these solutions are only realized in a single library.

In reflecting on our own experiences at the University of Houston, I wonder if perhaps we now need to circle back to rely more heavily on our ERMS or next-generation solutions. We have explored and implemented a number of add-on solutions. I will admit to working with several systems cobbled together to try to reach beyond the limits of our primary ERM. I am beginning to think of these add-ons as patches. They address specific needs, but are they really part of the bigger solution?

These many individual library efforts have provided valuable improvements to electronic resources management and are helping to set a direction for our library management systems that will support the work of electronic resources librarians.

The work of creating metadata for electronic resources continues to evolve, and significant progress has been made by libraries and vendors alike. At times partnerships with vendors have been formed. When the library community needed to update cataloging procedures, a new set of guidelines was crafted for the vendor participants by library professional groups, library organizations, and the Library of Congress. The result was a structure that encouraged vendors to adopt these library best practices.

Unfortunately, electronic resources metadata creation cannot be single-sourced. Out of necessity, vendors have played a major role in metadata creation, revision, and maintenance. Libraries have stepped up to help fill in the gaps for the smaller vendors that lack the ability to supply their own metadata. Libraries have found several ways to accomplish this task, ranging from creating bibliographic records to requesting customization options from vendors and creating ILS-specific customizations.

Maintaining bibliographic records for electronic collections has become a major challenge due to the growing volume of content that libraries are acquiring, and also due to the frequent updating that methods of access require. Libraries rely on services like 360 MARC to keep track of these frequent changes to collection set content. Batch updating of bibliographic records is scheduled on a weekly, biweekly, or monthly basis. Smaller vendors have discovered that libraries not only expect monthly files of new titles, but also monthly files of deleted titles. The magnitude of records that are updated each month is beyond what any library can manage on a record-by-record basis. Vendor-supplied files of bibliographic records for deleted or expired titles allow libraries to automate the deletion process.

I hear librarians discussing their library's project to evaluate the new library management systems in order to determine the best fit for their organization. Are we missing the point of migrating to a new system? Is our goal simply to retrofit the new system platform in order to replicate the library's existing policies and procedures? If so, are we limiting functional improvements based on the library's existing practices?

The development of community-managed knowledge bases is a very promising approach for the maintenance of an expanding volume of collection sets, e-books, and other resources that are now taking a major portion of our acquisitions budget. Community-managed knowledge bases allow vendors and libraries to continue the work that needs to be done, but now more of our users will benefit from this combined effort. At present libraries are primarily contributing to a specific vendor-supported knowledge base, or perhaps to the open knowledgebase (GOKb).

In conversation with a colleague at a recent conference, our discussion turned to metadata maintenance of electronic resources and the benefits of a community-managed Knowledge base. Surprisingly, he became alarmed at the thought of the library not owning its metadata. I had reasoned that since we don't own most of our electronic collections, why would we want to own the metadata? It was perhaps a reminder that some ideas require more time for buy-in. I believe that libraries can be more successful in electronic resources management if they work towards the greater good. No single library or even a statewide consortium can meet the many demands of providing access to electronic resources. Libraries must be part of a larger initiative to combine our efforts at the national level, and preferably even at the international level.

NOTES

1. "TERMS: Techniques for Electronic Resource Management," https://library.hud.ac.uk/blogs/terms/.
2. Lisa Mackinder, "The Seemingly Endless Challenge: Workflows," *Serials Librarian* 67, no. 2 (2014): 160, doi:10.1080/0361526X.2014.940481.
3. Ibid., 158–60.
4. Ibid., 159–60.
5. Ibid., 159.
6. Wendolyn C. Vermeer, "Evolving Technical Services Workflows in a Demand-Driven Acquisitions Pilot," *Serials Librarian* 69, no. 3/4 (2015): 298–308, doi:10.1080/0361526X.2015.1118719.
7. Ibid., 302.
8. Ibid., 308.
9. Christopher Cronin, "From Testing to Implementation: Managing Full-Scale RDA Adoption at the University of Chicago," *Cataloging & Classification Quarterly* 49, no. 7/8 (2011): 626–46, doi:10.1080/01639374.2011.616263.
10. Ibid., 631.
11. Ibid., 643.
12. Eric Hanson and Bonnie Parks, "RDA Training and Implementation at the University of Chicago: An Interview with Christopher Cronin," *Serials Review* 39, no. 2 (2013): 136–40, doi:10.1016/j.serrev.2013.04.012.
13. Program for Cooperative Cataloging, "MARC Record Guide for Monograph Aggregator Vendors," 2006, www.loc.gov/aba/pcc/documents/vendorguiderevised.pdf.
14. Becky Culbertson, Yael Mandelstam, and George Prager, *Provider-Neutral E-Monograph MARC Record Guide* (Washington, DC: Program for Cooperative Cataloging, 2009), www.loc.gov/aba/pcc/bibco/documents/PN-Guide.pdf.
15. Program for Cooperative Cataloging, *MARC Record Guide for Monograph Aggregator Vendors,* 2nd ed., prepared by Becky Culbertson et al. (Washington, DC: Program for Cooperative Cataloging, 2009), www.loc.gov/aba/pcc/sca/documents/FinalVendorGuide.pdf.
16. Kristin E. Martin and Kavita Mundle, "Notes on Operations: Cataloging E-Books and Vendor Records: A Case Study at the University of Illinois at Chicago," *Library Resources & Technical Services* 54, no. 4 (2010): 230.
17. Ibid., 235.
18. Kelly J. Thompson, "What If I Break It? Project Management for Intergenerational Library Teams Creating Non-MARC Metadata," *Code4lib Journal* 28, no. 1 (2015), http://journal.code4lib.org/articles/10395.
19. Jeanne M. K. Boydston and Joan M. Leysen, "ARL Cataloger Librarian Roles and Responsibilities Now and in the Future," *Cataloging & Classification Quarterly* 52, no. 2 (2014): 235–36, doi:10.1080/01639374.2013.859199.

20. Ibid., 237–38.
21. Ibid., 239.
22. Ibid., 243.
23. Eric M. Hanson, Xiaoyan Song, and Kristen Wilson, "Managing Serials Data as a Community: Partnering with the Global Open Knowledgebase (GOKb)," *Serials Review* 41, no. 3 (2015): 146, doi:10.1080/00987913.2015.1064853.
24. Ibid., 147.
25. Ibid., 151.
26. Jill Fluvog et al., "Meeting the E-Resources Challenge through Collaboration: An OCLC Perspective on Effective Management, Access, and Delivery of Electronic Collections," *Serials Librarian* 68, no. 1–4 (2015): 169, doi:10.1080/036152 6X.2015.1016857.
27. Ibid., 170.

Working with EBSCO Discovery Service

Regina Koury

As an academic library, the Idaho State University Library supports the mission of Idaho State University (ISU)—a Carnegie-classified doctoral research and teaching institution, with an enrollment of more than 13,000 students. Since the ISU Library has been committed to adding new technology to aid ISU faculty and students with study and research for some time now, implementing a new discovery service product was not our library's first rodeo. In 2014, after a three-year contract with Ex Libris for Primo, Primo Central Index, and SFX A-Z list and link resolver expired, the ISU Library chose not to renew it. Our decision was made due to the level of support offered by Ex Libris and the failure of EBSCO and Ex Libris to improve metadata sharing. The problem of metadata sharing was particularly important given that the majority of the ISU Library's databases are hosted on the EBSCOhost platform.[1] The ISU Library chose to subscribe to the EBSCO Discovery Service (EDS) and A-Z list and link resolver instead. The chapter below outlines our library's migration and day-to-day experience in troubleshooting.

MIGRATION

Since the ISU Library had experience in implementing the Primo discovery service, migrating to EDS was not a challenge. Additionally, the level of service for EDS was consistent with what our library was used to while working with other EBSCO services, such as the A-Z list and EBSCOhost databases. Since EDS is offered as a cloud-based hosted solution, our library is only responsible to set up and fine-tune some administrative options for EDS. Our Electronic Resources and Systems staff was a natural choice for the implementation team, and they already worked closely with other library departments. Before rolling out the discovery service for patrons to use, our library needed to decide on such issues as the local name used for the service, its placement on the web page, discovery service description, what content to include, customization (e.g., display of results, branding, etc.), authentication, and advertising.

NAMING, PLACING, AND DESCRIBING THE DISCOVERY SERVICE

The ISU Library did not have problems in voting on and choosing our new discovery service's name: OneSearch. The discussion ensued when trying to decide on OneSearch's location on the library's web page. Some staff argued for the library catalog to continue being the first tab, since it had historically been placed on the library's main web page, as with the setup of our previous discovery service. Others felt passionately about putting the OneSearch tab before other tabs because of its Google-like functionality. And then there were those who felt that the Academic Search Complete database, an EBSCO-host multidisciplinary database used frequently to teach freshmen, was more appropriate as the first tab. They noted that Academic Search Complete did not return as many search results as OneSearch and would not overwhelm the patron. The decision was finally passed to the library's Executive Committee, which decided to add OneSearch as the first tab on the library's web page.

Another discussion centered around explaining what content is available through OneSearch. By 2014, both library personnel and patrons knew that not all content is indexed in discovery services. Originally, our library's web page included a note explaining what OneSearch searches, with emphasis in bold on "not all" content, with a question mark leading to the OneSearch LibGuide.

Two years later, the statement in bold seemed to be too negative and unnecessary, and with the library migrating to a new content management system

Figure 4.1 | **OneSearch description note**

(CMS) for the web page, the library's web page management committee voted to remove that wording and substitute it with a general statement: "Get started with a quick search of the catalog and multiple databases" (see figure 4.1).

The problem of embracing new technology, including new ways of searching, is not unique to the ISU Library. Hubbard has discussed the difficulties of adapting discovery services and bringing staff on board. Libraries have historically been late adopters of new technology, a mentality which no longer has survival value. Unless we adapt to the current needs of users, libraries will end up on the wrong side of history.[2] Page outlined the benefits of a discovery tool for every kind of researcher that outweighs the negatives. These include a Google-like or simplified search experience for undergraduates, the ability to discover other databases that relate to their field, and then transitioning to searching in the native database or subject index for advanced research.[3]

CONTENT SETUP

Parallel to decisions about naming, placement, and description, the library had to make decisions on what content to include in the discovery service, such as the A-Z list content, records from the library catalog and institutional repository, and electronic resources available for inclusion through EBSCO's EDS administrative module. Configuring content is important because it drives seamless linking and relevant information retrieval by patrons in the discovery service.

Technically, the library's A-Z Journal content migration was easy and was taken care of by EBSCO tech support. Library catalog content migration to EDS was completed by file transfer protocol (FTP) after the library filled out an EDS Custom Catalog form. The EDS Custom Catalog form required information about our library's existing integrated library system (ILS), including metadata; for example, MARC fields used for holdings and identifying e-books and audiobooks, deep links for ILS records, and the real-time availability of library catalog items in EDS, using the Z 39.50 service. The library also needed to create a list of catalog locations to include in EDS and make sure to exclude suppressed or withdrawn records and any other undesired locations. These records are then sent via File Transfer Protocol to EBSCO using upload instructions they provided. The library set up guidelines for updating new records (not deletes) daily, though it might take a few days for the records to show up in OneSearch. On the fifteenth of each month, the library sends an entire database to EBSCO so that any deleted records are removed when it is processed and included in OneSearch. With the institutional repository at ISU still in its infancy, the library did not have any records to migrate.

EBSCO also provided a document entitled "EBSCO Discovery Service (EDS) E-Resource Analysis" which consisted of "Major," "If via EBSCOhost," "Complete," and "Other" worksheets. Another document, "Understanding Your EBSCO Discovery Service (EDS) E-Resource Analysis," explains what these definitions mean:

> The "Major" worksheet contains all of the major publishers, information providers, and products that are providing metadata to EBSCO. This list also includes all of the resources from the library's e-resource list that would be fully or partially covered by EDS.

> The "If via EBSCOhost" worksheet contains all of the resources from the library's e-resource list that may be fully integrated into the EDS and that does not involve the use of any additional software solution. This integration is only possible when these databases are accessed on the EBSCOhost platform.

> The "Complete" worksheet contains all of the resources from the "Major" worksheet as well as additional publishers, information providers, and products where metadata is discoverable via EDS. Since this list is so vast, EBSCO is unable to provide added detail about the scope and nature of the metadata for every resource.

> The "Other" Worksheet contains resources that are not yet covered directly by the EDS index, but that can be integrated using alternative technologies, including widgets.

Additionally, EBSCO provides the library with several files to complete, including the "EDS E-Resource Analysis Worksheet," which the library completes and forwards to EBSCO. This document lists all library-subscribed electronic resources, whether full text or indexes only, and their URLs.

CUSTOMIZING

The library is provided with log-ins for EBSCOadmin, where in EDS admin there are several options to customize the patron's experience with search, viewing search results, and linking:

> **Search:** Under this tab the settings show the search options available to libraries, and this is pretty straightforward. The library chose to default to a basic keyword search screen, to show "did you mean suggestion" (in which the search tool offers alternative suggestions for search terms entered by the user, e.g., if one were to type "maayya," EDS might offer, "did you mean "maya?"") and not to require the use of uppercase Boolean operators (AND, OR, NOT), and so on. There is also a section on limiters, which allow the library to narrow the focus of the search so that the information retrieved from the databases is limited according to the values the library selects: for example, full text, catalog only, and so on. The library did not choose any of the limiters, nor did the library ask for the catalog records to be treated as full text. The argument was that ISU patrons expect instant access to "full text," and print books do not provide that.

> **Databases:** Here the library can add new EDS Partner databases, as well as the library's EBSCO subscriptions. The library chose to enable only library-subscribed, purchased with one-time money, and fully open-access databases. This choice drove the decision to not enable adding new content automatically, in order to avoid adding anything the library does not have full access to.

> **Viewing Results:** This section allows the library to choose a page layout with different numbers of columns (the library chose three). The library also chose to enhance catalog records, meaning using FRBR (Functional Requirements for Bibliographic Records) information on the detailed record page, and so on. This is where the library can also add and modify widgets for resources that are not yet covered directly by the EDS index. The library had done so for the REDBOOKS advertising database,

and the health science-related ClinicalKey and Joanna Briggs Institute databases.

Linking: This allows the library to apply any CustomLinks, Persistent Links, or SmartLinks access to the profile. Here the library added a custom link for an interlibrary loan form via ILLiad, and EBSCO Support helped set it up to show for items not in the catalog or the A-Z list.

Delivery Options: Under this tab, there are settings that allow the library to set permissions to print or e-mail search results. The library changed the default EBSCOhost e-mail address for technical support so that messages were directed to a shared Electronic Resources e-mail address, which resulted in a patron's ability to reply and get to the right troubleshooting person at the library.

Multilingual Options: There are several options in this tab. The library chose to turn on this option allowing patrons to switch the interface to any of thirty foreign languages, and an option allowing patrons to translate the HTML full text "on the fly" in any of the thirty foreign languages.

Branding: Under this tab there are several options, such as adding an Ask-a-Librarian link, customizing colors, and adding the library's custom image. The library worked with the campus Marketing and Communications Department to approve graphics and colors.

Viewing Publications: This tab is displayed for the Publication Finder (replacement of A-Z List in 2015) interface to work in the EBSCO Discovery Service (EDS) interface when Holdings Management is enabled, which the library enabled. The library also enabled viewing publications landing page, auto complete keyword, and "browse by discipline" options.

There is certainly no "one size fits all" approach to customizing, and libraries have to make individual decisions of what to enable or not, keeping patrons' best interest at heart.

AUTHENTICATION

The library uses EZproxy for authenticating off-campus users. The original setup with OneSearch was done in a way so that patrons would conduct a search in OneSearch, get to the search results, and then log in to view an article via EZproxy.

In 2016, the EBSCO EDS Partners discussion list community reported a problem with guest log-ins, and so the library changed the setup for off-campus authentication. As of now, ISU-affiliated patrons, after conducting a search, are taken immediately to the EZProxy log-in page, where after authenticating, they are taken to the results list. Non-ISU-affiliated patrons, after conducting a search, are also taken immediately to the EZProxy log-in page, where they are presented with a Guest link to continue to search results.

ADVERTISING

The rollout of OneSearch happened in the fall 2014 semester and was advertised on the library's Facebook page and news blog. Additionally, the University Library Committee, an advisory committee to the university librarian and dean, and consisting of faculty from various departments, graduate and undergraduate student representatives, and staff representatives, was updated with the news of a new discovery service.

DAY-TO-DAY TROUBLESHOOTING

After initial implementation, the fine-tuning and customizing of OneSearch continued. A lot of library troubleshooting of OneSearch access problems stemmed from metadata issues. Working with metadata is important in order to provide patrons with seamless access and enable them to retrieve relevant search results. There is an ongoing need for the vendor's agreeing to share metadata, in order to make it discoverable and clean. The National Information Standards Organization (NISO) has several groups whose work is dedicated to improving metadata sharing.

The ODI (Open Discovery Initiative) Standing Committee was created and undertaken to help ensure that all three participants in the metadata supply chain (the library, the content provider, and the discovery provider) could enjoy mutual transparency about what metadata elements are provided and used for discovery throughout the process. This can happen through libraries advocating for metadata exchange and publishers getting on board.[4]

The KBART (Knowledge Bases and Related Tools) Standing Committee manages and supports the KBART Recommended Practice (NISO RP-9–2014). In November 2016, NISO announced that five publishers (Greenleaf Publishing, Harvard University Press, IEEE, Oxford University Press, and

Project MUSE) have joined this effort to supply metadata that conforms to phase two of the recommended practice, KBART: Knowledge Bases and Related Tools (NISO RP-9–2014). The committee reported that conformance with KBART indicates that the format and content of data supplied by these publishers observe practical recommendations for timely exchange between content providers and knowledge base vendors.

The following sections describe some specific issues encountered by the ISU Library in working with OneSearch.

ASSOCIATED PRESS (AP) VIDEOS

In August 2015 AP Video Carousel, videos related to the search terms when users searched for other materials, would display in the search result list. They were free to subscribing institutions and the collection was described by EBSCO as "footage from 1930 to the present, updated monthly, approximately 60,000 videos covering a variety of topics studied in schools and colleges." The library staff feedback was that these videos were taking up valuable "real estate" space on the search results screen, so they were removed completely. At this point the library's website management committee is setting up user testing for ISU students to determine their feedback and find out if there is a need to bring AP Videos back, and perhaps display them on the side or at the bottom of the search results page.

DOI

Just recently a library patron was puzzled by why a keyword search on "DOI" works in OneSearch in some cases but not others. Just as it was about to e-mail support, the library checked an EDS Partners list—a mailing list used to communicate among the EDS partner libraries for troubleshooting, plus features that EBSCO is reviewing in EDS, and found a reply.

> Currently there are 67 databases that support DOI as a keyword search. If Library has any of the databases in the EDS profile, you'll get results for a DOI match. Some examples of databases with DOI keyword search include: MEDLINE, PsycINFO, Academic Search, Business Source, etc.
>
> A few databases support DOI as a keyword search ONLY when the full-text expander is ON (also Search within full-text). This issue will be fixed, as DOI on these databases also should be searchable as a keyword when the full-text expander is OFF.

Hundreds of other databases support DOI search by using a search tag. The vast majority of these databases use the DO search tag. Twelve use the DI search tag, including INSPEC. If a DOI keyword search fails, you can run the search again using the DO and DOI tags. E.g., DO 10.1007/s11277–015–2357–7 OR DI 10.1007/s11277–015–2357–7.

EBSCO EBOOKS

Due to the library's limited budget, most e-books are purchased individually and are not subscribed to as a collection. The library catalogs individual e-books from EBSCOhost in the library catalog with purchase orders and an 856 access link attached to each bibliographic record. Due to the library's limited budget, most of those e-books have one user simultaneous access limit.

Additionally, the library activated eBook Collection (EBSCOhost) in EBSCOadmin for those individually purchased e-books. EBSCO maintains records in OneSearch for all of the library's purchased *records in that collection*, which are accessible to the library's users. The reason why our library activated this collection in admin profile is because it is cross-searchable across multiple EBSCOhost databases.

The library noticed that only EBSCOhost, not Ebrary or Gale eBooks from the library catalog, did not show in OneSearch search results. The reason why the library would like to see them in OneSearch is because the concurrent usage limits display right on the results page, where patrons can see it right away. In comparison, e-books from the eBook Collection (EBSCOhost) do not display concurrent usage limits right away: patrons have to go to the detailed record screen to see that.

After communicating with EBSCO support, the library found that EBSCO had EBSCO/NetLibrary suppression enabled for the OneSearch catalog. Whenever the following criteria were met, the record was removed from loading into OneSearch: IF 856 contains "netLibrary" OR IF 049 contains "N$T" IF 938 contains "EBSC" OR IF 856 contains "db=nlebk|db=nlabk." Since NetLibrary and EBSCO e-books are included in EDS subscription, EBSCO filters them out automatically as part of the OneSearch catalog design. In the library's catalog, the 856 link contained "db=nlebk|db=nlabk" and met that criteria. At the library's request, EBSCO removed this default filtering to ensure that uploaded records could be seen in the live database.

LIBRARY CATALOG
Bound with Issue

The ISU Library has monograph titles that have been bound together. For the most part these are monographs that were published in series, such as occasional papers of the Idaho State University Museum, USGS Bulletins, and so on. The library made an effort to link these together in a process called "Bound with" in the catalog. This process allows all titles in the bound volume to show as "Checked Out" in the catalog when the volume has been borrowed by a patron. It was discovered that many of the individual titles are not included and thus not searchable in OneSearch. At this time, only the first title in the bound volume will show in OneSearch.

RESEARCH STARTERS

EBSCO describes Research Starters as a service that "offers short, citable summaries and authoritative overviews of more than 64,000 of the most popular topics available through EDS and is free to EDS libraries."[5] Once the patron searches, for example, on "gun control," a short entry will display at the beginning of the search results. It provides background information on the topic, with content pulled from sources, such as Salem Press and Encyclopaedia Britannica.

SEPARATE PROFILES

EBSCO support provides the creation of EDS profiles, which is a free service. For example, the library's Health Sciences Library embraced OneSearch, but wanted to create a profile with subject-specific resources for health science students. EBSCO support created a separate, customizable profile and a link for the library web page. Additionally, EBSCO support also created a sandbox where library administrators could test changes before rolling them out for patrons.

SERIES SEARCH

A question from our library's Interlibrary Loan Department asking to adjust EDS settings to include series statements in its keyword searches brought up a discussion with EBSCO Support. Titles in series that are cataloged separately and have series statements (440, 490, and 830 MARC fields) and that are in the library's collection were not coming up in OneSearch, which was presenting a problem for ILL. EBSCO support replied that while they do have series

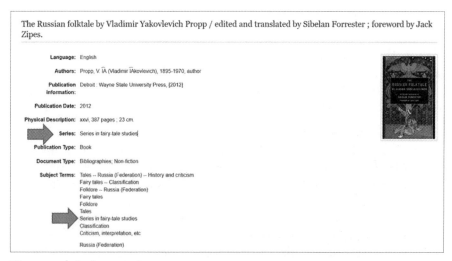

The Russian folktale by Vladimir Yakovlevich Propp / edited and translated by Sibelan Forrester ; foreword by Jack Zipes.

Figure 4.2 | **Series mapping**

information mapped to display in the series field in EDS, specifically the 440, 490, and 830 fields, which can be found with a keyword search, they do not give series titles as much weight as subject or title when determining relevancy ranking. EBSCO also reported that they have an enhancement request to index the series title, much like subject terms are indexed in EDS with a hyperlink. In the meantime, the library took EBSCO Support's suggestion to map series titles with the subject terms, which would link them together, and raise their relevancy ranking in the search results (see figure 4.2)

CONCLUSION

Once a library has completed implementation of a discovery service, fine-tuning and customization continue. To keep up with updates and to stay current with changes to content included in EDS, the library team working with EDS subscribes to the EBSCO Discovery Service Content Update Newsletter, EDS Partners Listserv, EBSCO Blog, and EDS Wiki, and attends EBSCO Users Group Meetings.

Of special note is the level of support and customer service provided by EBSCO. During the library's implementation and troubleshooting process, EBSCO tech support was there for us throughout. Customer service included WebEx meetings with EBSCO engineers, and on-site visits with EBSCO reps coming to the campus and holding an education hour to address our library questions. The latter event took place not once, but several times during the year.

While the library is aware that there are issues with discovery services, the library is also aware of the benefits for our patrons. The experiences of other libraries working with EDS may vary from ours, but the ISU Library is satisfied with EDS.

NOTES

1. Regina Koury, "Tracking Vendor Response to Library Concerns: The Case of an SFX Installation at Idaho State University," *The Serials Librarian* 69, no. 2 (2015): 142–54.
2. John Hubbard, "From OPAC to Search Engine: Making the Case for Discovery," Discovery Tools Now and in the Future, 2014, https://www.youtube.com/watch?v=EWqoaBMepJ8.
3. Mary Page, "Discover EDS: Tales of Implementation and Use," 2012, Charleston Library Conference, http://dx.doi.org/10.5703/1288284315108.
4. NISO Open Discovery Initiative, "Information for Libraries to Increase ODI Conformance among Vendors, www.niso.org/standards-committees/open-discovery-initiative/information-libraries-increase-odi-conformance-among.
5. Research Starters, https://www.ebscohost.com/discovery/content/research-starters.

5

Managing Discovery Services

Case Studies at Simon Fraser University (Summon) and Acadia University (Primo)

Leanna Jantzi, Jennifer Richard, and Sandra Wong

The progression in libraries from disparate finding systems that needed to be searched separately, for example library catalogs, abstracting and indexing tools, and databases, to federated search, and then to web-scale discovery (WSD) systems has been well-discussed and considered. Google and other web search engines have also had an impact on library users' concept and application of search.[1] The tension between user expectations and behavior on the one hand and the capabilities of WSD and those who develop and maintain these systems on the other is defining current electronic resource management (ERM).

User interaction and the promise of WSD has brought the role of ERM to the fore in libraries. ERM is changing workflows and impacting department structure.[2] Web-scale discovery and substantial collections of electronic resources have blurred the distinction between technical and public services. Increasingly, libraries view technical services and public services as working together on ways to best implement and present WSD.[3] Moreover, staff members in technical services are finding themselves part of decision-making processes that implement, maintain, and improve WSD.[4]

It is difficult to argue that Google and other search engines have not had a direct impact on libraries and library users. A single search box that returns a consolidated list of results, with links that lead directly to information, has become a standard expectation and created a familiar environment for all searchers:

> The advent of Google made one-box searching easy with result sets that seemed to be precisely what the searcher had in mind. Thus, the "Googlized" library patron was born. This patron—our patrons—will no longer tolerate anything more complex than a single search box and a single, integrated results set.[5]

And, of course, as Thomsett-Scott and Reese note, "the development of Google Scholar in 2005 was definitely another impetus for librarians to move from federated searching to something faster and more comprehensive."[6]

Not only have users' expectations changed, so has their pattern of search. Prior to WSD, a complete (or very close to complete) citation was required in order for a journal article to be found. Now, with WSD, only a partial citation is needed (perhaps one author and a fragment of a title) and the item can be surfaced in WSD. Therefore, libraries' A-Z journal lists are moving to the background of public use while the knowledge bases that populate A-Z lists remain integral to WSD services.

Now, rather than relying upon a complete refinement of a research query, users of WSD use multiple, simple keywords to fulfill their information need, reflecting the same environment of a web search engine. Moreover, users can conduct a search that produces a long set of results, but can then refine these using the facets available.[7] This post-search refinement is the direct opposite of the long-held search formula of refining and narrowing a query pre-search. As Georgas found in a study of undergraduate students, "there was little query reformulation."[8] Students also had a "high use of format terms within queries"[9]—an opportunity to leverage the format facets of a WSD service.

These user behaviors and expectations, combined with the possibilities of WSD, have raised new questions that are being considered in technical services, all informing how a WSD system is maintained and improved: How often and frequently is the central index updated? How stable is the relationship between the central index and the library's holdings? What is the quality of the metadata in the index? Are format types properly represented? How efficient and accurate is linking? Are current workflows and configurations best suited for this "new" work?

In this chapter, the authors will present two case studies that investigate many of these questions and discuss not only the implementation of WSD (in one case, within a consortium), but the implications of managing knowledge bases outside of the selected WSD service, issues of linking and access, and the changing roles of all library staff in the environment of WSD.

SUMMON AT SIMON FRASER UNIVERSITY LIBRARY

Simon Fraser University (SFU) is a medium to large university offering a comprehensive range of undergraduate and graduate degrees and is located in the Metro Vancouver region of British Columbia, Canada. In fiscal 2015/2016, the SFU Library's collection budget was just over ten million Canadian dollars, and the library spent approximately 80 percent of this budget on electronic resources.

In late 2009, the SFU Library started a small task group to investigate discovery layer options for the purpose of finding a unified interface to search the library's collection of print and online resources. The task group recommended Summon and by fall 2010, Summon became the default search option on the library's home page. The SFU Library also intentionally branded this new service Fast Search on its home page.

The SFU Library was able to automate a daily delivery by File Transfer Protocol (FTP) of catalog updates which included MARC records for physical materials such as print books and media, as well as records for digital resources including e-books, digital collections, and streaming audio and video. However, the library's electronic journal holdings had to be managed in the Serials Solutions Client Center, which also acted as the unified index for Fast Search/Summon. This situation meant that the library had to maintain two knowledge bases for its electronic journals, one for Fast Search/Summon indexing purposes and another for its public A-Z journal listing and link resolver. In time for the fall 2010 launch, a snapshot of the library's electronic journal holdings was activated in the Serials Solutions Client Center. However, the library lacked the staff to actively manage two electronic journal knowledge bases on a regular basis. The SFU Library's main A-Z journal listing and link resolver known as CUFTS, a homegrown and locally developed system, was given the priority. Back in 2010 and through early 2011, indexed-enhanced linking (also known as direct linking) was not yet available in Summon. At that time, all results from Fast Search/Summon were passed through the library's link resolver. Therefore, CUFTS took precedence as the library's primary knowledge base and link resolver, which was needed for link resolving in Fast Search/Summon and was already in use in many other licensed databases. By the time index-enhanced linking became available in Fast Search/Summon, the SFU Library had made a significant change to its discovery service options.

Library Search at SFU

Public service staff often lamented the overwhelming number of newspaper articles that seemed to dominate results in Fast Search/Summon. After analyzing the terms entered into Fast Search/Summon, the SFU Library discovered that users were frequently looking for known items, such as specific journal titles or databases. Users were also entering terms related to library services, such as building hours, library policies, and course reserves. These circumstances prompted the SFU Library to create a tool capable of searching multiple library resources. One year after the implementation of Fast Search/Summon, the library utilized the Summon application programming interface (API) in order to add another layer to the library's home page. Library Search replaced Fast Search/Summon as the default option on the home page in September 2011. Library Search offered users a three-column snapshot of results from different areas of the library's web-based resources, including Fast Search/Summon. Library Search could find specific journals, databases, material from the library's institutional repository, course reserves, and library web pages, as well as books and media, scholarly journal articles, and newspaper articles from Fast Search/Summon. Figure 5.1 presents the results from Library Search for "psyc 102," the common abbreviation for a course called Psychology 102.

With Library Search, students received a bento box display from different silos of resources from a single search, including course reserves as well as the librarian-developed guide to help students find information to complete assignments for Psychology 102. This same search in Fast Search/Summon would only produce a list of books and articles with words beginning with "psyc" and the number 102. For example, a citation to a meeting abstract called "Endocrine orbitopathy—A new psychosomatic illness? Preliminary research results on the psychosocial factors and quality of life in 102 EO patients" was the third item in Fast Search/Summon. This citation was the first one that contained both terms in the title. However, this reference would likely be of little use for a student taking an introductory psychology course. Indeed, Library Search continues to be the default search option on the library's home page since its launch in 2011.

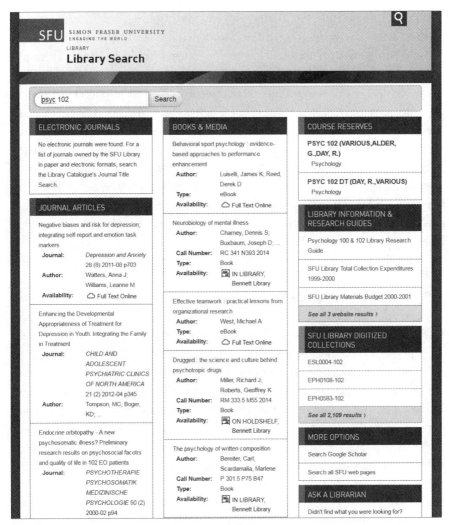

Figure 5.1 | **SFU Library search results from "psyc 102"**

Summon Management and Staffing Implications at SFU

The electronic resources librarian (ERL) worked in the Collections Management Office of the library and had sole responsibility for practically all of the library's electronic resources at the time, which involved licensing, acquisition, and ensuring access for authorized users. With Summon and the addition of a second knowledge base to manage, initial attempts were made to pass along some responsibility for managing the Summon knowledge base to technical services staff whose workloads were declining in areas such as check-in and binding. Unfortunately, familiarity with electronic journal publishers and platforms is needed in order to maintain a knowledge base. In the end, the library learned to live with inaccurate electronic journal holdings in the Summon knowledge base. The SFU Library's collection is large enough that activating many big deal journal collections and aggregator full-text resources was generally sufficient for the majority of users. Changes and corrections were made to the Summon knowledge base when errors were reported by patrons or public service staff. Initially, significant updates were performed yearly in January/February, when most journal transfers occurred. Then in 2015 and 2016, some automated updates were performed in bulk four times per year using data from the CUFTS knowledge base thanks to a solution provided by an SFU Library analyst, who found a way to update the status of Serials Solutions' knowledge base files programmatically.[10]

This situation of managing multiple knowledge bases due to the adoption of the Summon service emphasized the SFU Library's need to make strategic decisions regarding staffing for managing electronic resources. Continued growth in e-book acquisitions and other digital collections significantly increased the ERL's workload. Responsibilities related to electronic resource management needed to be distributed to other areas of the library outside of the Collections Management Office.

A few years later, in 2014, due to a retirement in the area, a vacant position in the Serials Check-in Unit was reevaluated and revised so that some duties performed by the electronic resources librarian could be delegated. This revised position would look after the daily maintenance of the library's electronic journal holdings in CUFTS, which in turn would update in Serials Solutions through the quarterly automated solution. This new position, called a "serials specialist," is now primarily responsible for managing CUFTS, the library's primary electronic journals knowledge base, and provides direct support to SFU students, faculty, and staff on accessing electronic journals. This has released the ERL so she can devote time to strategic activities related to managing electronic resources for the library. Even though the serials specialist resides in the Serials Unit, which is traditionally a technical services unit, a primary role for this position is to provide public service to both librarians and patrons related to resolving online access to electronic journals.

Communication/Troubleshooting

The SFU Library does not have a discovery services librarian or department. Summon was an orphaned service with no home in any specific traditional library unit. Implementation and configuration of the service were done by multiple staff in different divisions at the SFU Library, including Library Systems, Cataloguing, and Collections Management. Indeed, after initial implementation, Summon did not really require daily or weekly maintenance, aside from the occasional updates to the library's electronic journal holdings in the Summon knowledge base.

Solving problems related to Summon meant communicating across many library units, and being able to communicate such issues in a manner receptive to each department and its differing priorities. Users and public service staff would report unexpected behaviors from the discovery service, such as failed link resolving or broken links, inaccurate metadata, and missing or undiscovered content. Indeed, the results from discovery can be unpredictable. The unified index receives updates from many sources: the library's catalog and knowledge base, as well as content from publishers sending their metadata to the discovery service. Depending on the size of any update, it could take a few days to several weeks for Summon to process updates. The library has no control over how often and how frequently the central index is updated, so holdings in Summon may be out of sync with that of the library. One significant instance of such a delay in Summon updating caused users to find records to e-books in Summon that the library no longer had access to. A subscription to an e-book collection was canceled, so the library removed the catalog records, but these records continued to be found in Summon several months later. The SFU Library had to open a support ticket to investigate why these records continued to display in Summon even though the cancellation and removal of records had long since occurred. The solution came when the library sent a full catalog load as part of a regular quarterly update, and even then, the library was informed that it would still take two to three weeks for this update to be processed.

Frequently, these problem reports would end up in the e-mail in-box of the staff person generally thought to be responsible for making electronic resources available. Initially at the SFU Library, these reports went to the ERL. In 2014, responding to these general queries was delegated to the aforementioned new serials specialist. Anything that the serials specialist could not resolve or decipher would then be referred up to the ERL for assistance when necessary. Increasingly, this means that both the ERL and the serials specialist continue to provide a specific type of public service, even though both positions are generally in areas usually referred to as technical services rather than public services. The ability to correspond clearly and succinctly to patrons and other library staff as well as to publishers and vendors is a necessary skill. As listed in NASIG's "Core Competencies for Electronic Resources Librarians," effective communication is one of the seven core competencies outlined in that document. Competency 4: Effective Communication states:

> 4.1 Communicating effectively, promptly, and consistently, verbally and in writing, with a broad range of internal and external audiences: users, colleagues and staff, subscription agents, and vendors; the ERL must be able to tailor the message(s) to the circumstances and to the audience, as needed.[11]

In a largely digital environment and in a medium to large institution, where the management of electronic resources must be delegated to remain sustainable, the activities of technical services staff become more public service-oriented since they are frequently the staff who will provide and make accessible the online resources through the library's catalog, discovery tool, the A-Z journal holdings, and databases.

PRIMO AT ACADIA UNIVERSITY WITHIN THE NOVANET CONSORTIUM

Acadia University is a small, primarily undergraduate, liberal arts university located in rural Nova Scotia, Canada, and serving approximately 4,000 under-graduate and graduate students. The library has an acquisitions budget of approximately 700,000 Canadian dollars, and over 90 percent of that budget is spent on electronic resources.

Acadia Library is part of Novanet, a consortium of libraries representing all of the higher education institutions in the province of Nova Scotia. Novanet is made up of ten universities and one college system. Novanet provides support for a shared integrated library system and discovery service, Aleph and Primo from Ex Libris, in addition to a shared demand-driven acquisitions e-book project and a chat reference service.

The search for a WSD service for the Novanet consortium began in 2011 with the creation of a steering committee representing all of the libraries. Although Acadia University was not yet a full member of the consortium, the library was invited to participate in decision-making as an associate member. The steering committee invited four vendors to a Novanet Discovery Day to present their products. The participants were OCLC's WorldCat Discovery, ProQuest's Summon, EBSCO Discovery Service (EDS), and Ex Libris's Primo. All levels of staff were invited to attend and were encouraged to provide feedback during and after the formal presentations. After all of the product demonstrations, five further subcommittees were struck: Branding, Fulfilment

(Document Delivery and Interlibrary Loan Services), Systems and Technology, Central Index, and User Experience.

The impetus for launching a search for a new WSD service stemmed from a number of challenges identified with WorldCat Local at the time. By coincidence, all academic libraries in Nova Scotia happened to be subscribers to WorldCat Local between 2009 and 2014, although not all libraries were full members of the Novanet consortium. Dissatisfaction with WorldCat Local was palpable among the libraries in Nova Scotia. Libraries expressed frustration with the difficulties around known item searching, slow response times, and problematic results from federated searching. During evaluation, the steering committee and subcommittees all noted numerous advantages to selecting Primo. The current shared Aleph library system and Relais document delivery system would be integrated and interoperable with Primo. Fulfillment options would be seamless, such as the ability to request a book from another Novanet library directly. Users would be able to search course reserves in Primo. Relevance ranking, de-duplication, and FRBRized records were also offered in a Primo environment.

De-duplication and FRBRization are extremely important in a consortium setting. De-duping merges multiple records in order to combine and display holdings in a single record, as illustrated in figure 5.2.

Figure 5.3 shows a single entry for *Electoral College* by Lucius Wilmerding. Instead of separate records from each Novanet library as seen in figure 5.2, Primo has FRBRized the records into one result.

The FRBRization process groups similar editions or varying format types of the same work together. In this example, two editions of *Electoral College* are grouped. After the user clicks on the title or the link to "View 2 versions," the user is presented with two possibilities, as shown in figure 5.4. The first result is an edition published in 1964, and the second is the original work published in 1958 by Rutgers University Press. After extensive evaluation and testing, the

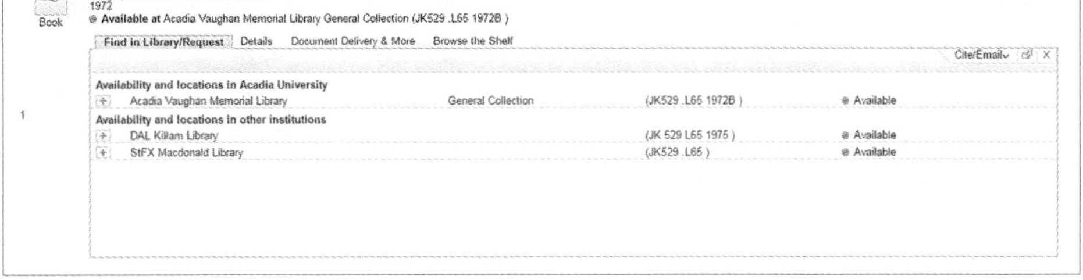

Figure 5.2 | **One merged record with holdings from three libraries**

Figure 5.3 | **FRBRized record display for** *Electoral College*

Figure 5.4 | **Display of the individual versions that were FRBRized**

steering committee and subcommittees recommended Primo to the Novanet Board of Directors.

Implementation and the Politics of Working in a Consortium

The implementation phase for Primo at Novanet libraries began in August 2014 with one representative interface and the expectation that a full public rollout would occur by the end of the calendar year. The same structure that was created for the selection and evaluation would be used for the implementation: an overall implementation steering committee with one member from each institution, and smaller task-based ad-hoc groups being formed as needed. The first task group created was related to link resolving due to the complexity of migrating different link resolvers into one resolver for ten libraries. This group assisted member institutions in the original setup of each library's instance of the SFX link resolver. SFX was licensed in conjunction with Primo, and Novanet expected participating libraries to use it since SFX came with Primo. However, individual libraries were responsible for selecting targets in SFX for managing their own electronic holdings. Acadia had recently migrated from OCLC's link resolver to SFU's CUFTS before Novanet adopted Primo. Thus, Acadia decided to continue to use CUFTS in addition to SFX. Acadia highly valued the CUFTS ERM included in the system for its public A-Z database and journal lists, and licensing modules. With no option for replacement of these services from Novanet, Acadia felt it was necessary to maintain two resolvers: CUFTS and SFX.

Site visits were scheduled halfway through the implementation to each institution and additional ad-hoc groups were formed to look at specific pieces: Fulfilment (document delivery and ILL), User Interface, Central Index, Marketing, Training/Instruction, and Course Reserves. These groups were advisory only. Outstanding issues continued following implementation: duplicate holdings for supposedly de-duplicated and FRBRized records, misleading labeling mainly in the area of available online access, and the ability to boost results for an institution's holdings.

The steering committee made several recommendations regarding interface design with the aim of having the separate institutional views be as similar as possible. This would also streamline usability testing. While there was general agreement by all in principle, in practice this did not occur. One institution immediately customized the initial simple search to mimic the advanced search page, and others made less drastic but still significant changes. Compounding the interface issue was the philosophical difference in opinion on how the discovery service should work. Many believed that users should cast a wide net and use facets to drill through their results. Others felt that the searching should start at what is available locally at their home institution and then expand if users did not find what they needed. Obviously, this difference had a great impact on the configuration of Primo, since many of the configuration options operated at the consortium level, not with the home institution.

Four months after launch, there were still significant outstanding issues, including title-level hold irregularities, configuration of course reserves, incorporation of institutional repositories and LibGuides, generation of Primo and SFX reports, print holdings in SFX, and modifications to the central indexing configuration. The official end of implementation for Primo finally came in June 2015, six months behind schedule. The catalyst for ending the implementation phase was the resolution of the two major issues for the consortium: title-level holds and disappearing locations. It is interesting to note that the majority of

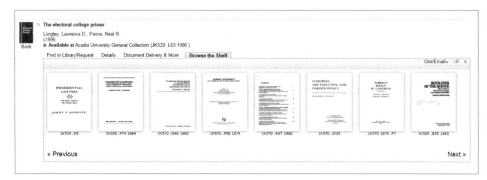

Figure 5.5 | **Browse the shelf feature**

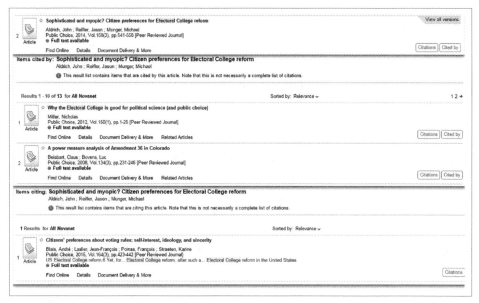

Figure 5.6 | **Citations and Cited By features**

Figure 5.7 | **Related articles or BX recommender feature**

such issues had nothing to do with Primo directly, but were actually Aleph configuration problems.[12]

Additionally, features that may be intriguing during selection and evaluation do not always turn out to be as impressive or useful in production. The ability to virtually "browse the shelf" sounds great. However, the default cover art coming from Amazon and Google Books is underwhelming; it consists of title pages, it seems, not covers. (See figure 5.5.) Better cover art service could have been implemented, but for an additional cost.

Two other services have been added since June 2015. These include cited by and citations services (figure 5.6) and the BX recommender service (figure 5.7). Though these services are commonplace and work well in databases such as PubMed and Web of Science, they seem to be underused within Primo. Statistics for the BX recommender reveal that usage is less than 1 percent at Acadia. Statistics for the cited by and citations options are not available.

Troubleshooting and Fail Points within a Consortium Installation of Primo

Chasing a one-size-fits-all solution creates a high number of potential fail points in a system, as noted by Novanet manager Bill Slauenwhite in a recent telephone conversation.[13] Fail points within the consortium WSD environment can include:

- errors in the original cataloging records from the native interface (eleven different cataloging departments with varying local practices)
- metadata errors in resolver data
- errors in the Primo Central Index (PCI)
- metadata errors in the sources within the PCI
- incorrect selection of resources within the PCI
- search errors in the interface itself
- parsing issues between the vendor databases and the WSD
- interoperability with open-access materials
- interoperability with institutional repositories

The initial testing by librarians responsible for electronic resources and the WSD service found failure rates of 30 to 70 percent on resolving successfully to full-text journal articles based on a number of random subject or keyword searches. After reconfiguration of the PCI, including the removal of several broad coverage products from the index, the likelihood of success increased. Primo documentation notes that 90 percent of EBSCO content is accessible through sources within the index (even though Ex Libris does not have agreements for indexing with EBSCO), but due to the poor quality of metadata in some of the sources, it was determined by Acadia that it was better to have fewer results successfully resolving to full-text content, than it was to cast a wide net with a higher number of errors.

Unfortunately, due to a number of delays, the consortium has not undertaken usability studies on the service yet. A brief review of search attempts indicate that patrons are looking for library resources or services that are not available in the WSD service, such as subject guides, tutorials and databases, and journals by title as noted by Simon Fraser University, resulting in the creation of their Library Search. Even with librarians teaching and directing patrons to the "journals" tab, patrons are still looking for journals within Primo. The librarians plan to review statistics and make the appropriate adjustments where possible to improve successful searches. Librarians and technical support staff at Acadia are considering the option of a bento box-style overlay, similar to SFU's Library Search, in the future.

Staffing and Workflow at Acadia with Primo

As observed in a 2013 survey for the ERM Report to the Council of Atlantic University Libraries, it appears that the management of electronic resources has been handled by the repurposing of staff from technical services, circulation, serials, acquisitions, and systems.[14] Changes in current job descriptions and the incorporation of the management of electronic resources into new job descriptions have occurred, although overall staffing levels have not increased at academic libraries in the region to meet the growing needs of electronic resource management.

As noted previously, each library within Novanet preserves autonomy, with most of the systems maintained and purchased separately; only the shared library catalog, discovery layer, chat services, and document delivery between the libraries are coordinated. Currently, one librarian and one staff member at Acadia are responsible for the management of electronic resources, with some support from the library technology specialist and the web and user experience specialist. The time dedicated to electronic resources by the one librarian is only a portion of a full-time position, since she is also responsible for liaison services to five departments, regular reference services, and additional research and service work as a faculty member. One other librarian is responsible for Primo at Acadia as one of her many responsibilities.

COMMON THEMES

While the management of two knowledge bases is a shared experience between Simon Fraser University and Acadia, there are some other common themes that appear, including staffing and workflow and the approach to maintenance and continual improvement, including troubleshooting.

At both SFU and Acadia, the responsibility for the management of electronic resources rests upon a few positions, and no brand-new positions have been created. However, at both libraries existing positions have been repurposed and redefined, demonstrating the overall impact of the shift from print to electronic resources. In what department or unit those redefinitions have occurred is different, which reflects the findings of Branscome, who investigated the management of electronic serials in academic libraries.[15] Survey results revealed a variety of approaches and strategies that reflected and addressed individual organizational needs.[16] Johnson also asserts that the management of electronic resources is an individual library decision: "No single model has emerged as the best way to manage the workflow and life cycle of e-content. Each Library must decide how to do this in the context of its current organizational structure, location of expertise, and number of available staff."[17]

Regular evaluation and reevaluation of WSD will provide a more responsive and current service. Of course, initial assessment and evaluation are required prior to acquiring a WSD service,[18] and continual assessment and usability studies need to be applied to the complete online library environment to ensure that the service is meeting the needs of users. This allows libraries to adjust search tools and their presentation in order to better reflect the behavior of users and their assumptions. For example, similar to SFU's and Acadia's experiences, other institutions have also found that users may enter location-specific or administrative queries into their library's single-search boxes, in addition to searches for known items such as database titles and research guides.[19] And, like SFU, some libraries have implemented bento box interfaces that offer a single-search box query, but produce results from a variety of library systems, including WSD, website, catalog, institutional repository, electronic journal holdings, and more.[20]

A common error that needs constant attention, evaluation, and troubleshooting is failed link resolving:

> The sharpest pain point is for end users of link resolvers and discovery tools, who may be incorrectly told their library has no access to the article they're searching for—or, perhaps worse, directed to a resource

they believe should be available, only to be faced with a pay wall or error message.[21]

As in the case of SFU and Acadia, with more than one knowledge base in play, in conjunction with the indexing of the WSD service, identifying the cause of an error and fixing the problem can be very complex. The introduction of direct linking in WSD, negating the need for link resolving, has addressed some of these issues, but problems persist. Those who manage the service need to work through a checklist of possible issues in an attempt to establish the root cause of the failed connection. Kornblau et al. suggest that "when choosing a discovery service, a library should consider which vendor's service allows for the most seamless access to its content."[22] However, in order to make the best possible match between the collection and WSD service, selectors need to know what metadata the WSD index holds. Writing in 2012, Kornblau et al. stated that "today, there is less flux and more transparency regarding indexing and content inclusion in Web-scale discovery services; yet, there is still a great need for librarians to influence publishers and content providers to share their metadata with all discovery services and for discovery vendors to make the content in their products even more transparent and interoperable."[23] Similarly, in a NISO Discovery to Delivery white paper, Breeding points out that WSD services have put processes in place to manage situations in which metadata is not available: "Libraries have to examine the coverage of a discovery service quite carefully to understand when a discipline-specific A&I database is included directly or whether it is covered indirectly through full-text or citation indexing."[24] Lastly, the trend of vendors offering the full suite of electronic resource management products (WSD, knowledge base, link resolver, and ERM) is arguably becoming standard: "Some libraries have already migrated away from link resolvers and knowledge bases previously in place to achieve better alignment with newly acquired discovery services . . . The differences among the link resolvers are increasingly trumped by broader integration concerns."[25]

CONCLUSION

In September 2016, the Simon Fraser University Library announced that Alma with Primo from Ex Libris was the successful vendor following a detailed procurement process for a new integrated library system to replace Millennium from Innovative Interfaces, which has been in use at the library for over twenty years. At the time of writing the SFU Library expects to go live with Alma and Primo in May 2017. The library's experience of implementing and managing Summon for six years highlighted the growing challenges of managing electronic resources. Managing multiple knowledge bases is unsustainable for a large library such as SFU. The responsibilities and tasks related to managing electronic resources should be delegated and distributed among all staff in technical services.

However, without Summon, Library Search might not have been developed or offered, and it would not be nearly as successful without the power of the Summon API. The SFU Library has high hopes that Library Search can continue in an Alma and Primo environment and looks forward to more unified electronic resource management. Indeed, with the adoption of Alma and Primo, the SFU Library has made the decision to decommission CUFTS and its associated services in 2017.

At Acadia and within the Novanet consortium, financial constraints will delay the adoption of a full library services platform (such as Alma) for an unknown period of time. Novanet has recently formed an ERMS Working Group to investigate potential solutions to managing electronic resource administrative and licensing data. Acadia changed to using only SFX as its link resolver in 2017.

The landscape of electronic resource management will continue to change along with the behavior of users and their expectations, as well as with advances in the technologies that create and support WSD. Libraries will change and adjust workflows, and those who manage the resources will need to continually strengthen their ability to be flexible and communicative.

NOTES

1. Helen Georgas, "Google vs. the Library (Part II): Student Search Patterns and Behaviors When Using Google and a Federated Search Tool," *portal: Libraries and the Academy* 14, no. 4 (2014): 503–32, doi:10.1353/pla.2014.0034; Tamar Sadeh, "From Search to Discovery," *Bibliothek Forschung und Praxis* 39, no. 2 (2015): 212–24; Beth Thomsett-Scott and Patricia E. Reese, "Academic Libraries and Discovery Tools: A Survey of the Literature," *College & Undergraduate Libraries* 19, no. 2–4 (2012): 123–43, doi:10.1080/10691316.2012.697009.

2. Beth A. Branscome, "Management of Electronic Serials in Academic Libraries: The Results of an Online Survey." *Serials Review* 39, no. 4 (2013): 216–26, doi:10.1080/00987913.2013.10766402; Amy I. Kornblau, Jane Strudwick, and William Miller, "How Web-Scale Discovery Changes the Conversation: The Questions Librarians Should Ask Themselves." *College & Undergraduate Libraries* 19, no. 2–4 (2012): 144–62, doi:10.1080/10691316.2012.693443; Mary M. Somerville, "Digital Age Discoverability:

A Collaborative Organizational Approach," *Serials Review* 39, no. 4 (December 2013): 234–39, doi:10.1080/00987913.2013.10766404.

3. Somerville, "Digital Age Discoverability," 234–39.

4. Ibid.

5. Roberta F. Woods, "From Federated Search to the Universal Search Solution," *Serials Librarian* 58, no. 1–4 (2010): 141, doi:10.1080/03615261003622957.

6. Thomsett-Scott and Reese, "Academic Libraries and Discovery Tools," 127.

7. Sadeh, "From Search to Discovery."

8. Georgas, "Google vs. the Library (Part II)," 521.

9. Ibid., 522.

10. Leanna Jantzi, Jennifer Richard, and Sandra Wong, "Managing Discovery and Linking Services," *The Serials Librarian* 70, no. 1–4 (2016): 184–97, doi:10.1080/036152 6X.2016.1153331.

11. NASIG, "Core Competencies for Electronic Resource Librarians," approved by the NASIG Executive Board, July 22, 2013, revised by CEC, January 26, 2016, www.nasig.org/site_page.cfm?pk_association_webpage_menu= 310&pk_association _webpage=7802.

12. Bill Slauenwhite (Novanet manager), e-mail to the author, October 7, 2016.

13. Bill Slauenwhite (Novanet manager), in discussion with the author, October 2016.

14. Jennifer Richard, *Report on the CAUL-CBUA Electronic Resource Management Study* (Halifax: Council of the Atlantic University Libraries, 2014), http://caul-cbua.ca/sites/ default/files/Grant%20Report%202012%20-%20J.%20Richard.pdf.

15. Branscome, "Management of Electronic Serials in Academic Libraries."

16. Ibid.

17. Peggy Johnson, "Working across Organizational Units to Acquire and Manage E-Resources," in *Developing and Managing Electronic Collections: The Essentials* (Chicago: American Library Association, 2013), 118.

18. Joseph Deodato, "Evaluating Web-Scale Discovery: A Step-by-Step Guide," *Information Technology & Libraries* 34, no. 2 (2015): 19–75, doi:10.6017/ital.v34i2.5745; Athena Hoeppner, "The Ins and Outs of Evaluating Web-Scale Discovery Services," *Computers in Libraries* 32, no. 3 (2012), www.infotoday.com/cilmag/apr12/Hoeppner-Web-Scale -Discovery-Services.shtml.

19. Cory Lown, Tito Sierra, and Josh Boyer, "How Users Search the Library from a Single Search Box," *College & Research Libraries* 74, no. 3 (2013): 227–41; Troy A. Swanson and Jeremy Green; "Why We Are Not Google: Lessons from a Library Web Site Usability Study," *The Journal of Academic Librarianship* 37, no. 3 (2011): 222–29, doi:10.1016/ j.acalib.2011.02.014.

20. Lown, Sierra, and Boyer, "How Users Search the Library from a Single Search Box," 227–41; Kornblau, Strudwick, and Miller, "How Web-Scale Discovery Changes the Conversation," 144–62.

21. Kristen Wilson, "The Knowledge Base at the Center of the Universe," *Library Technology Reports* 52, no. 6 (August 2016): 10–11, https://journals.ala.org/ltr/issue/view/606.

22. Kornblau, Strudwick, and Miller, "How Web-Scale Discovery Changes the Conversation," 152.

23. Ibid., 157.

24. Marshall Breeding, "The Future of Library Resource Discovery: A White Paper Commissioned by the NISO Discovery to Delivery (D2D) Topic Committee," February 2015, p. 41, www.niso.org/apps/group_public/download.php/14487/future_library _resource_discovery.pdf.

25. Marshall Breeding, "Knowledge Base and Link Resolver Study: General Findings, LIBRIS Nationella Bibliotekssystem," May 2012, p. 7, www.kb.se/dokument/ Knowledgebase_linkresolver_study.pdf.

From Electronic Resources Management to Library Services Platforms

L. Angie Ohler

ibraries have long been proponents of automation, but one area that remains a challenge is support for electronic resource management. With each step in the long history of library automation, expectations are that the next generation of technology will allow libraries to do work that has always been done, only faster. This chapter discusses how this expectation may in fact have been the reason behind the unrealized potential of electronic resource management systems (ERMS), and may further challenge the success of libraries in moving to new library services platforms (LSPs). As libraries contemplate this next migration, library professionals must reflect on how new technologies, particularly in the area of cloud-hosted services, may provide an opportunity to redefine the library's purpose and mission in a truly new way. Taking that opportunity will mean reclaiming the library's relevance with respect to its parent organization, rethinking and rebranding the services provided to library users, and most importantly, ensuring that the services libraries provide to their communities are understood to be something needed and valued by those communities.

Librarians and other library professionals have been talking about the revolution of print to electronic resource migration in libraries for the last thirty years, with the murmur becoming more of a roar these last twenty years as the proliferation of digital data moved from CD-ROMs to the Web, and then exploded in an ever-expanding universe of resources that users understand to be directly available to them anytime, anyplace, and all seemingly "free." But while libraries have been so focused on managing the ever-increasing number of tasks that migrating to electronic resource collections entails, as well as grappling with the crippling budgetary ramifications of an unsustainable rate of inflation for electronic journal content, something very important has been overlooked. This is not a revolution, but rather evolution.

The shift to managing electronic resources has sometimes happened in spite of, but more often in addition to, the traditional print workflows that libraries continue to perpetuate in both their support systems and organizational structures. Some libraries have implemented an ERMS along the way. Some have adapted the traditional integrated library system (ILS) to manage electronic resources. Most have done a bit of both, along with a myriad of other stopgap and homegrown tools cobbled together to manage what is an unsustainable workflow, given that more and more libraries spend the majority of their primary collections budgets on electronic resources. According to OCLC,[1] by the year 2020, 80 percent of collection expenditures will be for electronic resources, with the vast majority of libraries currently managing electronic resources using spreadsheets. Despite the many different iterations of organizational change that libraries have tried in response to the challenge of managing electronic resources, the technology needed to support electronic resource management always seems to fall short. There are those libraries that have embraced the move to a next-generation ILS, some more successfully than others. But the challenge here has never been just technological or structural. The final step in this evolutionary path is rethinking the type of services that libraries have traditionally provided to users, rather than simply improving the tools used to manage electronic, print, or any other kind of resource. Whether it's called a library management system, next-gen ILS, web-scale management solution, or library systems platform, perhaps the real indicator of how successful libraries will be in implementing this next step in the evolution of library automation is to understand what services are currently being provided to users, and why these should not necessarily be the same focus for the services provided to users in the future.

UNREALIZED POTENTIAL

A change in the environment always precipitates an evolutionary response. The evolution of the digital format as a vehicle for the delivery of information was certainly a fundamental environmental shift, but it was not an instantaneous one. Combined with the relative ease with which users can access information through online search engines and purchase products online with a click, it should be no surprise that user expectations for library services have evolved. Students and faculty often remark that "if it's not online, I'm not interested" and "I don't understand why the library doesn't have it, I just found it online for free from Google." In order to meet demand, library collections have become increasingly electronic, with workflows for managing electronic resources often in conflict with, or layered on top of, the work that library staff have traditionally done to support print-based materials.

With each iteration of new technology allowing library users more direct access to the information they seek without having to worry very much about the complicated processes by which library staff ensure access to those resources, it is often a shock to users (including many librarians and library administrators) to find that much of this process is still managed manually. Library staff are still what makes the difference between success and failure in terms of licensing, acquiring, cataloging, and maintaining reliable access to the library's online collections. The now famous diagram by Oliver Pesch[2] demonstrates the dizzying array of new tasks in which library staff still need support, work that became exponentially more complex in skill level, and which ultimately varied greatly in terms of the level of system support this new workflow received in the ERMS marketplace. So where did ERM systems go wrong, and why?

The Evolution of Standards

While no doubt the ERM Data Dictionary and the workflow diagrams of the DLF ERMI 1[3] and 2[4] projects were the key factors in pushing both the professional understanding of the needs surrounding electronic resource management as well as the marketplace development of system support to meet those needs, one critical challenge the industry has never overcome was the failure to adopt recognized formal standards based on them. Eager to get out ahead of their competitors, ERM system vendors labeled their products as "ERMI-compliant" while attempting to be all things to all customers. When they found themselves unable to meet all of the specifications that customers expected from their products, many marketplace vendors abandoned the development of ERM systems. Meanwhile, libraries could no longer justify the difficulty of implementing (or maintaining) an incomplete product, or find the funding for another product after a failed ERM system experience.

The work done by Kasprowski in 2008 to map best practices to emerging ERM standards and identify the initiatives and the organizations developing them finally gave the library world a sense of how to prioritize the many ERM data needs in a meaningful way using five distinct categories on which to focus in the future: (1) link resolvers and knowledge bases; (2) the work, its manifestations, and access points; (3) integration of usage and cost-related data; (4) coding license terms and defining consensus; and (5) data exchange using institutional identifiers.[5] Four years later, the NISO ERM Data Standards and Best Practices Review Steering Committee summarized the work to date and expanded the recommendations for each of these areas, suggesting that the industry focus its efforts on "practical projects of narrower scope [that] will have more positive impact than would an expanded ERM Data Dictionary."[6] Although some initiatives have fared more successfully than others in coalescing practices in the field, many of those identified by Kasprowski and the Steering Committee are today easily recognized as standards by the industry (Open URL, KBART, DOIs, SERU, COUNTER, SUSHI, and institutional identifiers such as the WorldCat Registry and Shibboleth).

The Qualified Success of ERM Systems

To the degree that ERM systems have been successful, however, a trend can be observed over time. Those standards and initiatives developed to address a specific focus of ERM need tended to be more successful than those systems that attempted to address everything all at once. An example of this is OCLC's automated holdings service, in which content providers send holdings information for a library's purchased content to OCLC, where that data is used to auto-populate the WorldCat Knowledgebase for that customer based on their WorldCat Registry identifier, which triggers a setting of the holdings in OCLC, and makes resources instantly discoverable for library users. This is particularly useful for libraries that use this service for demand-driven acquisition (DDA) selections, since titles can flow into the DDA pool and move to the purchased pool automatically with no intervention from library staff. Another trend that can be observed about the relative success of ERMS is that the libraries that were most successful in implementing an ERM system tended to be ones that were clear-eyed about their local workflows in relation to their most pressing ERM needs *before* developing or implementing a system solution. An example of this is the University of Notre Dame's development of CORAL, a system built foremost around the management of the licensing process and deliverables. The line between success and failure in each of these scenarios has one thing in common: a clear development of best practices with respect to ERM workflow and a solid understanding on the part of the library about where it sits within those best practices.

In a 2011 article on the results of their industry survey, Collins and Grogg described the state of ERM systems as "less like a silver bullet and more like a round of buckshot."[7] The survey's authors found that there were many options available to libraries, but none of them would solve every ERM need a library had. In the survey, librarians and vendors identified the problem of workflow management as the area most in need of ERM support, followed in order of importance by license management, statistics management, administrative information storage, acquisitions functionality, and interoperability. Workflow support had indeed become the unfinished business of ERM.[8] Despite the attempt documented in the workflow diagrams of the DLF ERMI 2 report, the library profession had not come to a common understanding about what ERM best practices should actually be, something that was equally as much to blame for the limited success of ERM systems as was the lack of system standards. Again and again, libraries found themselves in the situation of having purchased or developed an ERM system based on perceived needs, only to find that the system they now had failed to address the most pressing needs of staff on the ground. In an attempt to address this gap, the TERMS project was developed by Jill Emery and Graham Stone in 2011.[9] TERMS stands for "techniques for electronic resource management," and with its revival as Version 2.0, this good work will continue to help librarians address the core scope of services they need for ERM support before making decisions about a solution.[10] With the further development of ERM functionality already present in existing discovery systems and anticipated in library service platforms, it is clear that managing expectations about how a system will work in relation to the most pressing needs a library has for workflow support will continue to be the key to success.

COMBINING FORCES

In 2011 Collins and Grogg noted that despite being listed as sixth on librarians' list of top ERM priorities, interoperability was really the linchpin upon which all of the other ERM functionality that librarians had identified as needed would depend in the future.[11] They were not alone in noting the potential for new service-oriented architecture to finally free ERM from the constraints of the traditional ILS, although as Dawes and Wang noted, the new potential of this system architecture really depended on the willingness of libraries to reexamine their own internal workflows and let go of out-of-date practices in light of the new systems' potential efficiencies.[12] The idea of creating integrated platforms from the ground up, combining the ILS that data libraries still consider vital (purchase records, cost data, unique bibliographic data, circulation data) with knowledge bases (entitlements, holdings, discovery data) and the data libraries continue to manage rather awkwardly between ERM systems, spreadsheets, and homegrown databases (licensing terms of use, usage statistics, administrative data) is definitely the goal of the next generation of ILS products. But as Wilson points out, this Holy Grail of interoperability is hardly a straight line and does come with some drawbacks as libraries chart a course for their own future, namely those surrounding the decisions libraries will need to make between the efficiencies of interoperability vs. the independence of local control.[13]

Some things libraries will need to consider moving forward are (1) the risk of consolidating systems service with a single marketplace vendor, (2) their willingness to maintain data in different systems (back end vs. discovery being the biggest challenge here) in order to continue using products from multiple providers, (3) the shift in organizational culture and library workflow needed to accommodate agile development cycles, and (4) the sacrifice of local control and customization in order to benefit from the full potential of network-level efficiencies. The decisions libraries make along the way for any of these areas will also not happen in a vacuum, but rather in a rapidly evolving library marketplace increasingly dominated by large marketplace players consolidating services in a way that leaves many in the field uncomfortable and justifiably wary of how those mega providers will continue to work with, or against, each other.

From Separate Systems to Unified Architecture

At the heart of the move to "library services platforms" (LSPs), a term Marshall Breeding coined which has now replaced the term "next-generation ILS," is the technology of Software as a Service (SaaS) and the potential of cloud computing to replace the traditional client/server model for information technology. With SaaS, the customer is using a service that sits on a remotely hosted machine instead of software hosted on a local server. The benefit of SaaS is that updates to the system can happen more frequently, and require no assistance from library information technology staff to implement them. Cloud computing is defined by the National Institute of Standards and Technology as including the following functionalities: on-demand self-service, broad network access, resource pooling, rapid elasticity, and measured service.[14] SaaS is only one of three service models for cloud computing, the other two being Platform as a Service (PaaS) and Infrastructure as a Service (IaaS), all of which can be deployed in a cloud that is private, community-based, public, or in a hybrid model. All of this is to say that the different models are there, and have been for a few years now, but within the combination of these models are some decisions that libraries will have to make when considering what combination may be best for the library's needs.

Carl Grant highlights two features that libraries must factor into their procurement process and specifications.[15] First is understanding the benefit of true multi-tenancy, which is one instance of the system in the cloud serving multiple customers at the same time. While a vendor might use an SaaS architecture to support their services, there is a great deal of difference in the efficiencies of using one image of that software to push out updates for 500 customers sitting on that same instance versus a vendor who is hosting 500 different instances of that same software and has to spend staff and time updating 500 separate instances with the same update. The other feature Grant recommends libraries include in their procurement specifications is compliance with standard security certifications, considering carefully the security risks to which cloud computing could expose library data. Grant has been a vocal critic of what some in the field see as a growing inequality in the library marketplace over the degree to which libraries that embrace true multi-tenancy systems will reap the full benefit of the aggregated services and more importantly, aggregated data collected at the cloud level, versus those libraries that won't.[16] Libraries that embrace true cloud computing and free their staff to develop analytics will be able to engage in assessment activities such as mining user data to link student use of library services with higher grade-point averages and student retention versus students who don't use the library's resources, or link researchers' use of library services with the success of grants bringing external funding to campus. For anyone who might have missed the last thirty years of academic libraries reacting to funding cuts, these are precisely the proactive analytics that would finally show campus administrators that libraries are not the "cost center" of old but rather the true revenue generators for the entire campus.

Evolution in the Library Marketplace Landscape

Given the qualified success of those libraries that implemented an ERMS, many libraries continue to use them, and likely will continue to do so until another system solution provides more completely for the ERM needs currently being met by them. Given the much longer history of integrated library systems and the wealth of data that libraries continue to manage in them, it's probably not surprising that libraries will continue to use these systems for some time to come. Despite the growing maturity of those library services platforms that have reached the marketplace, traditional ILS vendors are not simply going to abandon their products, and it's likely there will be a number of simultaneous approaches in the marketplace for some time. Grant neatly summarizes these approaches as (1) starting over, (2) evolutionary, and (3) open.[17]

Starting over are products like OCLC's WorldShare Management Services, Ex Libris's Alma, and the now defunct Intota by Serial Solutions. These systems start with a new design from the ground up, breaking from the past functionality of traditional integrated library systems, and they are generally agreed to be true library services platforms. Traditional ILS vendors are pursuing an evolutionary approach, exemplified by products like Innovative's Sierra and SirsiDynix's use of BLUEcloud to deploy new interfaces and functional modules to its existing Symphony and Horizon customers, reutilizing their more recent generation of products and layering those with new technology to expand the products' functionality. And lastly, open systems such the now defunct Kuali OLE (Open Library Environment), rebranded as FOLIO (The Future of Libraries Is Open) with EBSCO's more active partnership, seem to chart a path that is a bit of building from the ground up while also embracing an evolutionary path.

Since the emergence of the library services platform, the library industry has also seen business mergers that are increasingly blurring the lines between traditional ILS vendors, book and serial vendors, and content providers. ProQuest's acquisition of EBL/ebrary, Serial Solutions, Coutts, and Ex Libris is one example of this, as is EBSCO's acquisition of YBP Services and the lead role they now play in FOLIO. As Marshall Breeding noted in his latest "Library Systems Report" for *American Libraries*, one effect of these kinds of mergers is the likely trend away from stand-alone ILS companies, which will simply not have the resources to compete in a marketplace dominated by such multiheaded giants.[18] Additionally, with these mergers there is now another contrast in the LSP development approach as exemplified in the two new super-companies; whether or not discovery will be (re)bundled with resource management or remain interchangeable should the library choose an alternative company for a library services platform.

THE PROBLEM OF TRANSITION

As one might expect from the variation in approaches present in the development of library services platforms against a marketplace increasingly defined by rapid business consolidation, there is also a growing sense of apprehension about which direction to pursue. Some libraries are understandably hesitant to commit too fully to any one product, while simultaneously recognizing that the longtime pursuit of best-of-breed products to support ERM work is unsustainable given the potential of true cloud-computing solutions to free up staff from otherwise redundantly updating multiple systems with the same information. This is especially true if libraries do not accurately assess the risks of waiting too long for the market to mature, staying with legacy tools longer than they should and falling behind in terms of their inability to leverage new technologies to more easily manage and assess their electronic collections. There are certainly risks and rewards with each development approach. As with the ERM system development trends, the degree to which a library understands these risks and rewards in relation to its own resource management needs and organizational aptitude for change will be the single most important condition for success.

Finding the Right Fit

So, what is it that libraries need to know about themselves in relation to different LSP development approaches and the volatility of the library marketplace? The following are some scenarios capturing what each path looks like in terms of the organizational culture, aptitude for change, and risk tolerance for a library that might match each LSP development approach.

Ground-Up Library Services Platform

While libraries that pursue the ground-up approach will ultimately benefit from true multi-tenancy in that they will no longer have to use IT staff resources to update systems that were previously hosted on local servers, there are some tradeoffs for that efficiency. Because these systems are built from the ground up and are still developing while in production, they are not fully formed when released into the marketplace. This means that they are unlikely to be a system that can address multiple competing needs within the broader marketplace of libraries until some time has passed and they further mature. Since these systems often lack the needed functionality in the early phases of development, libraries who are early adopters of them must match their greatest needs with those solutions being prioritized for early development. Matching the library's greatest needs with those functionalities prioritized in early development is crucial. One good way to do this is to become a development partner, ensuring that the vendor will focus on your library's needs as the segment of the library marketplace they wish to serve first. And even then, something to keep in mind for libraries pursuing this path is the need to continually assess staff resources in relation to workflow. Cloud-hosted solutions, particularly those that are true multi-tenancy, will not have the options for customization that locally hosted and developed systems did. This means there *will be* a moment (or many) when the library will have to confront its own legacy workflows in relation to how far away they are from those best practices that are now becoming expected standards of the profession and the marketplace.

Evolutionary Integrated Library System

Libraries that pursue the evolutionary approach are not yet ready to embrace the risks of being on the cutting edge of innovation, and they don't yet see enough gains in revolutionizing their workflow versus the staff and financial costs expended to get there. For library staff and library users accustomed to system interfaces they know well and that have served them admirably for a long time, the need for change is not yet apparent. The costs of moving too quickly into something that doesn't work well, or a product that fails, is simply too risky. For many library administrators, the risk of upsetting their user community by upending the library's reputation as a steady community resource is too great. Instead, they will defer the efficiencies gained from cloud computing services until later, choosing to continue expending staff resources to support systems that risk falling further behind, and that continue to force redundancies on ERM staff who must continue focusing on work that is rapidly becoming automated in cloud-computing library service platforms. The real risk here is waiting too long and being left behind. If many other libraries have moved to LSPs and successfully develop new services with data and staff resources they now have more readily available to them, then the libraries that don't make this transition quickly enough will suffer by comparison. Academic libraries already see this. Faculty members who come from other academic environments typically have expectations for the library's services based directly on their experience with libraries at other institutions, and they are not shy about letting the library know when they find something deficient.

Open System

The key thing that any library pursuing an open system development needs to understand is how its staff resources relate to the scope of the development. If a library has limited IT staff to help develop a community-sourced product, or support it after implementation if not a true multi-tenancy cloud-hosted system, then this is likely not the best option to pursue. Additionally, even if a library has IT programmers to spare, does it have the functional staff to support the testing and further development cycles before the system goes into production, or even afterwards? And since building from the ground up often means being unable to address all the functionality needed at the same time, a library that embraces this direction has to understand that needed functionality may not be there at the time of implementation and staff will likely need to duplicate their work by investing in homegrown solutions or continuing to use other systems in order to support those areas that are not yet being served. Additionally, libraries need to consider other financial costs. Using the now defunct Kuali OLE as an example, if the development work is initially funded by membership fees and/or limited grant funding, this model may not scale, since libraries with already limited resources may be unable to invest either money or staff time in a project that may ultimately advance too slowly to achieve market buy-in after commercial products have already matured in the marketplace.

Some Additional Concerns

Given the consolidation in the marketplace between different sectors of the library business, the issue of content neutrality may weigh heavily in library decisions and risk assessment. With consolidation at the product, fulfillment, and system level, there are serious concerns about the lack of content neutrality. If a vendor is simultaneously a library's vendor for product, supply, and system support for both resource management and discovery, this could be a problem should the library find fault with one area in this suite of services and wish to introduce a competitor for that area. That kind of consolidation in the industry makes libraries very nervous, particularly given the experiences they have had with consolidation in the journal publishing industry and the subsequent increase in costs that monopolies tend to generate. There is also a fair amount of skepticism in the library world about the altruistic role of the last remaining large content-neutral provider, OCLC. Yet, at least there, libraries do have direct input given that the basis for that organization is to act on behalf of its membership, and libraries that wish to make the most of that influence do have opportunities to provide it. Which brings us to the opposite end of the spectrum: businesses controlled through equity ownership. We have seen the devastation that equity ownership and the need for shareholder profits have done to longtime and trusted library marketplace suppliers. What's to stop a large super-services vendor from being acquired by an equity investor, reducing its research and development capabilities, and refocusing its priorities since it now works to send much of its profit to its new parent company? What happens if the stress of that is too much for the company and it goes under? A library pursuing an all-in super-vendor LSP may want to consider creating a disaster plan should that vendor go under and the library simultaneously risk the loss of its main source of support for both acquiring collections and managing them.

The Assessment and Selection Process

Aside from being aware of the traits that each library services platform development path might require, libraries need to make this decision using real data and real methodologies. Luckily, there are models out there. The importance of approaching vendor selection through the lens of a sound environmental scan, needs assessment, and cost-benefit analysis cannot be overstated here. It's also important to do all of these things within a formal Request for Proposal (RFP) process in which detailing the scope of service and functionality expected can go a long way toward eliminating the shock of realizing that the system for which the library has contracted does not in fact serve the majority of the library's needs. There are a couple of core factors to keep in mind here.

The first factor in considering a move to an LSP is assessing whether or not there is a consensus on the need for change. Conversations with stakeholders need to happen early, along with an honest assessment of what library users want, and what these new systems are likely to provide to them. Talk to other libraries that have already implemented an LSP and find out what the advantages and hurdles were for them. Talk to colleagues in other parts of the library or campus environment about what systems they use and whether it would be beneficial for their work were it easier to connect to an LSP, or if an LSP were to replace their current system. Talk to colleagues in your consortium about what common needs you might have that could be directed into a structured discussion about how to move as a group to identify solutions to those needs.

The second factor to consider is the complexity of the current ecosystem in which libraries exist. Today libraries are likely to employ systems to manage print (ILS and OPAC), to share print (ILL and union catalogs), an institutional repository, an ERM system for managing licenses or calculating usage statistics, link resolvers, knowledge bases, and proxy servers to manage electronic resources, discovery systems, and content management systems for supporting electronic resources. Add on to this any collection assessment tools that libraries are using. As Forsman notes, this complex environment requires that libraries looking to move to an LSP map their own current systems landscape, noting the dependencies of each, and especially paying attention to those areas in which the systems used work together *only* because of the people employed to make connections between systems that otherwise are not interoperable.[19] For Gallagher, it's also very important that libraries consider a variety of options for migration, first taking note of whether or not they have the financial or human resources to make the shift to an LSP, and second by employing a cost-benefit analysis to identify areas where cost savings will become greater over time and after the initial investment in migration.[20] Having a solid understanding of the financial processes involved in your institution's procurement process is an absolute must, as is understanding what university systems need to be considered when integrating an LSP into the university's payment operations, and identifying stakeholders in other parts of the library impacted by the move to an LSP. Doing market research, keeping up with the rapid changes in products and players, and requesting demos all help with the decision-making process. Additionally, it's important to collect feedback from stakeholders for any demos done, especially since those who don't normally work directly with managing library resources may have insights that haven't been considered, or concerns that might otherwise be overlooked.

Early Adopters

For those libraries considering the leap to a library services platform vendor, it can be enlightening to hear from real libraries that have already made this move. Bucknell University was one of the first libraries to implement OCLC's WorldShare Management Services (WMS).[21] In responding to the offer from OCLC to become an early adopter, Bucknell performed a cost-benefit analysis, working with its vice president for library and information technology.[22] Since the library shares IT support with the campus, this was one of its most vital stakeholders. While Bucknell is one of the largest liberal arts universities in the United States, with 3,400 undergraduate and 150 graduate students, the campus size and the library size are very small compared to the large Association of

Research Libraries members of other major universities in the United States. For a small library looking to save staff time in relation to system costs, an LSP might be the best solution.

Even though Bucknell may be small, many of the efficiencies it hoped to achieve with the move to WMS are certainly the same ones that drive much of the decision-making in larger campus and library environments: (1) reductions in staff, especially staff in technical services and information technology, make it difficult to continue the maintenance and upkeep of legacy systems or legacy system workflows; (2) an increase in costs as different systems for managing library resources have to be layered on top of one another to achieve different aims with respect to resource management or discovery; and (3) a desperate need to provide more patron-driven services to library users who expect to have resources available to them at the point of need and are not happy with waiting for the library to acquire those materials through traditional acquisition purchasing models. Looking at a couple of other libraries that have made the transition to WMS, this same scenario seems to be the impetus for change and the benefits most cited. In addition to the cost savings of no longer locally hosting an ILS or spending staff time maintaining that system, the University of Nebraska Omaha Library cited saving staff time in cataloging and e-resource management as successes of its move to WMS. Cataloging, acquisitions, and ERM staff benefited from direct updates to the knowledge base through OCLC's automated metadata processes, using publisher and vendor data for library purchases to automatically update the library's knowledge base, which then triggered updating the holdings in OCLC and making the resource instantly accessible for library users through the library's WorldShare Discovery catalog.[23] While there are certainly distinct benefits to the automated efficiencies experienced by Bucknell and the University of Nebraska Omaha, there are also clear tradeoffs for larger libraries when it comes to this same product. As Bordeianu and Kohl detail, the University of New Mexico (UNM) Libraries experienced some significant adjustment in workflows after they migrated to WMS as part of the broader seventeen-member LIBROS consortium.[24] Although UNM Libraries noted the same benefits of staff savings in both information technology and cataloging, the lack of needed functionality in other areas such as acquisitions was hard to overcome. Additionally, the libraries' staff had to adjust to the fact that twinned with the WorldShare Discovery interface, any problems with electronic resources were much more visible to users when something in the resource chain had gone wrong, and addressing those problems in real time with users who were unhappy without an immediate fix was a struggle.

Sharing IT Support: A Contrast in Consortia

Libraries have a long history of sharing IT support within consortia, the aim of which has historically been the cost savings of group purchasing for at least the system itself in terms of the software and maintenance, but sometimes also the hardware and the IT staff who support the system if centrally located for all member libraries. The primary reasons why many libraries formed consortia were a desire to form union catalogs and share bibliographic data in order to streamline searching and borrowing between member libraries. In the case of consortia in which libraries share a single administrative instance of their system, sharing bibliographic data can also benefit the functions within acquisitions and cataloging since libraries can use the same records for both setting up orders and holdings within the ILS. Given the variety, history, and degree of cooperation among different consortium models, the complexity in this area of the library marketplace is proving to be one of the most challenging for library services platform providers to develop. That said, an analysis of three different consortia, the history and structure of their cooperation, and the decisions they have since made about LSPs might shed some light for other groups wondering how to navigate this next group decision.

PALNI

The Private Academic Library Network of Indiana (PALNI) is a consortium made up of twenty-three private academic institutions across Indiana. With a range in full-time equivalent (FTE) size from 50 to 5,000, the consortium is primarily made up of small- to medium-sized colleges and universities with a primary focus on undergraduate education. Given the relative size of the schools in relation to each other, and their history as private institutions, it is perhaps not surprising that their cooperative relationship has a long history of deep collaboration. The PALNI website presents some wonderfully informative information about the group, detailing the members, governance, organization, mission, and strategic plan, as well as the history of the group.[25] PALNI's origin was a successful Lilly Endowment grant during the 1980s to create a union catalog among the private academic institutions of Indiana, an endeavor that led to the creation of the State University Library Automation Network. By 1990, what would become the PALNI libraries agreed that they needed to form their own independent college library resource-sharing network rather than risk losing out to the priorities of much larger libraries in a state university-dominated system. After receiving IRS nonprofit status in 1992, the group officially moved forward as PALNI with their first online library automated system in 1994. With the help of another Lilly Endowment, the group contracted for its first integrated library system with Ex Libris, and by 2004 they had bundled the full suite of Ex Libris's ILS and ERM-related products, including Aleph, Metalib, and SFX. By 2010, a number of factors led the group to consider even deeper collaboration with each other, including expanding beyond a shared union catalog and a cooperative contract for an ILS. Two key decisions were made that likely contributed to the later course of action the group would take for a group library services platform.

The first decision PALNI made was contracting with Ex Libris for Primo Total Care (the vendor's fully hosted cloud service discovery layer), a decision that meant PALNI libraries were making a conscious decision to move away from the model of individually hosted systems. The factors leading to that decision and the process by which they selected the product are well documented.[26] But it is the subsequent post-migration article by the same authors a year later that highlighted many of the challenges they'd faced with respect to moving to a hosted service and that would no doubt later influence the LSP decision.[27] In migrating to Primo, PALNI libraries discovered divergent workflow practices between different libraries which had resulted in divergent implementations and use of Aleph over many years. These differences had to be normalized, and the libraries reported that a lot of data cleanup was necessary in order to ensure that the data fed into the new shared discovery layer would be consistent. Additionally, the libraries experienced the same pushback from librarians and users with respect to the Primo interface, resulting in only five of the libraries implementing it as their primary default search interface, and triggering a much deeper conversation about how well the interface met or did not meet user expectations.

The second decision that would act as a catalyst for the group's move to an LSP was hiring staff for a centralized office. In 2010 an executive director was hired to oversee the operations of the consortium, along with a digital communications manager to help them communicate effectively with each other, brand and market their services, and assist with usability and user experience studies. By 2011 PALNI was clearly struggling with the Primo decision, and they decided to create two part-time coordinator positions to help with resolving some of the internal data problems they'd encountered. A systems coordinator and a cataloging coordinator were drawn from existing library staff and would continue to be employed by their home institutions, but would spend half their time working for PALNI. No doubt the experience of standardizing workflows across previously independent technical services staffs contributed greatly to the libraries' 2013 decision to contract with OCLC for WorldShare

Management Services. Given the efficiencies documented above by the libraries that also implement WMS, this was a solid choice for a group of smaller libraries that did not have large technical services staffs, and would be looking to redirect local IT staff toward other institutional priorities. Since the decision to go with WMS, PALNI has phased out the two part-time member library personnel positions and has now added four additional full-time central office positions—-an assistant director, a knowledge base/license manager librarian, an office administrator, and a scholarly communications/open access librarian.

Orbis Cascade Alliance

The Orbis Cascade Alliance is a consortium of thirty-seven academic libraries across the states of Oregon, Washington, and Idaho. The current consortium was formed from the merger of two previously separate consortia in 2003—-Orbis and Cascade. Resource sharing has long been a key trait of the group, particularly for the former Orbis consortium, and is what led both consortia to merge and then migrate to a single instance of Innovative's INN-Reach union catalog and interlibrary loan system used in tandem with each library's independent implementation of Innovative.[28] Following a contractual dispute with Innovative, and heeding a desire to further explore efficiencies in resource sharing beyond their own membership, the Alliance decided to explore an initiative in 2008 with OCLC to implement a resource-sharing union catalog called Summit which prioritized the member libraries' holdings in WorldCat and better facilitated circulation transactions within each member library's ILS operations. The Alliance was also interested in OCLC's next-generation ILS development leading to what would eventually become WorldShare Management Services.

By 2010, the consortium members were beginning to think more deeply about even further collaboration, believing that it would be beneficial to the group if they pushed collaboration beyond public services and began building shared technical services, including collection development, vendor files, serials holdings information, and electronic resource licenses.[29] They had also done an assessment of ILS costs among each of their members, itemizing software, hardware, and local staff support costs, which later was the foundation against which they could calculate the cost-benefit of migrating to a hosted LSP. The Alliance was also unhappy with what they had found with OCLC's developing WMS product. Specifically, they were concerned about the data security of moving user data and other sensitive information to a vendor-hosted system, and they were frustrated with the methods then in place for migrating library holdings data into WMS, a process that many of the members felt placed too much of a burden on member libraries.[30]

After an exhaustive Request for Information (RFI) and subsequent RFP, the Alliance announced in 2012 that they had selected Ex Libris's Alma with Primo for their shared LSP and discovery solution. This meant a shift in workflow and systems for many members. At the time of migration, the Alliance members would move from three different integrated library systems and four different discovery platforms. The libraries' parent campuses range in size from small colleges with 1,000 FTE students to major research universities with 45,000 FTE students. The likelihood of common workflows and best practices among libraries with that degree of campus differentiation may be difficult to find. Added to this was the Alliance members' long history of independently hosted systems, which meant that a certain level of customization in workflow support for each library was possible. Fu and Carmen document some of the challenges the member libraries went through in cleaning up their ILS data in preparation for migration, as well as resolving issues after the migration, highlighting the communication and leadership necessary for key personnel responsible for the bulk of any member library's migration efforts.[31] In fact, Stewart and Morrison cite coordination between consortium members as one of the primary challenges of the Alliance's migration, as library staff had to learn to design workflows in coordination with staff in other libraries, while at the same time grappling with the perpetual beta testing of a system still in development.[32] The largest of the Alliance libraries, the University of Washington Libraries, was surprised to find that Alma lacked basic acquisitions functionality such as templates for ordering, and it did not yet have an ERM module. In this respect, the experiences of libraries implementing Alma were no different than those cited above that have implemented WMS.

USMAI

The University System of Maryland and Affiliated Institutions (USMAI) is a seventeen-member library group representing primarily those colleges and universities that receive state funding for higher education through the University System of Maryland (USM). The group represents institutions ranging in size from small colleges to a large research university with an FTE of 36,000. It also includes great variation in institutional focus, including specialized libraries for health sciences, law, a center for environmental sciences, and a university specializing in distance education and online degrees. Additionally, the group includes a semi-independent campus offering degrees and classes using a mix of resources and faculty from nine of Maryland's public universities. Starting in 1982, four of the state universities began a cooperative contract for a shared library information management system (LIMS). After the state system's name change to the University System of Maryland in 1997, the consortium re-chartered to form the University System of Maryland Library Information Management System. By 2000, the group included two additional state universities and colleges not formally part of the USM, and it became the University System of Maryland and Affiliated Institutions. In 2003, USMAI embarked on its third cooperatively purchased library system, migrating to Ex Libris's Aleph, and expanded this to include the ERM tools SFX and Metalib. By 2012 the group had also investigated a hosted version of SFX, but it could not reconcile the lack of local control and loss of customization with the potential IT efficiencies offered by a hosted service.

Unlike other consortia, USMAI has a long history of centralized computing services. The staff who manage the ILS and ERM tools are housed at the state's flagship university at College Park. With the migration to Aleph, the group decided it would implement the system on a single administrative instance shared by all member libraries. As a result of this uniquely centralized system, the group's resource-sharing decisions often went beyond agreements on lending and borrowing, and further into developing best practices for sharing bibliographic records in core technical services areas for cataloging and acquisitions. What this relationship yielded over many years was a more or less constant awareness of how far any one library could stray from the centralized standard, and a comfort level with systems and interfaces that had benefited from many years of customization, provided that all members agreed to the changes needed. At times, the relationship was difficult should any library's needs stray too far outside the norm of the IT support needed for the rest of the members. As documented by England and Lowe, USMAI also has a long practice of cooperative electronic resource purchasing, something the consortium began in the late 1990s.[33] The USMAI model here was no different than with its ILS support. The consortium had never become an independent legal entity, nor had it applied for IRS nonprofit status. Instead the group functioned as a buyer's club, paying part of the salary of a licensing librarian housed with the IT staff at College Park who was expected to split her time between College Park and USMAI. This same librarian was also negotiating on behalf of the larger Maryland Digital Library (MDL) representing fifty-four libraries across the state of Maryland and of which USMAI was also a part. With the Great Recession of 2008 and the retirement of the licensing librarian, both USMAI and MDL had to work together to find an alternative support model after College Park was told by its own campus administration that the vacant licensing librarian position would not be filled due to an indefinite hiring freeze.

Around this same time, USMAI was in the process of deciding on a discovery system to layer on top of the traditional shared Aleph catalog. While the majority of the libraries ultimately settled on implementing EBSCO's Discovery Service (EDS), College Park decided to commit to OCLC's WorldCat Local, eventually fully implementing the WorldCat Knowledge Base, and migrating to the OCLC link resolver and WorldCat Discovery Services interface. Although moving to a discovery layer was challenging for all of the USMAI libraries, the largest challenges remained migrating data initially into the interface, continuing to maintain multiple knowledge bases for the same e-resource content, and struggling with user and librarian expectations for what a discovery interface should be. In the case of College Park, the decision to make use of OCLC's new automated metadata processes saved significant acquisitions and cataloging staff time since e-book resources for both purchases and DDA selections could be activated in the knowledge base, and holdings were updated in OCLC and were instantly visible to users through the discovery catalog. This efficiency led College Park to discontinue exporting full-copy cataloging records in the local Aleph catalog for e-books after moving to WorldCat as its new public-facing interface for users. College Park, like other libraries, continues to experience the struggle between weighing the value of new efficiencies versus the challenge of missing functionality and uneven development cycles.

By 2010, the flagship university at College Park had decided to implement Kuali Financials as its next campus financial system, leading the libraries to decide it should become a founding member of the nascent Kuali OLE (Open Library Environment) development. This decision meant another disconnect for College Park, which would potentially implement the OLE system independently of USMAI. By 2013, USMAI decided to move forward with an RFI to explore marketplace-ready options that would support the needs of the consortium as a group, and were willing to consider Kuali OLE. However, the result of the RFI proved that all of the systems of possible interest to the group were too early in their development cycle, and none had yet developed the kind of consortium resource-sharing and ERM functionality that the USMAI group had hoped to find. Given the findings, USMAI decided not to move forward with a formal RFP to entertain contractual bids from LSP providers, and instead decided to extend its contract a while longer with Ex Libris for Aleph. Although the USMAI Council of Library Directors approved a 2015 proposal to allow the centrally located systems librarians at College Park to spend a percentage of their time participating in hands-on testing and evaluation of the Kuali OLE software, they were not allowed to participate fully in the development of the system. There was also great concern expressed at this time by the functional experts in cataloging, acquisitions, and circulation about the degree to which the OLE development seemed to focus on print management, a focus that College Park staff felt was not a good fit, given that nearly 80 percent of the yearly collections expenditures were now for electronic-only resources. After another environmental scan in late 2015 yielded no additional prospects, USMAI agreed to six-month intervals between revisiting this decision, only to decide in late 2016 that it would indefinitely delay any procurement actions on a next-generation system in order to wait for the products in the marketplace to mature fully. Meanwhile, after the demise of Kuali OLE, College Park decided not to participate in the new open-source development, FOLIO, led by EBSCO.

Given the degree to which this group of libraries was accustomed to centralized computing services, the OLE development might have seemed a good choice since it would have potentially offered the flexibility of open-source product development without the loss of local control and customization that are typically seen in cloud-hosted LSPs. But even then OLE might not have been a long-term solution in the sense that it would be locally hosted, and would continue to require the libraries to invest in local IT programming and staff. After the demise of OLE, the USMAI decision to wait for further development of consortium functionality in commercial products is certainly understandable, but waiting has its downsides too. First is the potential for the USMAI libraries to be left behind when compared to other libraries that have already implemented LSPs. As seen with the libraries that have made this move, the migration does involve a significant rethinking of local practices and workflows. One effect of delaying is that the USMAI libraries will not have a chance to influence the direction of the marketplace and systems providers for what eventually will become industry best practices and new standards. Another result of waiting is that the libraries will miss out on opportunities to redeploy staff to other organizational priorities, delaying further the potential for successfully translating their value in the parent organization into additional funding opportunities and new library services.

LOOKING AHEAD
Ongoing Challenges and Opportunities

While it is true that transitioning from integrated library systems to library services platforms has a great deal of potential to solve some of the more vexing problems libraries continue to face in managing electronic resources, there is so much more potential for opportunities to be gained here than merely a better way to manage resources. Finding the right fit, and charting a course that makes sense culturally and organizationally, are vital for the success of any library in this new marketplace. While not implementing an LSP is an option, it also introduces some risk in allowing legacy workflows to dictate a library's future, and limit its potential for developing new services. Learning from the hard lessons of the ERM system developments, and particularly confronting the profession's own responsibility for the lack of standards and best practices that led to stalling efforts in that area, are essential. If libraries manage the transition to library services platforms more reflectively, and become more consciously aware of the need for standard practices and normalizing local workflows, there is a very good chance that the library profession may benefit from the opportunities to solve the much larger relevancy and funding problems that plague libraries.

The Power of Time

While not always completely accurate, the predictive capabilities of Marshall Breeding have become somewhat legendary in the library technology field. In a paper based on a 2011 presentation made at the IX Conferencia Internacional sobre Bibliotecas Universitarias in Mexico, Breeding made a number of five-year and fifteen-year predictions about the future of library information technologies.[34] Many of his predictions for 2016 have come true, while others are clearly close to it. Library collections, particularly in the area of journal content, are now almost exclusively electronic for many libraries. Very few libraries have the wherewithal to continue duplicating content in both print and electronic format for journals. Most are becoming equally concerned about the "double dipping" of content published both in paid subscription models and available via open access initiatives while unable to identify quickly or easily these duplicate versions of the same works. E-books have certainly gained popularity among academic libraries, with many libraries that can no longer afford expensive print approval plans moving almost exclusively to demand-driven acquisition models for book content in an effort to better target the specific needs of their users. Libraries have almost universally embraced and implemented new discovery systems, although the degree to which these systems and their interfaces meet the expectations of a broad market of libraries and users continues to be a debate not quite resolved. Library services platforms have entered the marketplace, disrupting in many ways the local understanding of workflows and the traditional development cycles that libraries were accustomed to, given the more evolutionary approach of integrated library system development. And while locally hosted integrated library systems may be around for a while longer as the library marketplace makes this leap, it is true that the preference for locally managed servers for library systems is becoming the minority approach. Breeding expects LSPs to reach full maturity by 2026, with most of the models based on open source software that is dominated by subscriptions to hosted services, and evaluated by the system's quality of support, functionality, and relative power of application programming interfaces or APIs it offers.

Breeding notes the role that open high-quality linked metadata and progress toward the semantic web will have on improving the user experience, which he hopes will be routine by 2026 and reduce the dependencies on commercial producers of both metadata and content. As documented by Antelman and Wilson, the role of projects like the Global Open Knowledgebase (GOKb) can immediately help libraries to identify duplication between content published in subscribed collections and the same content published in open access initiatives.[35] In many ways, the GOKb project to build a community-sourced knowledge base freely available to libraries, content providers, and metadata providers suffered from its association with the Kuali OLE project and the perception that it would be a competitor to the commercial knowledge base and metadata providers in the marketplace. The reality is that embracing open linked-data systems can only improve the efficiencies for all marketplace players because it would allow them to refocus their energies on developing support for the process of scholarly communication and education rather than simply managing the products of it.

The Power of Relevance

Libraries have an image problem. If they are perceived by the larger communities they serve as irrelevant, they continue to risk dwindling resources and an inability to shake the impression on the part of their funding organizations that they are cost centers rather than revenue generators. Organizations fund what they perceive to be of value. In response, it's not just the systems that help libraries manage electronic or other resources that must change. If the only outcome of the move to library services platforms is to enable libraries to manage the same resources, but faster, then the library profession will have squandered the opportunities this technological change could finally bring. Library missions must change, libraries must do a better job of identifying what their core services should be, and they must stop maintaining services that are no longer core to their new mission. "For us to move forward in doing new things, we have to squeeze and extract from these peripheral services the money, time, and people resources they currently consume and redirect them toward our core services. The 'core' is where we create differentiation and thus ultimately add value for our members and end users."[36] In discussing the future of library systems, Carl Grant believes the power of new library services platforms is the degree to which libraries can use them to reinvent themselves, remake their brand, and regain a reputation of relevance to the communities they serve.

For instance, libraries should be pushing library services platforms to focus on helping to provide a place for knowledge creation, not just discovery. Find a tool that makes information and data discoverable, yes, but then go one step further and provide a space for that user to recombine what he has found with other data to produce more sophisticated analyses, create new works, and then seamlessly feed that new scholarship into open access systems for review, publication, and dissemination. Libraries should deliberately disassociate from the image of themselves as warehouses for books, and instead find creative ways to reinvent space and stock them with systems and tools that routinely allow students and faculty to create rather than consume information.

Given the frequent discussions about the detrimental role that fake news has had on public discourse, there is no doubt a need for educating the general public in the skills necessary for critical thought, exposing them to opposing viewpoints, and making the environment in which knowledge is made and who might fund or profit from it more transparent. Pushing library systems to include this kind of sophisticated context for data and information sources could make libraries the trusted resource for providing this kind of contextualizing service to the larger society.

Mining the aggregated data about library users, their needs, and their experiences could also be another potential success of library services platforms for libraries. Although operationalizing user data is common in the business sector to justify the creation and funding of new services for customers, and to tailor services around unique customer markets, it is something that libraries have been slow to embrace. As Murray, Ireland, and Hackathorn have shown, finding a concrete way to link student use of the library with student retention can do wonders for the library's image and funding opportunities because it taps into the same measures that university administrators use to define their own success when presenting the case for increased higher education funding to state legislatures.[37] In the library used in their study, the authors found that the use of the library's communication center had a positive correlation with student retention and directly translated that into a successful bid for additional funding for the center itself, a model that is now also being used for the library's writing center.

While libraries have long struggled with both the technological and organizational challenges of electronic resource management, the potential of new library services platforms to help them overcome these challenges is so much more than just a better way of managing the resources. If libraries are to embrace the potential of new cloud-computing technologies and LSPs, understanding how local workflow must give way to standardized efficiencies and capitalizing on the staffing surplus this could create, the possibilities for reinvention are only as limited as the will to try something new.

NOTES

1. OCLC, "Meeting the E-Resources Challenge: An OCLC Report on Effective Management, Access and Delivery of Electronic Collections," 2010, www.oclc.org/content/dam/oclc/reports/pdfs/OCLC-E-Resources-Report-UK.pdf.
2. Oliver Pesch, "ERMs and the E-Resource Life-Cycle" (PowerPoint slides), 2009, figure 21, rhttp://tinyurl.com/ERLifeCycle.
3. Timothy D. Jewell et al., *Electronic Resource Management: Report of the DLF ERMI Initiative* (Washington, DC: Digital Library Federation and Council on Library and Information Resoruces, 2005), https://old.diglib.org/pubs/dlf102/.
4. Tim Jewell, *DLF Electronic Resources Management Initiative, Phase II: Final Report* (Washington, DC: Digital Library Federation and Council on Library and Information Resources, 2008), https://old.diglib.org/standards/ERMI2_Final_Report _20081230.pdf.
5. Rafel Kasprowski, "Best Practice and Standardization Initiatives for Managing Electronic Resources," *ASIST Bulletin* 35, no. 1 (2008): 13–19.
6. NISO ERM Data Standards and Best Practices Review Steering Committee, *Making Good on the Promise of ERM: A Standards and Best Practices Discussion Paper,* a NISO White Paper (Baltimore, MD: NISO, 2012).
7. Maria Collins and Jill E Grogg, "Building a Better ERMS," *Library Journal* no. 4 (March 2011): 22–28.
8. NISO ERM Data Standards and Best Practices Review Steering Committee, *Making Good on the Promise of ERM.*
9. Jill Emery and Graham Stone, "TERMS: Techniques for ER Management," 2011, http://6terms.tumblr.com/post/9997650918/what-is-terms.
10. Jill Emery, Graham Stone, and Peter McCracken, "Getting Back on TERMS (Version 2.0)," 2016, https://library.hud.ac.uk/blogs/terms/.
11. Collins and Grogg, "Building a Better ERMS."
12. Yongmin Wang and Trevor A. Dawes, "The Next Generation Integrated Library System: A Promise Fulfilled," *Information Technology and Libraries* 31, no. 3 (2012): 76–84.

13. Kristen Wilson. "Introducing the Next Generation of Library Management Systems," *Serials Review* 38 (2012): 110–23.

14. Peter Mell and Timothy Grance, "The NIST Definition of Cloud Computing," NIST Special Publication 800-145 (Gaithersburg, MD: National Institute of Standards and Technology, 2011).

15. Carl Grant, "The Future of Library Systems: Library Services Platforms," *Information Standards Quarterly* 24, no. 4 (Fall 2012): 4–15.

16. Carl Grant, "The Approaching Divide in the Provision of Library Services...," Thoughts from Carl Grant, August 21, 2013, http://thoughts.care-affiliates.com/2013/08/the-approaching-divide-in-provision-of.html.

17. Grant, "The Future of Library Systems: Library Services Platforms," 4–15.

18. Marshall Breeding, "Power Plays: Library Systems Report 2016," *American Libraries* 47, no. 5 (2016): 30–43.

19. Daniel Forsman, "Change as a Service—Challenges and Effects of a New Paradigm for Library Systems and Content Infrastructure," *Library Management* 33, no. 8/9 (2012): 498–510.

20. Matt Gallagher, "How to Conduct a Library Services Platform Review and Selection," *Information Today* 33, no. 8 (2016): 20–22.

21. OCLC, "Bucknell University," 2016, www.oclc.org/member-stories/bucknell.en.html.

22. OCLC, "Bucknell University and OCLC WorldShare Management Services: Who Says You Can't Have It All?" 2012, http://schd.ws/hosted_files/scelcpz2016/c6/Bucknell_Case-Study.pdf.

23. Rene J. Erlandson and Jeff Kuskie, "To Boldly Go Where Few Have Gone Before: Global E-Resource Management in the Cloud," *The Serials Librarian* 68 (2015): 215–22.

24. Sever Bordeianu and Laura Kohl, "The Voyage Home: New Mexico Libraries Migrate to WMS, OCLC's Cloud-Based ILS," *Technical Services Quarterly* 32, no. 3 (2015): 274–93.

25. PALNI, 2016, www.palni.org/.

26. Noah Brubaker, Susan Leach-Murray, and Sherri Parker, "Shapes in the Cloud: Finding the Right Discovery Layer," *Online* 35, no. 2 (2011): 20–26.

27. Noah Brubaker, Susan Leach-Murray, and Sherri Parker, "Implementing a Discovery Layer: A Rookie's Season," *Computers in Libraries* 32, no. 3 (2012): 13–19.

28. Marshall Breeding, "Case Study," in *Resource Sharing in Libraries: Concepts, Products, Technologies, and Trends*, by Marshall Breeding (Chicago: American Library Association, 2013), 30–31.

29. Alan Cornish, Richard Jost, and Xan Arch, "Selecting a Shared 21st Century Management System," *Collaborative Librarianship* 5, no. 1 (2013): 16–28.

30. Al Cornish, "OCLC Web-Scale Management Services Presentation Montana Shared Catalog, Fall 2010 Membership Meeting," presentation handout, OCLC Web-Scale Management Services, 2010, https://research.libraries.wsu.edu/xmlui/bitstream/handle/2376/2652/wmsCornishHandout.pdf?sequence=1.

31. Ping Fu and Julie Carmen, "Migration to Alma/Primo: A Case Study of Central Washington University," *Chinese Librarianship: An International Electronic Journal,* no. 40 (2015): 1–14.

32. Morag Stewart and Cheryl Aine Morrison, "Notes on Operations Breaking Ground: Consortial Migration to a Next-Generation ILS and Its Impact on Acquisitions Workflows," *Library Resources and Technical Services* 60, no. 4 (2016): 259–69.

33. Lenore England and Randy Lowe, "ERM Ideas and Innovations," *Journal of Electronic Resources Librarianship* 28, no. 3 (2016): 186–92.

34. Marshall Breeding, "Current and Future Trends in Information Technologies for Information Units," *El Profesional de la Informacion* 21, no. 1 (2011): 9–15.

35. Kristin Antelman and Kristen Wilson, "The Global Open Knowledgebase (GOKb): Open Linked Data Supporting Electronic Resources Management and Scholarly Communication," *Insights* 28, no. 1 (2015): 42–50.

36. Grant, "The Future of Library Systems: Library Services Platforms," 4–15.

37. Adam Murray, Ashley Ireland, and Jana Hackathorn, "The Value of Academic Libraries: Library Services as a Predictor of Student Retention," *College and Research Libraries* 77, no. 5 (2016): 631–42.

7

The Library in the Information Marketplace
Cost Containment Strategies

George Stachokas

T. Scott Plutchak presented a lecture, "Breaking the Barriers of Time and Space: The Dawning of the Great Age of Librarians," at the Medical Library Association Conference in Minneapolis on May 16, 2011. I did not have the pleasure of attending in person, but thanks to digital information, I know that Plutchak compared the contemporary information age with its digital information resources to the revolution of the printing press inaugurated by Gutenberg in the fifteenth century. Even though it took only about fifty years to perfect the basic technology of printing, it took considerably longer for society to adapt to the new technology. The full consequences of this adaptation ranged from mass literacy to revolutionary changes in industry, government, and warfare that built the modern world as we know it. Plutchak, in my opinion, rightly assumes that libraries have yet to adapt to electronic resources. In his own words, "What was required for a mature print culture was the transformation of the legal, political, social and cultural frameworks that were necessary to take advantage of those innovations."[1] One of the most important frameworks is the contemporary marketplace for information resources. As libraries continue to advance, pursuing all manner of improvements in collections and services, how do we pay for it all?

The state of the information marketplace for libraries in recent times continues to put most institutions at a distinct disadvantage. As Stephen Bosch and Kittie Henderson note in their recent "Periodical Prices Survey" featured in *Library Journal,* the average annual cost of journals for different scientific disciplines ranged from $5,105 for chemistry to $1,687 for agriculture.[2] Furthermore, for 2017, Bosch and Henderson forecast a 5.2 percent average price increase for titles included in the Arts & Humanities Citation Index, 7.2 percent for titles included in the Social Sciences Citation Index, and 5.6 percent for titles in the Science Citation Index.[3] Most academic librarians are already very familiar with the dilemma raised by annual subscription costs for electronic journals that exceed inflation, combined with flat, nearly flat, or declining library materials budgets. Subscription fees for databases sometimes reach six figures at major research libraries in the United States, and the cost of e-books, while roughly comparable to print books, still generally exceeds print book costs, especially when online content is made accessible to an unlimited number of simultaneous users. In addition, some e-book packages are priced for as subscription packages with a purchase model that resembles expensive databases.

Saving money on electronic resources acquisitions requires a careful determination of what is needed to serve particular academic programs, a complex process that is beyond the scope of this chapter. Good license agreements and thorough collection analysis based on the best available quantitative and qualitative information are also necessary, but these topics are addressed by other chapters in this book. This chapter provides a discussion of major trends, business models, general engagement with vendors, and the negotiation process.

AFTER THE GREAT RECESSION

The Great Recession of 2008 hit higher education particularly hard, and had enduring negative consequences that are global in scope. For many academic libraries of all sizes, this was a time of budget cuts, salary freezes or reduced raises, the elimination of open positions, and the enforced cancellation of many electronic serial subscriptions. The title of an article published in *Library Journal* announced to the world that "Large ARL Libraries Struggle" on June 1, 2009.[4] Nicholas et al. analyzed the findings from a global survey with 800 respondents conducted by the Charleston Observatory in 2009, along with a focus group study of sixteen librarians from British universities, in order to better understand the full negative impact of the Great Recession on libraries. A total of 27 percent of academic librarians reported budget reductions of more than 10 percent. Another 16.8 percent reported reductions of less than 10 percent, while 39.4 percent reported flat budgets. This meant that over 80 percent of academic librarians faced flat or declining budgets in 2009.[5] One key impact of these grim budgetary realities, particularly in the United States, was to help accelerate the change from print to electronic formats, with 62.5 percent indicating that their libraries planned to shift more subscriptions to electronic formats in order to help reduce costs.[6]

Charles Lowry analyzed the results of a survey of 123 Association of Research Libraries (ARL) members for their responses to the crisis in fiscal year 2008–2009 and fiscal year 2009–2010. Many academic libraries that had been spared in 2008–2009 experienced deeper cuts in 2009–2010, while others that had already been cut received little relief. A total of 77 percent of 74 responding ARL members experienced budget reductions ranging from 0.01 to 22 percent in 2009–2010.[7] A total of 56 ARL members reported the following strategies for reducing the cost of acquisitions in 2009–2010: 54 percent, the highest ranking, canceled serial subscriptions; 41 percent reduced monograph purchases; 30 percent canceled database subscriptions; and 21 percent shifted journals from print format to online or electronic-only formats.[8] Regarding staffing reductions, 66 percent of 70 responding libraries eliminated vacant positions in this period; 43 percent froze new hires; 28 percent laid off staff; and 25 percent encouraged their employees to pursue early retirement.[9]

While ARL members certainly endured a great deal of pain during this period of time, the impact on smaller, non-ARL libraries was much worse, as confirmed by data from the National Center of Education Statistics. Regazzi's study of changes in 2008–2010 builds on his previous analysis of long-term trends from 1998 to 2008. Very small libraries experienced a 19 percent reduction in staffing from 1998 to 2008, and this continued through 2010. Spending on electronic serials from 1998 to 2008 rose by 110 percent in very small libraries, but was 699 percent greater in large libraries. Expenditures continued to rise on electronic serials in large libraries from 2008 to 2010, but the increase was 0 percent in very small libraries. Large libraries lost about 7 percent of their total staffing from 1998 to 2008, with another 3 percent loss from 2008 to 2010, but very small libraries lost 19 percent of their total staffing from 1998 to 2008 and 21 percent from 2008 to 2010. Small libraries also lost 20 percent and 10 percent of their staffing in these respective time periods, with losses for medium libraries more closely approximating larger libraries at 9 percent from 1998 to 2008 and 3 percent from 2008 to 2010.[10] Regazzi identified three major trends during the period of 1998 to 2008 that were accelerated during the Great Recession from 2009 to 2010: (1) large libraries continued to separate themselves from all other libraries in terms of the scope and scale of their information services; (2) library operations shifted from labor- to more capital-intensive operations, from print to electronic format in collections, and from an emphasis on physical space to virtual space; and finally (3) the overall productivity of library staff increased while the unit costs for information resources tended to go down.[11]

REVISITING THE BIG DEAL

Beyond an acceleration of the transition from print to electronic formats, libraries also began to investigate different business models for electronic resources more intensively in the aftermath of the Great Recession. One early and sustained point of contention has been the "big deal," the large journal packages that many large libraries and consortia have negotiated with publishers in order to maximize access to electronic journals while driving down unit costs. An installment of "The Balance Point" published in *Serials Review* in 2012 included the views of thirteen different contributors from the publishing world, academic libraries, and consortia. While opinions differed regarding the value of the big deal, potential survival and prospects for replacing big deals varied among participants. There was a general recognition of the economic pressures driving libraries to consider different options. Some suggested greater reliance on interlibrary loan, pay-per-view or just-in-time acquisitions, smaller packages, and single-title subscriptions. Others also raised open-access options, driven partly by practical concerns regarding pricing, but also equity and access to information. Most agreed, however, that the big deal was still a functional reality for many libraries and consortia.[12]

Research Libraries UK (RLUK), the equivalent of ARL in North America, pursued a dual-track strategy in 2010–2011 to pressure Wiley and Elsevier to reduce the cost of their big deal journal packages. Plan A consisted of three demands by the 21 member libraries agreed upon in October 2010: (1) a return to 2007 fees, effectively a 15 percent reduction in the overall cost of the packages, (2) the ability to make payment in British pounds sterling, and (3) a waiver of the requirement to make full payment in advance. Plan B was a kind of cooperative collection development scheme in which member libraries would balance subscriptions to the most highly used and highly desired titles with document delivery using the British Library's Document Delivery Center as well as RLUK member library collections.[13] Having appointed a steering committee for the Affordable Subscriptions for Periodicals Initiative (ASPI), RLUK librarians began to analyze the potential costs, benefits, and risks of switching to select title subscriptions and document delivery. Interestingly, ASPI did not accept the usage statistics provided by Wiley or Elsevier. They considered only 65 percent of Elsevier usage to be a reliable measure of demand, while Wiley's usage statistics were thought to be inflated by 10 percent. Factoring in an anticipated 14 percent annual increase in usage, ASPI made projections of future demand. Based on data from other libraries and other sources, ASPI also assumed that actual document delivery requests (DDR) would fall short of lost downloads, with an estimated 35 DDR for every 100 full-text downloads. While negotiations with the two publishers continued, ASPI organized a document delivery workshop for participating libraries, determined that print subscriptions rather than electronic format were the best investment for document delivery, and worked to put together title lists for each library. Ultimately, Plan B was never implemented due to success in achieving most of the terms of Plan A, which saved RLUK members an estimated £20 million.[14] It is possible that the visible attempt to implement Plan B helped to influence Elsevier and Wiley to come to more agreeable terms, but since Plan B was never implemented, it would be difficult to assess its long-term viability.

The University of Oregon and Southern Illinois University Carbondale (SIUC) decided to leave their own big deals with Elsevier and Wiley due to the financial impact of the Great Recession. In fact, SIUC also decided to leave its big deal with Springer. By canceling these deals, SIUC users lost access to 242 Elsevier titles, 597 Wiley titles, and 1,100 Springer titles. These titles accounted for 40,000 downloads, but Jonathan Nabe notes how 82 percent of the canceled Springer journals received only one download per month or less.[15] With at least one year of data for analysis, Nabe found that ILL requests were submitted for only 27 percent of the canceled Wiley titles, and only 9 percent were requested more than once. By another measure, for the most highly used 25 percent of the canceled Wiley titles, there were only 71 ILL requests for titles that had previously had 7,770 downloads.[16] Protests from users were described by Nabe as "minimal," but when these did occur, sharing data and asking users to find alternative titles to cancel usually resolved any concerns. Canceling the big deals resulted in $300,000 of annual savings, and attempts by vendors to slap additional penalties onto SIUC were mostly prevented through negotiations.[17] David C. Fowler noted how the University of Oregon took a somewhat different tack by replacing its Elsevier big deal package obtained through the Orbis-Cascade Alliance consortium with a mini-consortium arrangement with Oregon State University and Portland State University based on a smaller shared title list that represented around 90 percent of their combined usage.[18] The savings were smaller than SIUC had experienced, but were sufficient to stabilize their materials budget when taken in conjunction with cuts to Wiley subscriptions. Chemistry and physics faculty expressed the most concern, but providing pay-per-view services was considered in order to address needs in these areas as a supplement for interlibrary loan. The Wiley big deal was canceled outright and replaced by single-title subscriptions to 297 journals.[19] Both Jonathan Nabe and David Fowler were comfortable reporting in 2015 that their respective institutions continued to benefit from the choices made from 2008 to 2010. Both universities reported limited impact on interlibrary loan requests and were satisfied with the overall impact on their materials budgets and the research activities on their respective campuses.[20]

Mary Ann Jones et al. have reported a less positive experience in canceling their Wiley-Blackwell and Springer big deal packages at Mississippi State University (MSU). Pressed for time and needing to address a $500,000 budget cut in fiscal year 2012, MSU librarians had to rely almost exclusively on usage statistics. Access to 2,800 journals was lost and the impact fell disproportionately on some disciplines, particularly in the social sciences. Jones and her colleagues concluded that their experience confirmed the need to gather qualitative information in addition to quantitative information before selecting titles for cancellation, especially the input of subject specialist librarians and faculty who teach and conduct research on campus.[21]

Iowa State University (ISU) used an evaluation model based on cost per use and interlibrary loan costs to evaluate big deals with Springer and Wiley. Library personnel began gathering data in 2010 in anticipation of the 2012 renewal of their Springer package. Titles with a cost per use exceeding $17.50, a figure taken from an ARL ILL cost study conducted in 2003, were identified by Acquisitions Department staff as candidates for possible cancellation in consultation with subject specialist librarians. Some titles, particularly those with a high-impact factor, were re-subscribed to later by the library, indicating the value of using this metric in conjunction with other data to evaluate journals that staff planned to consider for future cancellation. Interestingly, there was little increase in overall ILL activity.[22] ISU Library staff later applied lessons learned to the renewal of their Wiley big deal in 2014. Based on their experience at ISU, Wayne Pedersen recommends that libraries calculate the cost per use for all big deals at their institution for comparison, while remaining cognizant of important differences in online platforms. Pedersen also recommends that libraries gather local ILL data, consult with subject specialists regarding specific titles, make sure to document clearly all criteria used in the evaluation of journals, monitor the consequences of cancellation—including ILL activity—well into the future, and establish a fund to acquire titles that have excessive ILL demand, as well as create a system for identifying journals that are not being used at the level expected for an active subscription.[23]

Some of the immediate concerns regarding big deals were likely driven by the shock of the Great Recession and its impact on funding for higher education, including academic libraries, but for many librarians, the big deal is just another business model that requires evaluation relevant to the needs of local users. As Sarah Glasser points out, the big deal may or may not be a good deal. An analysis of five big deal packages conducted by Hofstra University in 2012 found that all but one was a good deal for that university. One important measure of value was the low cost of use, ranging from $4.59 to $9.44 per download, but what was decisive for Hofstra was that in all but one case, the cost for subscribing to highly used individual titles exceeded the cost of the entire package.[24] Glasser was careful to note that in the event of cancellation, subject specialist librarians and faculty on campus would have to be consulted, and while metrics are useful, one must understand their limitations.[25]

The Maastricht University Library in the Netherlands evaluated its big deals and found that it saved up to 40 percent with their packages, in comparison to the cost of single-title subscriptions regarding its core title lists by subject discipline. Parameters included in the library's evaluation were a list of core titles as determined by academic faculty, usage statistics, a list of current titles, a list of future titles (when available), list prices for all titles, and impact factors. The library chose to leave out usage per user or faculty or by subject, the number of articles published by their own faculty in the journals under evaluation, the percentage of titles used in the package(s), and the total of the list prices for all used titles in the packages.[26] Some institutions have taken an even more comprehensive approach. For example, Kansas University (KU) has used COUNTER usage statistics, usage from their institutional repository, impact factor, Eigenfactor, Project MESUR (Measures from Scholarly Usage of Resources), overlap analysis, altmetrics, e-mail, web/click statistics, discovery tool statistics, OpenURL statistics, usability studies, and other surveys in the efforts to evaluate big deals.[27] KU librarians also developed a formula for estimating potential interlibrary loan costs for unsubscribed journals based on the total number of unsubscribed titles, annualized usage of unsubscribed titles (prior to cancellation), average copyright fees per article set at $45, estimated staff cost of $7 per article (presumably based on local staffing), and the fact that the first five articles were freely available as per CONTU guidelines.[28] Mitchell Scott has calculated a ratio of 17 to 1 for COUNTER uses to ILL request based on the University of Wisconsin-Milwaukee's usage data for Elsevier, Springer, and Wiley journals from 2006 to 2008.[29] The University of South Alabama used a comparison of cost per use for journals in packages vs. single-title subscriptions, pay-per-view costs, and ILL fees to evaluate its subscription models.[30] Duke University, the University of North Carolina at Chapel Hill, and North Carolina State University have all attempted to take a deeper look at return on investment by using a cost-per-cited-reference (CPCR) based on citation data from Scopus. Their use of CPCR was intended to reduce reliance on cost per use in analyzing library spending on subscriptions, and while this is imperfect, the authors of the study recommended the continued use of CPCR in collection evaluation.[31]

The Canadian Research Knowledge Network, a national library consortium in Canada, applied a weighted-value algorithm measuring quality, utility, and value to evaluate big deal packages across multiple institutions, with the conclusion that these large packages were indeed cost-effective for most member libraries. The data points used included usage, faculty publications, impact factor, source-normalized impact per paper (SNIP), cost per use, and cost per SNIP. Furthermore, the utilization of multiyear contracts combined with the purchasing power of very large regional and national consortia were successful in regulating price increases for their member libraries.[32] A study of the licensing of large journal packages or big deals between 2002 and 2012 revealed that most ARL members continued to subscribe to big deals, mostly negotiated through consortia, although cost increases and provisions for interlibrary loan or lack thereof were matters of concern. Other observed trends were an increase in open access titles and a further decline in print serials subscriptions.[33]

OTHER BUSINESS MODELS

A discussion with five thought leaders regarding the big deal compiled by Carlen Ruschoff in 2014 concluded that the big deal was far from dead, but its role in the information marketplace was likely subject to change given the emergence of more open-access titles, the HathiTrust initiative, and other coalitions. Finally, a conversation was needed between publishers and librarians to help find more viable models. Rick Anderson, in particular, questioned the long-term viability of the big deal given that most library materials budgets were flat and could not handle even modest annual cost increases.[34] This is true, but it also raises the issue of why library budgets remain flat and it begs the question, what can be done about it? This issue will be discussed later in this chapter, but, suffice it to say, the big deal is one of many business models that are likely to remain in some form. Big deals may even become more of an issue for other types of electronic resources such as e-books. Steven Shapiro of Montclair State University raises concern about the emergence of e-book big deals, arguing that librarians save money and preserve their professional discretion through patron-driven acquisition, demand-driven acquisition, and evidence-based acquisition models, as well as selective individual title purchases, rather than relying on the judgment of publishers.[35] Shapiro's concerns about the discretion of individual librarians in building collections echoed earlier concerns about journal packages, and it remains to be seen if more cost- and value-driven metrics will be applied and/or developed to analyze e-book big deals.

Consortia were at the forefront in developing big deals, and they continue to play a critical role in helping libraries save money on electronic resources acquisitions. Drawing on an MBA and a background in the soft drink industry, Tom Sanville, executive director of OhioLINK from 1992 to 2010, understood economies of scale and applied his knowledge and experience to help develop big deals that sharply drove the unit cost of information down.[36] However, even Sanville began to consider an orderly retreat from the big deal in 2004 in response to high annual cost increases.[37] As George Machovec of the Colorado Alliance notes, big deal packages remain highly attractive to libraries and are difficult to cancel. Machovec calls for publishers and other vendors to accept more standardized terms and conditions such as interlibrary loan rights without the need for recurring negotiations, but above all greater flexibility in terms of the configuration of packages and the ability to secure group discounts even when member libraries prefer to choose different options.[38] Finally, just as individual libraries are increasingly challenged by e-books, many consortia also see e-books as a growing challenge. The member libraries of OhioLINK are increasingly converting stacks' space to other uses and buying more e-books, as well as expanding distance education programs, but licensing restrictions, particularly on resource sharing, and the high cost of some business models make consortial acquisitions more difficult. Frustration at lack of access to e-books by users in member libraries led to the removal of all non-sharable e-resources from their union catalog in 2016.[39]

Apart from big deals, libraries also increasingly made use of patron-driven acquisitions (PDA), demand-driven acquisitions (DDA), evidence-based acquisitions (EBA), and pay per view (PPV) in the wake of the Great Recession. Most PDA programs allow libraries to advertise thousands of titles directly to users through metadata, with actual purchases triggered by usage. Although just-in-time acquisition has also been used for print resources, only with electronic resources does the model genuinely deliver an information resource immediately upon a user's request. Depending on the parameters of the individual program and underlying licensing, users can browse and even make sure that they need or do not need to use specific titles before the library is obligated to pay the full cost of an item. When used in conjunction with interlibrary loan services, just-in-time purchases can be cost-effective alternatives to resource sharing between libraries.[40] A survey of Indiana library directors with 28 respondents in 2014 found high levels of support for PDA e-book programs that mirrored similar findings from a contemporary survey of 8 CIC library collection development officers.[41]

Pay-per-view services, particularly for online journals, require consideration of whether the service will be mediated by library staff or made directly available to users. The Florida Institute of Technology (FIT) decided to test PPV options in 2010 after a significant budget cut, designating funds for Wiley and Elsevier deposit accounts in 2011. The Evans Library at FIT started with a mediated program using the Wiley Online Library with a streamlined workflow in Illiad, but then switched to unmediated access in June 2011. Duplication of requests, sometimes from the same user, averaged 30 percent per month after the change to unmediated access. Users also sometimes selected full-text content that while not available through the library's subscriptions, was otherwise freely available online through institutional repositories, PubMed, or by other means.[42] Hosburgh concluded that for titles with low anticipated usage, PPV was a more reliable and convenient replacement for interlibrary loan services. However, given the average 30 percent duplication of unmediated PPV, mediated PPV or a better use of automated technology to reduce duplication would be necessary for libraries that cannot afford to pay more than once for identical content.[43]

Open access is sometimes cited as the ultimate answer to the problems of rising electronic serial costs for academic libraries. While it is not possible to address every aspect of this rich and interesting topic in this chapter, it is necessary to consider freely accessible electronic resources in terms of cost containment for academic libraries. There are different types of open access, but green open access, in which authors self-archive their articles in repositories where these can be freely accessed, and gold access, in which publishers make their online content freely available from their own websites, are the most common. Writing in 2012, David Lewis has argued that open access is inevitable. Based on data from sampling performed by Mikael Laakso et al.,[44] for the percentage of articles available in Gold Open Access (OA) from 2000 to 2009, Lewis uses an s-curve extrapolation to show that by 2020, an estimated 89.9 percent of articles are predicted to be Gold OA. Based on data from 2005–2009 only, Lewis uses another curve to estimate that only 43.2 percent of articles will be Gold OA in 2020, but 94.6 percent will achieve that status by 2025.[45] According to Peter Suber, "money already spent on journals by academic libraries is more than enough to pay for high-quality OA journals in every scholarly niche. We don't need new money, we just need to redirect the money we already spend."[46] Walt Crawford notes that "OA was idealistic" in its earliest phase of development between 1987 and 2001. Later, many journals started collecting article-processing charges (APCs), particularly after 2006. At the time of writing in 2015, Crawford noted that while some journals were charging just enough money to maintain operations, the average cost to publish an article in journals that did charge APCs was $1,045 while the average cost for all articles, including no-fee journals, was $630.[47] Clifford Lynch has expressed doubt about the ability of most colleges and universities to enforce the mandates necessary for depositing scholarly research in institutional repositories, as well as concerns about the funding for long-term curation and preservation of OA content in general.[48] John Wenzler argues that universal open access is dependent on libraries or other academic units being able to coordinate their activities systematically in collective action for the greater good. Given that academic libraries are separate entities with their own interests, cooperation on that scale seems highly unlikely. Wenzler believes that libraries will be paying too much for many journals for the foreseeable future, with the open access movement, at best, being a source of some freely available content and perhaps serving as a tool to encourage some publishers into negotiating better deals. Wenzler suggests some alternative strategies such as government regulation of journal pricing, which he admits is also unlikely, or for libraries to pool together their resources in order to manage large journal packages as cooperatives.[49]

In terms of cost containment, making high-quality, freely available electronic resources discoverable to their users is an important strategy for academic libraries. Some commercially available databases and other electronic resources merely duplicate government information, for example. As long as a freely available information resource meets academic requirements, is or can be made discoverable, and is acceptable in terms of overall usability or ease of use, it does not make sense to pay for duplicate content. However, libraries do have to be careful to avoid predatory open-access journals. Ayeni and Adetoro suggest that libraries consult sources such as the Directory of Open Access Journals (DOAJ), Journal Citation Reports, the SCImago journal ranking, and the Global serials directory, among others, to help evaluate OA journals.[50]

SUCCESSFUL VENDOR RELATIONS

Beyond selecting correct business models for electronic content whether that be a big deal, small collection, single-title acquisition, PPV, PDA/DDA/EBA, or interlibrary loan or other variation, librarians need to consider how they engage and negotiate with vendors because these important business relationships can save or lose money for academic libraries. Being on good terms with library vendors enables libraries to request extensions, duplicate copies of lost or missing documentation, and receive credits if last-minute changes must be made to orders that are beyond the library's control. However, the single most important reason is information. Vendor representatives are an indispensable source of information about what is available, what might be available, and how to approach their respective organizations in order to obtain the most content at the lowest possible price.

Outside of technical services and collection development, most librarians that I have encountered have not been particularly interested in working with vendors and undertaking some of the more difficult work involved, such as negotiation for pricing and licensing terms. Some have identified financial literacy as a problem for academic librarians in a rapidly changing society.[51] This is understandable considering that most academic librarians are professionals in the academic world and are generally not familiar with best practices in business or how to handle professional relationships that require representing organizations with different interests. The first step in any negotiation is gathering intelligence or doing your "homework," as Beth Ashmore, Jill E. Grogg, and Jeff Weddle point out in their book *The Librarian's Guide to Negotiation: Winning Strategies for the Digital Age*.[52] Since practical considerations are less visible in our professional literature than would be optimal, I thought it might be helpful to make some suggestions based on my own experience as an electronic resources librarian at ARL and non-ARL libraries, chair of the Resource Advisory Committee, and volunteer negotiator for the Academic Libraries of Indiana consortium.

Once an electronic resource has been identified as having value as a potential acquisition (meeting curricular, research, or other information needs of the user population), I try to learn all I can about the vendor or content provider as an organization. Investing in electronic resources is a risk, and one has to consider much more than price for potential acquisitions. Is the content provider a for-profit vendor, or is it associated with a nonprofit organization such as a university or government agency? What resources does it offer? Does it appear to be stable in its current configuration, or can one anticipate any changes such as mergers, sales, or some other reorganization that could impact available content, pricing models, or customer service? Since libraries are investing in electronic resources, it cannot hurt to check share prices and financial information, ownership changes, leadership and personnel changes, outstanding or notable legal cases—particularly anything involving intellectual property rights—news, press releases, and any noticeable turnover in sales representatives and other specialists.[53]

For providers of electronic resources, I always try to consider technology and customer service as well as business models. Is the same content available on more than one platform or from more than one source? Is the metadata good, bad, or indifferent compared to expectations? What is the reputation of the organization? Does the organization have any links or ties to my own organization beyond sales? Do faculty members at my institution publish in particular journals? Do any librarians at my institution sit on advisory boards? I also try to consult with my colleagues about how they have interacted with a given vendor organization and if they have any insight to share.

Next, I try to get to know the individual representatives of vendor organizations who will work with me. Getting along is very important even when we agree to disagree on particular acquisitions, business models, or other business matters. I try to maintain collegial, professional relationships but I also try to be cordial, responsive, and as helpful as I can be when working with vendors. As circumstances permit, I let vendor representatives know that I am just as interested in hearing what they have to say as I hope they are to what I have to say. I reassure them that I understand the aims of our organizations are different, but I neither resent nor misunderstand their need to pursue profit even though I myself have chosen to work for a nonprofit organization. As Rick Anderson notes, librarians should mirror the professionalism that they would like to see from vendors, including attending meetings on time, being responsive to e-mail messages and telephone calls, staying on task, focusing on business, and not allowing one's personal feelings to cloud one's judgment.[54]

I try to learn as much as I can about available business models, and what might be permissible or not, particularly with regard to how much personal discretion or influence the person I am speaking with has over a particular acquisition. Is he or she authorized to provide discounts? If yes, at what level? Does the person also work with consortia? How can my library get the best possible deal? Would the vendor be open to crafting an entirely new business model if I can demonstrate how it might work to the advantage of both organizations? Negotiation need not be adversarial or contentious in order to be effective. It is important to be able to say no or be able to walk away from specific offers while maintaining positive relations with vendors over the long term. As Peggy Johnson reminds us, "Starting with interests instead of positions opens the door to effective negotiation by making clear the basic problem to be solved."[55]

As a practical matter, I typically ask if a vendor's price quote is negotiable or not. Would it be possible to bundle a potential acquisition with another, even across formats? I also remind vendors of our total spend and ask if that might be taken into consideration. If we purchase a journal archive, might we expect a discount on a new e-book package? If we currently subscribe to multiple journals not included in a journal package, would the vendor be open to creating a customized package? Could we negotiate an agreement that would reduce or even freeze our annual cost increase for the next three, four, or five years? A common pitfall for some librarians, which I also try to avoid, is resources that are initially made available at lower costs, but soon rise in future years. Tracking and mitigating cost increases for existing subscriptions and financial obligations are as important as obtaining discounts on new acquisitions.

One has to strike an effective balance between advocating for the library while exploring ways to find mutual agreement. Getting along, of course, does not always mean going along. While invitations to dinner, service on advisory boards, and other interactions and collaborations with vendors can promote good business that ultimately benefits libraries, librarians must be careful to avoid compromising their fundamental institutional interests and make sure to address problems as these occur with professional candor.[56] Electronic resources librarians sometimes serve as professional diplomats of a sort, navigating the complex boundaries and intersections between academia and business in hard times. Academic libraries play a different role than commercial vendors in the information ecosystem, but they should still be ready to do professional business as required on behalf of their users.

Cost containment for electronic resource acquisitions begins with determining collection development needs and technological requirements. One then faces the challenge of finding the cheapest way to obtain the most content with the fewest possible restrictions on access, including considerations of outright ownership and perpetual access. As we have discussed, libraries during the past ten years have approached this problem using a wide variety of methods ranging from big deals to pay per view, demand-driven acquisitions, EBA, disaggregation and cancellation projects, and open access and freely available electronic resources, as well as smaller, more customizable arrangements with vendors. Choosing the right method in any particular case requires ever more complex and thorough collection analysis, as well as an understanding of the ever-evolving mission and strategy of the academic institution that the library services. The successful application of these business models also requires that librarians learn from the professional techniques and best practices of the business world, particularly in negotiating pricing and complex licensing terms with vendors. While the academic library cannot and should not be managed like a business, librarians must be able to do good business in order to make developing electronic collections financially sustainable in the long run.

NOTES

1. T. Scott Plutchak, "Breaking the Barriers of Time and Space: The Dawning of the Great Age of Librarians," *Journal of the Medical Library Association* 100, no. 1 (2012): 18.
2. Stephen Bosch and Kittie Henderson, "Fracking the Ecosystem," *Library Journal* 141, no. 7 (2016): 32.
3. Ibid., 38.
4. Norman Oder, Lynn Blumenstein, Josh Hadro, and Michael Rogers, "[newsdesk]," *Library Journal* 134, no. 10 (2009): 12.
5. David Nicholas, Ian Rowlands, Michael Jubb, and Hamid R. Jmali, "The Impact of the Economic Downturn on Libraries: With Special Reference to University Libraries," *The Journal of Academic Librarianship* 36, no. 5 (2010): 377.
6. Ibid., 381.
7. Charles B. Lowry, "Year 2 of the 'Great Recession': Surviving the Present by Building the Future," *Journal of Library Administration* 51 (2011): 41–42.
8. Ibid., 44.
9. Ibid., 45.
10. John J. Regazzi, "U.S. Academic Library Spending, Staffing and Utilization during the Great Recession 2008–2010," *The Journal of Academic Librarianship* 39 (2012): 219.
11. Ibid., 220–22.
12. Sharon Dyas-Correia, column editor, et al., "Is the 'Big Deal' Dying?" *Serials Review* 38 (2012): 36–45.
13. Mike McGrath, "Fighting Back against the Big Deals: A Success Story from the UK," *Interlending & Document Supply* 40, no. 4 (2012): 178.
14. Ibid., 178–84.
15. Jonathan Nabe and David C. Fowler, presenters, "Leaving the 'Big Deal': Consequences and Next Steps," *The Serials Librarian* 61, no. 1–4 (2012): 60.
16. Ibid., 61.
17. Ibid., 62–64.
18. Ibid., 67–68.
19. Ibid., 69–72.
20. Jonathan Nabe and David C. Fowler, "Leaving the 'Big Deal' . . . Five Years Later," *The Serials Librarian* 69, no. 1 (2015): 20–28.
21. Mary Ann Jones, Derek Marshall, and Sharon A. Purtree, "'Big Deal' Deconstruction," *The Serials Librarian* 64, no. 1–4 (2013): 137–40.
22. Wayne Pedersen, "The Big Deal, Interlibrary Loan, and Building the User-Centered Journal Collection: A Case Study," *Serials Review* 40, no. 4 (2014): 244–46.
23. Ibid., 248–49.

24. Sarah Glasser,"Judging Big Deals: Challenges, Outcomes, and Advice," *Journal of Electronic Resources Librarianship* 25, no. 4 (2013): 269–74.

25. Ibid., 274.

26. Angelique Dikboom, "Tackling Big Deals: The Experience of Maastricht University," *Interlending & Document Supply* 44, no. 3 (2016): 94–95.

27. Angie Rathmel, Lea Currie, and Todd Enoch, "'Big Deals' and Squeaky Wheels: Taking Stock of Your Stats," *The Serials Librarian* 68, no. 1–4 (2015): 27–28.

28. Ibid., 34.

29. Mitchell Scott, "Predicting Use: COUNTER Usage Data Found to Be Predictive of ILL Use and ILL Use to Be Predictive of COUNTER Use," *The Serials Librarian* 71, no. 1 (2016): 22.

30. Trey Lemley and Jie Li, "'Big Deal' Journal Subscription Packages: Are They Worth the Cost?" *The Journal of Electronic Resources Librarianship* 12, no. 1 (2015): 4.

31. Virginia Martin, Teddy Gray, Megan Kilb, and Tessa Minchew, "Analyzing Consortial 'Big Deals' via a Cost-per-Cited-Reference (CPCR) Metric," *Serials Review* 42, no. 4 (2016): 300–304.

32. Eva Jurczyk and Pamela Jacobs, "What's the Big Deal? Collection Evaluation at the National Level," *portal: Libraries and the Academy* 14, no. 4 (2014): 617–27.

33. Karla L. Strieb and Julia C. Blixrud, "Unwrapping the Bundle: An Examination of Research Libraries and the 'Big Deal,'" *portal: Libraries and the Academy* 14, no. 4 (2014): 603–5.

34. Carlen Ruschoff, "Reality Check, the Big Deal—Dead or Alive?" *Technicalities* 34, no. 2 (2014): 6–9.

35. Steven Shapiro, "The 'Big Deal' in E-Books," *Journal of Electronic Resources Librarianship* 24, no. 4 (2016): 287–89.

36. Kathy A. Perry, "Tom Sanville in Conversation," *Collaborative Librarianship* 7, no. 1 (2015): 30–37.

37. Jeffrey N. Gatten and Tom Sanville, "An Orderly Retreat from the Big Deal: Is It Possible for Consortia?" *D-Lib Magazine* 10, no. 10 (2004): 1.

38. George Machovec, "Library Networking and Consortia," *Journal of Library Administration* 54 (2014): 629–36.

39. Gwen Evans and Theda Schwing, "OhioLINK—Recent Developments at a United States Academic Library Consortium," *Interlending & Document Supply* 44, no. 4 (2016): 176–77.

40. Suzanne M. Ward, "Patrons: Your New Partners in Collection Development," *American Libraries* 45, no. 3/4 (2014): 13.

41. Robert S. Freeman, Judith M. Nixon, and Suzanne M. Ward, "Indiana Library Directors' Perceptions of E-Book Patron-Driven Acquisitions," *Indiana Libraries* 34, no. 1 (2015): 22–26.

42. Nathan Hosburgh, "Getting the Most Out of Pay-per-View: A Feasibility Study and Discussion of Mediated and Unmediated Options," *Journal of Electronic Resources Librarianship* 24, no. 3 (2012): 204–10.

43. Ibid., 210–11.

44. Mikael Laakso et al., "The Development of Open Access Journal Publishing from 1993 to 2009," *PLos ONE* 6 (2011): e20961.

45. David Lewis, "The Inevitability of Open Access," *College & Research Libraries* 73, no. 5 (2012): 501–2.

46. Cheryl LaGuardia, "An Interview with Peter Suber," *Library Journal* 140, no. 1 (2015): 19.

47. Walt Crawford, "Idealism and Opportunism: The State of Open Access Journals," *American Libraries* 46, no. 6 (2015): 32.

48. Clifford Lynch, "Updating the Agenda for Academic Libraries and Scholarly Communications," *Copyright, Fair Use, Scholarly Communication, etc.* 40 (2017): 126–29.

49. John Wenzler, "Scholarly Communication and the Dilemma of Collection Action: Why Academic Journals Cost Too Much," *College & Research Libraries* 78 (2017): 184.

50. Philips Oluwaseun Ayeni and Niran Adetoro, "Growth of Predatory Open Access Journals: Implications for Quality Assurance in Library and Information Science Research," *Library Hi Tech News* 34, no. 1 (2017): 20.

51. Glen E. Holt and Leslie Edmonds Holt, *Crash Course in Library Budgeting and Finance* (Santa Barbara, CA: Libraries Unlimited, 2016), 13–19.

52. Beth Ashmore, Jill E. Grogg, and Jeff Weddle, *The Librarian's Guide to Negotiation: Winning Strategies for the Digital Age* (Medford, MA: Information Today, 2012), 2–5.

53. Virginia Kay Williams and Kathy A. Downes, "Assessing Your Vendor's Viability," *The Serials Librarian* 59, no. 3–4 (2010): 322–23.

54. Rick Anderson, Jane F. White, and David Burke, "How to Be a Good Customer," *The Serials Librarian* 48, no. 3–4 (2005): 322–24.

55. Peggy Johnson, *Developing and Managing Collections: The Essentials* (Chicago: American Library Association, 2013), 91.

56. Locke J. Morrisey, "Ethical Issues in Collection Development," *Journal of Library Administration* 47, no. 3–4 (2008): 168–69.

Using LibGuides to Promote Communication between Public and Technical Services

Jennifer Bazeley

Communication in twenty-first-century libraries is a challenge that is made complex by organizational cultures, legacy practices and workflows, staff personalities, and ongoing technological changes. There is an enormous body of literature concerning the theory and practice of "organizational communication"—an article search on that phrase in Google Scholar yields more than 80,000 results, published as long ago as the early 1950s. The subset of that literature concerning communication within academic institutions, and specifically within academic libraries, is much smaller, though communication issues are no less challenging in this setting. In 1988 McCombs wrote: "The hidden dynamics of a university library are no less complicated than the human body. What makes it tick? What are its strengths and weaknesses? Given our current resources and the needs of our students and faculty, what can we do to improve the service we give?"[1] These questions are no less relevant today, thirty years later, than they were then. In Clampitt's book *Communicating for Managerial Effectiveness,* he suggests that four characteristics produce interdepartmental communication challenges: departments have different job duties, may not be physically located near one another, may have discrete budgets, and likely have separate authority structures. Of these, the first two tend to cause the greatest silo mentality in academic libraries and lead to breakdowns in communication. Differing job duties may be exacerbated by the use of jargon or specialized terminology, priority differences, and adherence to rigid departmental procedures.[2] Mautino and Lorenzen suggest that a focus on customer service may be valuable in overcoming these silos: "For academic libraries, the over-arching value of customer services provides inspiring and fundamental bedrock for all to embrace. It guides the activities of every department, from cataloging to circulation, behind-the-scenes or public. It could be said that embodying values, attaining goals, and achieving organizational initiatives can happen most effectively through cooperation and collaboration between departments, processes which are significantly enhanced by successful interdepartmental communication."[3] While all units within an academic library serve the same ultimate purpose in fulfilling an institution's mission and providing access to information to patrons, the ways in which each unit has historically done so have required drastically different (and in some cases unique) expertise and skill sets.

THE RIFT

Differences have historically produced the tallest barriers between the public and technical services departments of academic libraries. There have been numerous articles and chapters published over several decades that discuss why technical and public services departments have difficulty communicating. Of note is the fact that while these articles describe the challenges and frustrations that public and technical services librarians face in communicating with each other, almost all of them acknowledge that the end goal for these librarians is the same: service to the end user. In a discussion of these communication challenges, it's important to remember the positive, which is that most librarians, regardless of their professional specialization, do respect the ultimate beneficiary of their work (the patron). In their chapter in *Rethinking Library Technical Services: Redefining Our Profession for the Future,* Boyd and Gould sum up succinctly: "Much of our work is not understood outside of the profession or, in some cases, by our own colleagues who work in other departments in our libraries."[4] This chapter, published in 2015, provides the same message that is seen in the literature from the 1970s onward, which is that a significant divide exists between technical and public services. In a 1983 article about the reorganizations of public and technical services at the University of Urbana-Champaign Library, Michael Gorman wrote: "One of the saddest results of the traditional technical/public services dichotomy is the profound, and often self-imposed, ignorance of, and indifference to, each other's expertise."[5] The organizational restructuring discussed in Gorman's article was aimed at increasing efficiency and accommodating technological changes within academic librarianship. He later stated: "the fundamental premise of this new stage is that modern technology, in particular the online catalog, does away with the rationale for the distinction between public and technical services professional librarians."[6] The evolution of technology in libraries that began with the online catalog forty years ago has been a double-edged sword for the public-technical services silos. Although the organizational restructuring Gorman spoke of was meant to ease the transition of the library catalog from an analog, print format (the card catalog) to an electronic format (the online public access catalog or OPAC), the transition still created new challenges in communication between public and technical services. Not every academic library was in a position to reorganize staff and reassign work while migrating from a print to an electronic catalog. In order to serve patrons, the electronic format forced librarians to acquire a new knowledge of technology in addition to the expertise needed for effective search strategies and information management. For technical services librarians who performed the work of moving the analog catalog into electronic format, this transition was built into their job. However, public services librarians had to rely on technical services librarians for education on how the new electronic catalog's format functioned.[7] As a result, technical services librarians had to learn how to communicate effectively with their public services counterparts. This pattern of education and communication has continued into the twenty-first century as libraries see an increasing majority of their content transition into electronic, online formats. In 2003 Jankowska wrote: "In this time of information overload, faculty and students need efficient and comprehensive access for their information-seeking processes; that requires the cooperative work of both public and technical services librarians. This cooperative work depends on good communication and social interaction between librarians. The traditional library organizational model, with major divisions for public and technical services, does not provide a common set of values that would be the foundation for effective communication and social interaction."[8] While this was undoubtedly true in 2003, it can be argued that the patron of 2016 has information needs that *do* provide public and technical services staff with a common set of values; these staff must understand library resources, especially online resources, in a much more aligned and expert way. As a result, the twenty-first century has seen the destruction of some of the traditional public-technical services silos as the vagaries of electronic and online resources force these departments to work more closely together. As Michalak states,

"The greatest force for technology diffusion has been the library's aggressive move to electronic books and journals . . . There remain few jobs in the library that do not assist in providing electronic access to something or use multiple information technologies."[9] Public services and technical services staff both have to understand the life cycle of electronic resources in order to help patrons, especially in regard to troubleshooting specific, often technologically related, information access problems. The role of technical services staff has shifted from a print-centric to an electronic-focused role, and now technical services staff must communicate and educate public services staff on these resources. This education, in part, is what aids in the breakdown of the existing unit communication silos that exist within libraries.

It's easy to discuss how technical services staff can and should break down departmental silos through education and communication efforts. While these efforts are underway at numerous institutions, there are still challenges involved with communication between public and technical services. Academic libraries have seen these challenges addressed in a variety of ways as library services and technologies have evolved, especially in the twenty-first century. As academic libraries acquire ever-increasing numbers of electronic resources, technical services departments are increasingly responsible for providing current information about those resources to public services staff. The methods by which technical services departments communicate internally have expanded in recent years as technology becomes more sophisticated and more available to a greater number of institutions and personnel. The literature illustrates that technical services departments have been innovative and have experimented with a wide variety of communication methods, some of which have gained a more mainstream popularity. In 1990 Gossen, Reynolds, Ricker, and Smirensky noted that "the existing means of communication in libraries may not adequately bridge the gap between the divisions. Formal channels such as library newsletters may be general in nature . . . departmental supervisors reporting on the activities in another department may rightfully edit details . . . information traveling the proper hierarchical chain may be lost or altered. Informal means of communication also cannot be depended on to be timely or necessarily accurate, nor should they be the sole lateral communication channel between librarians from different divisions."[10] They conducted a cross-training project at the University at Albany Library in 1988 which was intended to increase communication among librarians of different units. Their cross-training project allowed librarians to share with each other unique job responsibilities, special knowledge, and different approaches to similar tasks. The benefits of this cross-departmental exchange were technical, environmental, and professional and included increased understanding of policies and procedures across departments, increased understanding of patron needs, and most importantly, helped to bridge the gap between public and technical services by identifying common problems and experiences among all librarians. This shared understanding increased professional confidence by demonstrating what each librarian's role and importance was within the organization. The outcomes of this exchange ultimately benefited the library and the larger institution.[11]

COLLABORATION WITH TECHNOLOGY

At the same time that technological changes and electronic resources are creating new challenges in academic librarianship, the Internet and Web 2.0 tools have become increasingly accessible to and needed by academic librarians. These technologies offer new, flexible solutions for librarians to communicate with one another and share information to better serve the end user. Library or departmental intranets utilizing specific Web 2.0 tools (some in combination with other types of content management software) for communication and collaboration feature prominently in the literature between 2009 and the present time. The use of these newer technologies allows for consistent communication that is affordable, easy to update, use-friendly, centralized, flexible, rapid, and efficient.[12] An intranet or internal documentation that was previously static with no opportunities for two-way communication or group collaboration was transformed into dynamic resources that allow for current content, interactivity, and audience feedback. Wikis and blogs have been explored extensively by academic libraries since the mid-2000s for use in a variety of ways, including but not limited to as a place to store policies and procedures, workflows, departmental documentation, and as a means of communicating all of the above. As Costello and Del Bosque summarize in their 2010 literature review, "the literature clearly indicates that the potential for blogs and wikis to improve internal communication within a library organization exists. However, it also makes clear that simply using new technologies will not automatically improve existing communication problems."[13] One challenge noted with respect to the use of wikis and blogs is that some training of staff is required in order for contribution to occur; while most staff frequently read or use blogs and wikis, fewer staff contribute to them. Costello and Del Bosque surveyed their staff to learn how wikis and blogs were perceived by staff as a means of communication. Staff rated wikis as their second most preferred method of communication (after e-mail) and blogs as their fourth most preferred method. The reason for these lower preferences was in part related to staff wanting to be notified of changes to the wiki or blog; because staff had not completely integrated these Web 2.0 tools into their daily workflows, they wouldn't necessarily know when new information had been posted. While e-mail was identified as the easiest-to-use and most effective communication method, it was noted that it was only useful when recipients read the contents.[14]

As discussed above, libraries have been using stand-alone wikis or blogs to communicate among departments and track needed information for some time. There are also examples of the use of more comprehensive tools, such as Jive, Microsoft SharePoint, Google sites, and LibGuides, each of which offers a collection of tools that can be used together to better organize material. England and Diffin reported using both LibGuides and Jive technology to manage their electronic resource processes and workflows. The Jive technology allowed them to create a community site called ENGAGE, which provided the University of Maryland University College library with a broader method to communicate electronic resource information to its library and university communities, and to collect feedback from those communities.[15] Microsoft SharePoint is an enterprise-level package product that allows for document management and also integrates various Web 2.0 tools like blogs, wikis, and discussion forums. The Florida International University (FIU) Medical Library wrote about its implementation of SharePoint to create a library intranet in 2008. The FIU Medical Library's SharePoint intranet spanned multiple departments and included pages for cataloging and collections, digital access services, education, help desk, interlibrary loan, and reference. While the SharePoint software provides a variety of Web 2.0 tools (discussion forums, announcements, links, tasks, etc.), Kim and her colleagues found that most of these tools went unused, with staff heavily utilizing the document storage and sharing capabilities of the software instead. The staff's lack of familiarity with Web 2.0 tools appears to be the reason behind the low use of those tools; staff were much more familiar and comfortable with the document library functionality. Interestingly, staff reported that they didn't use SharePoint for communication but preferred e-mail because of its convenience. Generally speaking, SharePoint was not found to be intuitive to use by staff, did not integrate well with external tools (such as calendars), and did not have an adequate search functionality. Because the document library function was easier to use than the institution's previous iteration of an intranet, satisfaction with that function of SharePoint was very high. The Web 2.0 communication tools included with SharePoint simply did not fit into existing staff workflows as easily as e-mail, so there was little motivation for staff to learn how to use them.[16] Jensen reported on using Google Sites to manage electronic resources at the University of Alaska Fairbanks

Libraries, and their electronic resource management site was created with the following goals in mind: "have a centrally located place where all acquisitions information could be stored and made easily accessible; to have a highly searchable tool so that invoicing, licensing, fiscal, and administrative data (including statistics) are easy to find; and to assist with the purchase and renewal process, eliminating multiple steps and the flood of e-mail with every action."[17] While these goals do not specifically include internal communication, the creation of a central location and the elimination of floods of e-mails certainly implies a more efficient communication strategy.

The literature demonstrates that sharing information, deciphering jargon and professional terminology, and providing a means of two-way communication breaks down departmental silos and benefits the academic library as a whole. While there are numerous examples of how individual library departments or whole libraries have utilized the above technologies to address specific communication issues or workflows (e.g., library-wide blogs; troubleshooting, evaluating, and managing electronic resources; access services workflows and policies), there are few examples of technical services departments creating a comprehensive technical services portal to increase communication specifically with public services staff. At Miami University Libraries, the Technical Services Department has created a comprehensive tool to enhance communication and aid in breaking down the technical-public services silos.

CASE STUDY

MIAMI UNIVERSITY LIBRARIES
Using LibGuides

The Miami University Libraries (MUL) Technical Services (TS) Department LibGuide began in late 2009 as a collaboration between the coordinator of catalog access and acquisitions (who was at that time the electronic resources and serials librarian) and the former bibliographic systems librarian at MUL. The TS LibGuide was jointly maintained by these librarians until the bibliographic systems librarian left MUL in 2011 for a new position. Since that time, the coordinator of catalog access and acquisitions has maintained the guide with the support of TS Department staff. The guide has changed significantly since its first iteration and continues to evolve as needed, meaning that guide content presented in this chapter may change between the author's writing of the chapter and the publication of the book. Readers should also note that MUL subscribes to LibGuides and the LibGuides content management system

(CMS), and is using version two of LibGuides. Some features and functions discussed below may not be available to or may differ from those using the non-CMS version and/or version one of LibGuides.

Why a LibGuide?

Springshare was founded in 2007, and LibGuides became available to libraries shortly after that. Libraries' use of LibGuides has grown dramatically since that time; Springshare reports that 4,800 libraries in 78 countries currently utilize its LibGuides product (www.springshare.com/about.html). This rapid growth has allowed Springshare to evolve the product quickly and efficiently, and has also brought the cost of the product down, making this a more affordable solution for a wider variety of libraries. Although LibGuides was originally intended to create public-facing research guides, the library community has seen many experimental and innovative uses for the product that are unrelated to its original intended purpose. Many of these experiments have appeared in the literature between 2009 and 2016:

- Tenure and promotion process[18]
- Library website (public-facing)[19]
- Library intranet[20] (internal)[21]
- Special collections[22]
- Current awareness service[23]
- Professional development[24]
- Interdisciplinary collaboration (faculty learning community)[25]
- Outreach (virtual and distance students,[26] international students,[27] scholarly communication[28])
- Platform for student research[29]
- Electronic resource evaluation,[30] management,[31] access,[32] and troubleshooting[33]
- Technical services information (technical services LibGuide,[34] RDA LibGuide,[35] technical services procedures and policies[36])

As noted in the above list, there are only a few instances in the literature of LibGuides being used by technical services departments; the majority of non-public-facing use is specifically for the management of electronic resources. The only instances of technical services-specific LibGuide use appear in Bazeley and Yoose's 2013 article[37] (which details the original, version one iteration of MUL's TS LibGuide), a brief report about an RDA LibGuide created by the Virtual Academic Library Environment in New Jersey,[38] and a 2015 article appearing in *Against the Grain* by Mueller and Thompson detailing how they used LibGuides for technical services policies and procedures at Sam Houston State University Library.[39]

MUL has subscribed to the LibGuides product since 2009, which made the implementation of a TS LibGuide essentially a no-cost solution. The most basic reasons for choosing a LibGuide include ease of use and its flexibility in accommodating a wide variety of information and formats. On the administrative side, the MUL TS Department needed a solution that could be maintained within the department, which meant a system that didn't require specialized knowledge of coding or HTML. Like many TS departments, MUL's TS Department has shrunk significantly over the last five years, so the ability to quickly train staff with no HTML experience on updating the guide was an essential feature. Adding new content is quickly accomplished, and deleting or archiving old content is simple. The TS Department also wanted a simple method of backing up shared content, and creating backups of LibGuides content is a simple process. Built-in LibGuides functionality allows for the creation of an HTML backup of all pages, as well as the option to export all LibGuides data in XML with just a few clicks. On the public side, MUL's public services staff were already intimately familiar with LibGuides, meaning there was almost no learning curve in their adjustment to a TS LibGuide as a means of interdepartmental communication.

Conceptually speaking, choosing a LibGuide provided opportunities for TS staff to learn how to utilize a piece of software that they might not have otherwise been exposed to, and it also gave TS librarians an integrated way of advocating the work that the TS Department does to other library stakeholders. In *Rethinking Library Technical Services: Redefining Our Profession for the Future,* Mary Beth Weber argues that "the need to advocate for one's work has taken on added importance. What are some of the ways that technical services librarians can advocate for their work? A first step is to promote their work so that others fully understand what they contribute to the library overall and the implications of what would happen should that work cease to be provided. When others understand a process and its outcome, they are better prepared to support that work, particularly when that work has a direct influence on the outcome and success of their work."[40] A technical services LibGuide provides not only essential information but a much-needed advocacy platform for a department that is often hidden from public view. Later in the same chapter, Weber states, "Your work should be understood by others in the library and not viewed as a shadowy backroom practice reserved for the socially inept."[41] The TS LibGuide can serve as a neutral platform to enhance communication and advocacy.

The flexibility of the LibGuides software may be its most attractive quality. Although guides are owned by a single account holder, ownership can be transferred to other LibGuides users in the event that an administrator or editor leaves the department. The software can accommodate numerous types of content, including RSS feeds, widgets, graphics, links, and embedded documents and files. Content, format, and layout changes are incredibly easy and can be made from any computer with an Internet connection. This ease of use and flexibility means that it is incredibly easy to maintain static content while also keeping dynamic content current. Guides can be public or private and can be password-protected if necessary, features that are useful in protecting sensitive information that may be shared by a TS department. MUL's TS Department felt that the features and functions of LibGuides would allow staff to communicate information rapidly and efficiently, in an organized and hierarchical manner. Using a LibGuide for commonly requested questions and information allows the TS Department to receive fewer repeat e-mails and phone calls, and frees up valuable staff time.

About Miami University

Miami University, founded in 1809, is a large residential, primarily undergraduate school with some graduate programs at the master's and doctoral levels. Its main campus is located in Oxford, Ohio (35 miles north of Cincinnati, Ohio), with three regional US locations in Hamilton, Middletown, and West Chester, Ohio, and one European location in Luxembourg. Miami University's full-time student enrollment is approximately 19,000. The university's main campus has four libraries: King Library, which is the main library (and where the TS Department is housed); the Amos Music Library; the Business, Engineering, Science and Technology (B.E.S.T.) Library; and the Wertz Art and Architecture Library. Miami University is a member of the OhioLINK consortium, which includes approximately ninety-two libraries across the state and provides patrons with access to an enormous variety of consortial e-resources. Library staffing consists of 42 librarians and 40 full-time staff. Of the 42 librarians in the system, 28 perform public services duties. The TS Department consists of four and a half full-time librarians, five paraprofessional staff, and one student worker. The TS Department is a centralized operation and is responsible for the acquisition and cataloging of all formats and materials and the oversight of the entire electronic resource life cycle, at both the local and consortial levels.

TS LibGuide Design Considerations and Scope

When creating the TS LibGuide, the department kept in mind several broad design parameters. In order to allow for problem-solving, the guide had to allow for the dissemination of information as well as serve as a means of two-way communication between technical and public services. To better serve the needs of internal TS LibGuide users (i.e., public services staff), guide creators identified two distinct audiences within public services: those who work at public service desks and do virtual reference, and subject selector librarians who perform collection management and development tasks. Content identified for inclusion in the LibGuide was broadly categorized between these two populations. TS staff consciously decided that the TS LibGuide would not be used as a tool for managing the complete life cycle of e-resources since MUL already had an e-resource management system that accomplished those tasks. As Bordeianu and Lubas pointed out in their chapter in *Workplace Culture in Academic Libraries,* every department of an academic library has its own dialect and jargon, and one of the first steps in communicating is to learn each other's dialects.[42] TS staff were consciously aware of the need to avoid (or explain) any TS dialect or jargon within the LibGuide. TS also discussed the idea of opening up the TS Department's PBWiki, which houses all departmental processes and procedures, to all library staff, but ultimately decided that the information there was too jargon-heavy to be useful to staff outside of the department. Finally, TS staff identified both static information (related to processes, procedures, and workflows) and dynamic information (about projects and problems) for inclusion in the guide.

In deciding on the scope of information to be included, TS staff looked at both the type of information that the department regularly provided to external staff as well as the type of information that was most frequently requested by external departments. This method of identifying important content has been noted by others in the literature—the University of New Mexico Libraries reported that their technical services department provided education to public services librarians based on questions routed through their internal request system, major changes to cataloging codes, and the implementation of a new discovery tool.[43] Every technical services department has a list of frequently asked questions that surface repeatedly, and identifying those questions helped to determine scope and create information priorities and hierarchies. While this broader scope dictated early iterations of the TS LibGuide, the guide has changed and evolved significantly over the last seven years, based on feedback from staff as well as assessment of LibGuides usage statistics. In implementing an access services intranet, Chu observed that "the acquisition of relevant content for the Web site became a learning process that defied careful schedule planning . . . since information vital to developing knowledge and opening communication in the unit was based on ongoing sensitivity to changing workflow procedures and staff dynamics . . . Implementation of the Web site was about staying in tune with the workplace to actively provide value to its users—the library staff."[44] The MUL TS Department has observed these same trends in its TS LibGuide implementation and evolution.

At the present time, the scope of the TS LibGuide encompasses seven areas:

1. Contact information for and basic job duties of TS Department staff
2. Product news and updates
3. Forms for requesting and reporting
4. Information about acquisitions, serials, and e-resources (often categorized by local versus consortial purchasing—an area of confusion for many staff)
5. Electronic resource usage statistics
6. Library tools and software
7. Archived material

Preliminary Steps—Other Tools

Before implementing the TS LibGuide, TS librarians set up and adjusted department-wide accounts and identified free tools to work in tandem with the LibGuide. A departmental Google account was created and shared with all TS staff. As Adam Murray noted in his 2008 article, Google Docs and Spreadsheets are incredibly useful in managing and sharing information related to electronic resources because they can be edited by multiple people and shared with others as read-only documents.[45] Google Docs and Spreadsheets were preferred formats for integration with LibGuides for these reasons, and moreover, they can be easily embedded into LibGuides using Google's "publish to the web" feature. MUL's TS Department uses Google Drive to store e-resource usage statistics, gift-tracking spreadsheets, embedded forms and associated response spreadsheets, and miscellaneous e-resource and serial lists that require sharing. In 2013 Miami University became a Google Apps for Education institution, making the sharing of the TS Department Google account even simpler. In regard to preserving data stored in Google Drive, users have the option of installing the Google Drive desktop application, which backs up data from a

Google Drive to the hard drive of a computer (or computers) automatically. In regard to storage and space concerns, there is little to fear. Currently, free Google Drive accounts allow for fifteen GB of storage, which is more than ample for spreadsheets and documents. MUL's TS Google Drive currently stores all of the library's electronic resource usage reports (approximately 240 spreadsheets, most of which have between three and eight worksheets) and a wide variety of miscellaneous other documents, all of which requires only one GB of the fifteen allotted free GB in the account. The Gmail account associated with the departmental account is utilized to funnel notifications from Google forms used for electronic resource problem reporting and list requests to the appropriate staff within the TS Department.

A departmental WordPress account was also created in order to implement and maintain a basic (free) WordPress blog with a very simple theme. The WordPress blog is used to aggregate news and updates and to generate RSS feeds for the "News and Updates" tab of the TS LibGuide. A free Word-Press account provides sufficient storage space (3,072 MB) to hold blog posts. Between 2009 and 2016, the TS account utilized 8.14 MB of the allotted storage space, which includes over 1,100 blog posts and numerous vendor logos/graphics. While using a WordPress blog this way may seem very labor-intensive, it actually creates efficiencies once it is set up. WordPress has a "Post by Email" feature that allows WordPress blog users to generate a unique e-mail address that allows them to e-mail posts to their blog. When TS Department staff receive an e-mail about an e-resource update, trial, or news of interest, it is simply forwarded to the WordPress e-mail address that is unique to our blog and is automatically posted. The WordPress e-mail system also allows the addition of topics and tags to e-mailed posts, which allows posts to be sorted by topic without ever having to go into the blog. Because posts have specific topics attached to them, WordPress allows the creation of RSS feeds for those categories—this is a simple way to separate e-resource update posts from e-resource trial posts on the TS LibGuide. While WordPress blogs are generally public-facing and indexed by search engines, WordPress has a feature called "Discourage search engine indexing," which does a good job at keeping this content out of search engines. This feature is helpful for users who are concerned about sensitive information (e.g., log-in credentials for trials) being available on the Open Web. The TS Department has not experienced any issues with WordPress blog content being discovered and abused by the public.

Several adjustments were required within MUL's LibGuides accounts before the TS LibGuide was created. Librarians involved in creating and maintaining the TS LibGuide were given administrator privileges in LibGuides because it allowed for more efficient oversight of the TS LibGuide, including the ability to set up new accounts for TS staff or change privileges for existing users. TS librarians also created a LibGuides sandbox—in this case, a separate LibGuide tab that is hidden from public view and used to test new features, functionality, and content.

"Home" Page

MUL's TS LibGuide is a private LibGuide, which means it doesn't display on MUL's public-facing LibGuides interface and is not indexed by search engines. Links to the LibGuide are provided to staff via the library's intranet and other internal, password-protected sites. Links to relevant TS LibGuide pages are also included in occasional e-mails to all staff when needed. The "Home" page of the TS LibGuide (see figure 8.1) follows standards and best practices dictated by MUL for all LibGuides, as well as two additional features. Standard features are a profile box for the owner of the LibGuide in the top left position and a "Quick Links" box in the top right column that is essentially a linked table of contents to the rest of the LibGuide. Below these standard boxes are a box of links to catalog resources (discovery layer, OPAC, consortial catalog, and A-Z list) and a box with links to external resources useful to librarians (library and information science-specific databases and cataloging tools such as Cataloger's Desktop, ClassWeb, and RDA Toolkit).

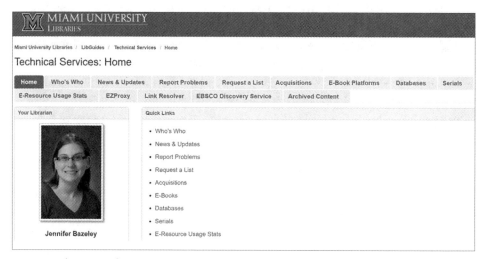

Figure 8.1 | **MUL TS home page**

Figure 8.2 | **Technical Services Who's Who**

"Who's Who" Page

While MUL has a staff directory on the library website that includes department names and titles, it is often difficult to know who to contact in the TS Department based on that information (Coordinator of Collection Access and Acquisitions, a title used in TS, is not as obvious as Art and Architecture Librarian, a title used in public services). Additionally, because TS staff don't work at any public service points, they are not always well known by staff in other library departments. This page of the TS LibGuide (see figure 8.2) offers TS Department contact information organized by the type of question a user may ask, and chosen categories were based on the questions the department most regularly receives from other staff. Categories include everything from "ER, Serials, OhioLINK Questions" to "Physical Processing" to "Textbooks on Reserve." In this way, the LibGuide intends to direct staff with specific questions to the right contact for the function. Where possible, multiple contacts for each issue are provided, although since the department has shrunk over the last five years, the incidence of overlapping contacts on this page has greatly increased.

"News and Updates" Page

This page uses a variety of tools (with an especially heavy reliance on RSS feeds) to aggregate current information from different sources into one page. Potential customizations include how many items should display in the box at a time, and whether links are routed through an institutional proxy server, which can be useful when linking users to journal articles that may require an institutional subscription to access (e.g., the TS Department uses this setting for the "Recent LIS Articles" box). The left column displays three boxes: "E-Resource

Updates" (information about changes to vendor or publisher sites, vendor site maintenance and downtime, and anything related to library-owned or subscribed resources, retrieved via RSS feed from the TS WordPress blog); the "E-Resource Trials" box (information about trials to electronic resources available throughout the year, retrieved via RSS feed from the TS WordPress blog); and "LIS Journals" (a BrowZine widget that links to library and information science titles in MUL's collection via BrowZine). TS staff used to send e-mails to MUL staff via internal electronic discussion lists with information about trials and electronic resource updates, but those e-mails tended to get lost in staff in-boxes. By aggregating all of this information on one LibGuides page, staff don't receive an overload of e-mail from the TS Department. The right column of the page offers three different boxes: "TS News" (general information from TS staff and TS vendors that is not electronic resources-related, retrieved via RSS feed from the TS WordPress blog); "OhioLINK Blog" (an RSS blog feed maintained by the OhioLINK consortium which publishes news and notes of interest to OhioLINK members); and "Recent LIS Articles" (an aggregated RSS feed of library and information science journal articles retrieved via RSS feed from EBSCO journal alerts). In order to provide staff access to library and information science articles of interest, MUL used to physically route professional journals to library staff using a cumbersome paper process and interoffice mail. That physical journal routing system was replaced by the LIS articles box. This box is generated by creating RSS alerts for peer-reviewed LIS titles available to us via EBSCOhost, and then aggregating those RSS alerts using ChimpFeedr (www.chimpfeedr.com/). ChimpFeedr is a tool that aggregates content from multiple RSS feeds, and MUL uses it to collocate multiple RSS alerts into a single RSS feed that can be used in the TS LibGuide.

"Report Problems" Page

Like the Colorado State University (CSU) Libraries, MUL is using LibGuides to help with troubleshooting electronic resources.[46] However, where the CSU Libraries' electronic resources troubleshooting guide is public-facing, MUL's is intended for internal use by public services librarians. The "Report Problems" page (see figure 8.3) is an essential part of the TS LibGuide. This is where TS staff provide links to forms for staff to report electronic resource access issues (for both locally and consortially purchased resources) as well as catalog errors. Like many other libraries,[47] the MUL TS Department depends in part on our catalog users (both staff and patrons) to report catalog errors for correction. Unlike other libraries, the "Report a Catalog Error" form is currently intended

Report Problems

- E-Resources Access Problem Form
  Use this form during **regular business hours** to report all e-resource access problems.
- MU Libraries Feedback
  Use this form on **evenings and weekends** for **Miami** e-resource access problems.
- OhioLINK Problem Reporting Form
  Use this form on **evenings and weekends** for **OhioLINK** e-resource problems.
- Report a Catalog Error

Resources

- Check a URL for EZProxy Coverage
- Download Miami University VPN Software
- EBSCO Products System Alerts
- Is It Down Right Now?
- OhioLINK Connection Info Link
- OhioLINK Databases A to Z
- OhioLINK Staff Page (OStaff)
- Online Journals A - Z

Figure 8.3 | **"Report problems" page**

only for internal staff use. The page is kept clean and simple by providing links to forms rather than embedding the forms on the page. The "Report Problems" box attempts to provide clarity on dealing with problems depending on the day the problem occurs. Most TS staff do not work during evenings or on weekends, which means that problem reports follow a slightly different path during those times. The TS Department's "E-Resources Access Problem Form" is recommended for local or consortial electronic resource problems (during regular business hours) or nonurgent problems (at any time), while MUL's more general "Feedback Form" is recommended during nonbusiness hours, especially if a problem is very urgent. The OhioLINK consortium provides their own problem-reporting forms for consortially managed resources, and a link to those forms is also provided in this box.

"E-Resources Access Problem" Form

When this link is clicked, the user is taken to a simple Google form interface (see figure 8.4). The form is intended to gather all of the information needed to begin troubleshooting an electronic resource access problem. Some problems may be too complex for a form, but most of the time, TS staff are able to begin

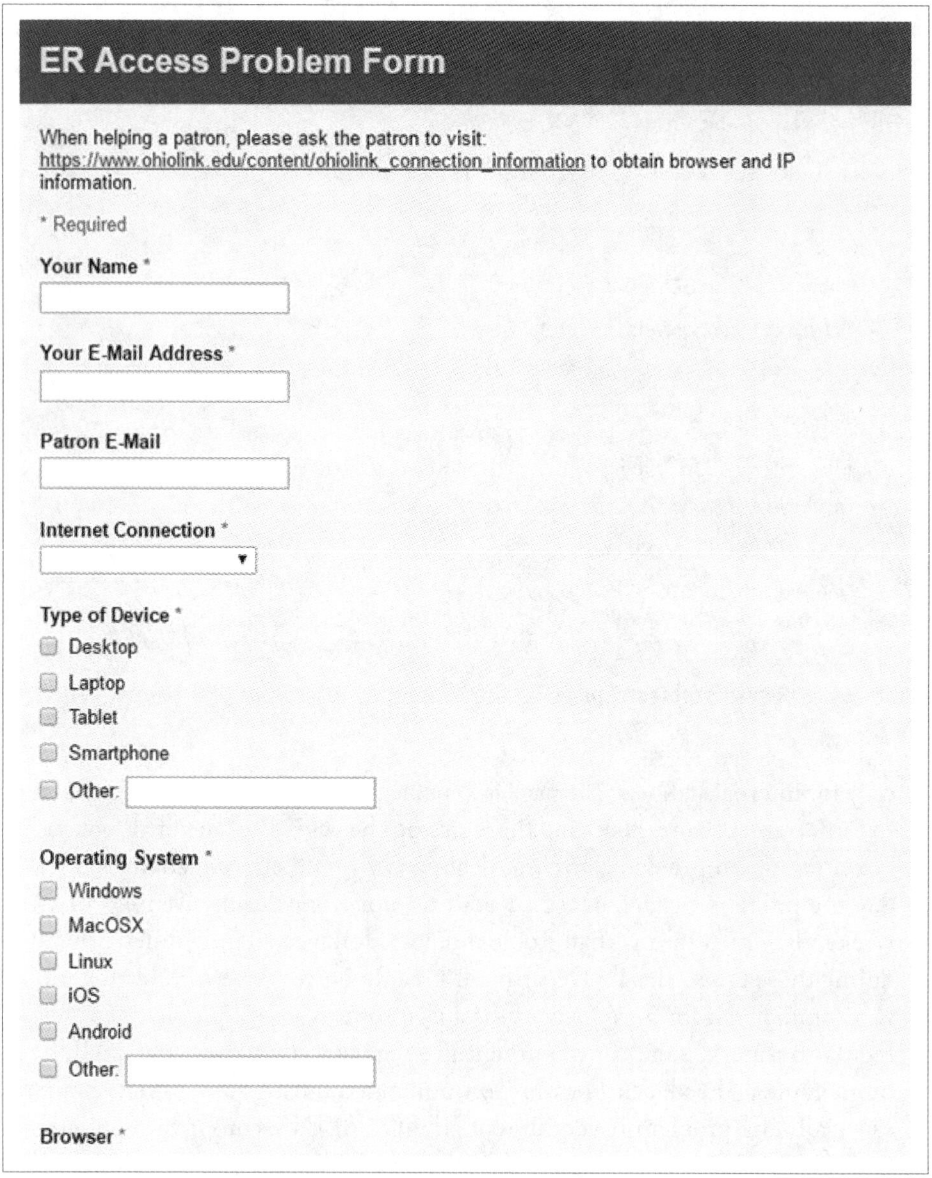

ER Access Problem Form

When helping a patron, please ask the patron to visit:
https://www.ohiolink.edu/content/ohiolink_connection_information to obtain browser and IP information.

* Required

Your Name *

Your E-Mail Address *

Patron E-Mail

Internet Connection *
▼

Type of Device *
☐ Desktop
☐ Laptop
☐ Tablet
☐ Smartphone
☐ Other:

Operating System *
☐ Windows
☐ MacOSX
☐ Linux
☐ iOS
☐ Android
☐ Other:

Browser *

Figure 8.4 | **"E-Resources Access Problem" form**

troubleshooting from the submitted information. This type of Google form is very easy to create within Google Drive. Once the form is created, a link to it is generated by clicking on the blue Send Form button that shows in the upper right side of the Google form. Once the user submits a form, her submission goes into a Responses spreadsheet that resides in the TS Department's Google Drive. Google forms include the option of setting up a confirmation e-mail (by installing and utilizing the Google Form Notifications add-on) that goes to the submitter, to let her know that her form was received. The TS Department set up the Responses spreadsheet so that the submission of the form and subsequent update of the spreadsheet triggers an e-mail notification to the TS Gmail account. Setting up a notification trigger in the Google spreadsheet is done by going to "Notification Rules" under the Tools menu. In the TS Gmail account, filters have been set up that forward these messages to the appropriate staff in the TS Department. Once the notification is triggered and goes into that departmental Gmail account, these filters forward the notification out to the appropriate staff. The e-mail notification is short, simple, and does not allow for any customization. The e-mail includes a link to the spreadsheet where the form responses are recorded, which provides one-click access to the problem report in the responses spreadsheet. In the responses spreadsheet, the columns correspond to the questions asked in the form. Initials and Notes columns are not part of the form but are filled out by TS staff, who place their initials in the Initials column to indicate that they are working on the issue. The problem details and solution (if any) go in the Notes box for future reference. At one time, this spreadsheet was made available to all librarians and staff, but it was discovered that they found it confusing rather than helpful. Once a TS staff member has resolved a problem or identified a solution, that person e-mails the submitter and patron to let them know. For library staff who are willing and able to do their own troubleshooting, a "Resources" box at the bottom of the right column provides links to resources for self-help troubleshooting, such as a link to see whether an e-resource is properly configured to work off campus, a link to a site that provides end-user IP address and browser information, and a link to EBSCO system alerts.

"Request a List" Page

The "Request a List" page uses an embedded Google form for staff who want to request a list from MUL's integrated library system (ILS), which is Innovative Interfaces' Sierra. Because this is a shorter form (and the only form on the page), it is ideal for embedding in a box on the LibGuide. Requests for lists like this used to arrive primarily by exchanging multiple e-mails with staff. Using this form instead of e-mails allows library subject selectors and other requesters to know what criteria and information are available to them from Sierra, and also forces them to specify what type of information they are interested in receiving in the final spreadsheet. Embedding Google forms into LibGuides is incredibly simple. When creating a Google form, instead of using the "Send Form" button to generate a link, users go to the "File" menu and choose "Embed," then copy the HTML code. In LibGuides, a new box is created and from the "Add/Reorder" dropdown, "Media/Widget" is selected. This is where the code that Google generated is pasted. Like the "E-Resource Access Problem" form, submissions from this form also go into a Google spreadsheet, and then trigger an e-mail notification to the TS Gmail account. This form also utilizes the Google Form Notifications add-on, which sends an automatic e-mail confirmation to the submitter. Filters set up in the TS Gmail e-mail account then forward that message to multiple staff in the TS Department. Staff place their initials in a specified column to indicate who is working on the requested list. Completed lists are e-mailed to the requester within one to two business days.

"Acquisitions" Page

The "Acquisitions" page (and its five subpages) are intended for librarians who are subject selectors/liaison librarians, and they feature information about fund activity reports, rush orders, acquisitions contacts, and an embedded Google spreadsheet that lists the fund codes used in Sierra as well as the corresponding librarian liaison. Below the "Acquisitions" page in the LibGuide hierarchy are five subpages that include ordering information for books, e-books, and videos, as well as pages on acquiring and reviewing gifts and donations. Information on video acquisitions has become increasingly important because MUL has expanded its video purchases to include streaming video and patron-driven acquisition video acquisition models. Information on gifts and donations is also a necessity for MUL public services librarians, since they may only work with donations a few times a year but are usually the primary contact point for donors.

"E-Book Platforms" Page

Due to the popularity of patron-driven acquisition of e-books and the growing number of e-book purchasing models and platforms, a page for e-book platforms was necessary. The most frequently asked questions from subject selector librarians involve the features and functionality of the large variety of e-book platforms on which MUL purchases e-books. The "E-Book Platforms" page details both local and consortial e-book platforms and, most importantly, has a table that details all of the e-book platforms available to users and what basic features and functionality each offers (e.g., format of e-book, downloadable, number of simultaneous users, software required, and copy/print abilities). In addition to its availability on the TS LibGuide, the platform table has been reused by several subject selector librarians for their own public-facing guides. Under the "E-Book Platforms" page are subpages for several of the larger e-book platforms. Platforms such as ebrary and EBSCOhost require more detailed explanation because they are more complex and difficult to use than the publisher e-book sites that offer simple PDF downloads. Each subset platform page is laid out and formatted uniformly, with the same type of information given for each. This allows users to go from one platform to another and compare features across platforms more efficiently.

"Databases" Page

The "Databases" page offers lists of locally subscribed/purchased databases with campus/user limits, lists of all EBSCOhost databases (MUL and OhioLINK have invested heavily in EBSCOhost products, and the sheer number of EBSCOhost databases can be overwhelming), recently purchased or acquired databases, and a larger box that details recent database changes. These lists allow MUL staff to look up usage limits and see new purchases at any time, rather than waiting on a response from TS staff. On this page, Jing (a free screen-capture software) has proven to be very useful. For certain types of database problems, it is often easier to display a screenshot and a few sentences rather than attempting to describe a problem using only text. Error messages seen on database sites are generally more recognized by library staff when seen in context as a screenshot. This allows for more efficient troubleshooting at public service points. The "Databases" page also contains two subpages, one for OhioLINK consortially subscribed/purchased databases and a second for Kanopy streaming videos. Consortially subscribed/purchased resources may change with more frequency and less warning than locally subscribed/purchased resources, which makes a separate page dedicated to OhioLINK resources necessary. The Kanopy database provides access to thousands of streaming videos that are leased in a patron-driven acquisition model, and the TS Department gets frequent questions about how the model works, what is available through Kanopy, and how to embed and link to Kanopy videos. This page provides all of that information in one place and reduces the number of phone calls and e-mails received by TS staff about Kanopy resources.

"Serials" Page

Serials are by far the most confusing, most frequently changing, and most complex of the resources that libraries provide. The "Serials" page on the TS LibGuide and its subpages (BrowZine, Get It Now, SharedIt!, OhioLINK, Open Library of Humanities, Serials Policies) attempt to provide information in a self-service model to cover the most frequently asked questions about serials changes, models, and policies. The "Serials" page is where links to lists of serials changes (by fiscal year) and serials review materials are posted. Like the "Databases" page, the "Serials" page also contains a box with recent platform changes, new additions, and cancellations. This page has been exceedingly helpful for platform changes, especially at the end of each calendar year, when numerous journals and packages change publishers or platforms. Subpages on BrowZine (Third Iron), Get It Now (Copyright Clearance Center), and the SharedIt! (SpringerNature) services came about in response to regular questions about each. These subpages provide a place to aggregate information about a product or service, including where to go for vendor support, where to find usage statistics for the product, and specific information about how it has been implemented or used at MUL. For example, BrowZine is an app for browsing subscribed library resources in a shelf-like setting that is more intuitive than browsing a straight A-Z list. Faculty in particular like this app, and as a result, MUL's public service points receive questions about it. This subpage provides staff with a starting point to help faculty with BrowZine questions. A subpage devoted specifically to OhioLINK (consortially purchased) serials is necessary due to the complexity of consortial e-journal licensing and packages and a high frequency of questions about those packages. The frequency of change of e-journal packages (both changes within packages and the addition/cancellation of packages) at the consortial level makes this page essential, since it includes links to lists of titles in each package, as well as information on cancellations and new additions. A subpage on the Open Library of Humanities (an open-access journal platform) was added when MUL began supporting it in 2015. This initiative is important for librarians to know about both because it provides additional journal titles to our users and also provides open-access publishing opportunities to MU's faculty members. This information is essential for liaison librarians who work closely with humanities faculty. The final subpage of the "Serials" page contains information about serials policies that affect library staff, including but not limited to policies about setting up trials of e-journals, replacing missing journal issues, and acquiring/canceling journal subscriptions.

"E-Resource Usage Statistics" Page

The "E-Resource Usage Statistics" page is one of the most heavily visited pages in the TS LibGuide. Like most libraries in recent years, MU librarians are being asked to make more electronic resource decisions based on usage, which has meant increased requests for usage data. Usage data, whether COUNTER-compliant or not, is cumbersome to retrieve, collect, store, and disseminate. For these reasons, the TS Department created a system to handle usage reports before the availability of usage statistics software. This LibGuides page solves the problem of the dissemination of usage statistics to library staff. The initial creation of the page was labor-intensive, but once completed, the page only requires updates when a publisher, platform, or resource is canceled or added. The top box on the page notes caveats and disclaimers because usage data is inconsistent and full of exceptions. Included in this box are details that staff tend to forget between visits; for example, the fact that some vendors don't offer usage at all, the frequency of usage statistics updates, and how the spreadsheets open and display. The box also offers tips on determining what publisher or platform report to look at for a specific title, since reports are in most cases organized by platform. Finally, because the majority of reports offered are COUNTER reports, there is a second box that contains general information about the most current version of the COUNTER standard, so that users know what type of report they are looking at. This is especially useful for e-book reports, since there isn't consistency among e-book vendors in using BR1 and BR2 reports, which report on different types of use. Links to usage statistics are placed in four different boxes organized first by format (e-books, databases, e-journals, e-videos) and then by vendor (for packages) or name (for single databases or stand-alone titles). Coverage years of available statistics are indicated next to each entry as well as the COUNTER report type, if the vendor offers COUNTER reports. Links in these boxes open in Google spreadsheets, and users can view or download the spreadsheets if they are interested in compiling and manipulating statistics on their desktop. Statistics are organized by calendar year within each spreadsheet, with each year residing in a separate worksheet. Staff external to TS are not given the ability to edit these reports within Google, since this often leads to unintentional editing and formatting mistakes. Usage statistics spreadsheets are updated monthly by one of the TS Department staff members. MUL also subscribes to the EBSCO Usage Consolidation software, which is capable of producing aggregated usage reports for e-books, e-journals, and databases across vendors/ platforms. It also provides the ability to create subscription usage details reports and title usage summarized by platform/publisher reports. Because the reporting functions within EBSCO's Usage Consolidation software are not user-friendly to non-TS staff, these reports are retrieved by the TS Department from this software annually and linked to in a separate box on the "E-Resource Usage Statistics" page (see figure 8.5).

The purchase of e-books via patron-driven acquisitions (PDA) has gained significant traction as a purchase model at MUL over the last six years. Reports on PDA e-book triggers and usage can be significantly different from COUNTER reports. Because of this, the TS LibGuide "E-Resource Usage Statistics" page includes separate subpages for PDA e-book usage reports. MUL purchases PDA e-books from both EBSCOhost and ebrary, which can be a source of confusion to library staff. These subpages are another ideal place for utilizing embedded Google spreadsheets. On both the ebrary and EBSCOhost PDA subpages, embedded Google spreadsheets display PDA trigger reports (updated weekly) and turnaway reports (updated quarterly). Because the updates to these spreadsheets take place entirely in Google Drive, these subpages within LibGuides require little to no maintenance.

"EZProxy" Page

To staff outside of Technical Services, library tools and software such as EZProxy, link resolvers, and discovery layers can be incredibly confusing. To combat confusion, the TS Department created three pages in the TS LibGuide to offer general information about each tool and to better explain how each software works. Based on the frequency of questions and problems related to off-campus access, the TS Department has identified proxy access to electronic resources as one of the most confusing aspects of electronic resources to public services staff. The "EZProxy" page was created to help address this confusion, and it attempts to address the two problems that are encountered most frequently: first, that users can (and must) add the proxy prefix to subscribed electronic resource URLs to enable off-campus access, and second, that only one instance of the prefix is required at the front of a URL. Numerous instances of links with up to three proxy prefixes appended to the front of them were discovered in some public-facing LibGuides, which creates log-in loops for end users. This page also helps to address questions about locally created stable

EBSCO Usage Consolidation Reports

EBSCO Usage Consolidation software allows us to combine COUNTER-compliant reports from many vendors into one database and produce compilation reports.

- Subscription Usage Details (Cost Per Use for EBSCO Subscription Titles) 2012
- Subscription Usage Details (Cost Per Use for EBSCO Subscription Titles) 2013
- Subscription Usage Details (Cost Per Use for EBSCO Subscription Titles) 2014
- Subscription Usage Details (Cost Per Use for EBSCO Subscription Titles) 2015
- Title Usage Summarized by Platform 2011
- Title Usage Summarized by Platform 2012
- Title Usage Summarized by Platform 2013
- Title Usage Summarized by Platform 2014
- Title Usage Summarized by Platform 2015
- Title Usage Summarized by Publisher 2011
- Title Usage Summarized by Publisher 2012
- Title Usage Summarized by Publisher 2013
- Title Usage Summarized by Publisher 2014
- Title Usage Summarized by Publisher 2015

Databases

Adam Matthew (2016-) DBR1

AdSpender (2013-)

Alexander Street Press (April 2009-) DBR1

APA PsycInfo (2012-) DBR1

ArtSTOR (June 2004-)

Bibliography of Asian Studies (2009-2016) *[for 2016 forward, see EBSCO Database report]*

Birds of North America (2014-)

Business & Industry (Gale) (2009-2015)

Cabell's Directory of Publishing Opportunities (current year only) *Note: self-service; must be on campus to view usage*

Chadwyck Healey Databases (2008-)

Chadwyck Healey Databases COUNTER (2009-) DBR1

Children's Literature Comprehensive Database (2013-)

Columbia Gazetteer of the World (2014-) DBR1

Figure 8.5 | "E-Resource Usage Statistics" page

URLs that automatically push users through the MUL proxy server without requiring the addition of the proxy prefix.

"Link Resolver" Page

Link resolvers are truly "behind-the-scenes" products, and while library staff use the public-facing menu of MUL's link resolver regularly, few of them understand how it works or what its limitations are. Several years ago, MUL transitioned from a consortial, locally created link resolver to a commercial product. This change elicited many questions from staff about display and functionality issues, which was the genesis of this page. The "Link Resolver" page in the TS LibGuide addresses the basic functionality of the link resolver, describes the limitations of the software (in some cases, platform-specific limitations), offers information about how services like Google Scholar and PubMed utilize linking, and provides links to usage statistics generated by the link resolver.

"EBSCO Discovery Service" Page

The TS LibGuide page on MUL's EBSCO Discovery Service implementation serves two purposes. It started as a place to manage the implementation process for the discovery service, which began in 2012. This page was used to keep library staff informed about the implementation personnel and time line, and to compile lists of known issues and solutions. Once the implementation was complete, the page remained in the TS LibGuide and was updated to include subpages for discovery service usage statistics as well as information on how to build discovery layer search boxes.

"Archived Content" Page

After several years of utilizing LibGuides in these ways, the TS Department recognized that some material was outdated (specifically electronic resource updates) and no longer useful to staff external to TS. The creation of an "Archived Content" page allows the department to remove outdated information from the primary pages, keeping them shorter and simpler, while still maintaining the content for those within the TS Department who might need it. Archiving information in this manner also allows the department to track changes over time, making staff less reliant on the institutional memory of the staff who worked on these changes originally. Lastly, but still importantly, archiving the content this way allows for the preservation of LibGuides usage statistics associated with the boxes and links, in the event that this usage is needed for reporting.

Adoption by Public Services Staff

The literature about implementing Web 2.0 tools like a LibGuide for communication indicates that it isn't technological barriers that inhibit staff from utilizing it, but a lack of organizational effort in the implementation of such tools.[48] Several changes in how the MUL TS Department communicated to public services staff were made to encourage use of the TS LibGuide. E-mail announcements for things like electronic resource free trials and noncritical electronic resource updates or announcements were discontinued, and were instead placed only on the "News and Updates" page of the LibGuide. If staff want to find out about free trials or read about noncritical vendor maintenance, the LibGuide is their sole source of information. Critical information about widespread system outages is still sent out via e-mail, as well as posted on the LibGuide. The coordinator of collection access and acquisitions strongly encouraged public services staff to use forms found in the LibGuide for problem reporting and to request lists of materials from MUL's Sierra ILS. Staff were told that using the provided forms instead of e-mailing TS staff directly would provide a quicker response time, since multiple staff monitored the forms. The presence of a self-service portal for electronic resource usage statistics on the LibGuide has also served as an excellent motivator for public services staff who need usage reports immediately. When a public services staff member contacts a TS Department staff member with a question, if the information required can be found on the TS LibGuide, the TS staff person simply provides the link to the TS LibGuide page to the requester. Newly hired public services librarians become generally acclimated to LibGuides since they all receive a LibGuides account and basic training in creating and maintaining LibGuides. Additionally, the coordinator of collection access and acquisitions provides a two-hour introductory session to each new public services librarian on electronic resources and serials that heavily utilizes TS LibGuide content. This orientation is meant to provide new staff with immediate knowledge of the self-service content available to them on the TS LibGuide. The above strategies have been in place for over six years and have made the TS LibGuide a fixture for many public services staff.

Assessment: LibGuides Statistics and Google Analytics

Looking at the statistics provided by Springshare for each page in a LibGuide has helped to guide the TS Department in updating content. Statistics for specific pages are checked regularly to determine if anyone is looking at them, and if so, how many times each page has been viewed. If a specific piece of content sees no use over a semester-long period or more, then the TS Department considers archiving or deleting it. LibGuides statistics display data both textually and graphically, and each view can be downloaded for use in reports. Usage reports can be customized for a period of time selected by the LibGuides user in increments of days, weeks, or months. Also noteworthy is that usage of a LibGuide while a staff member is logged in to her LibGuides account doesn't count towards these statistics, so the work that TS staff do on the TS LibGuide while logged in doesn't artificially inflate the numbers seen in the usage statistics. This usage data has also been helpful for TS librarian annual reports, promotion and tenure documents, departmental statistics, justifying the cost of MUL's LibGuides subscription, and justifying the use of staff time in the TS Department. Since the inception of the TS LibGuide in 2010, the guide has had 7,219 total page views. The year 2013 saw the guide's lowest usage, with only 786 page views, and 2014 saw the guide's highest usage, with 1,374 page views. The most-used pages on the guide for all years are the "Home" page and the "Electronic Resources Usage Statistics" page. While the LibGuides statistics are informative, they don't necessarily illustrate the depth of the usage. For institutions that want a more in-depth look at LibGuides usage, Google Analytics can be easily integrated into an institution's LibGuides account. MUL set up Google Analytics on its LibGuides in 2015, and data gathered by Google corresponds to what we see in our LibGuides stats but provides a much greater level of granularity. The TS Department hopes to use this more detailed information to further refine the content of the LibGuide.

Non-Successes

Because the MUL TS Department has been using a LibGuide for more than five years, the department has been able to identify and revise or eliminate the guide's less successful features and content. Original iterations of the LibGuide included feedback boxes for library staff using the guide to provide feedback to the guide's owners. These were utilized only a few times over two years and so were eliminated from the guide to allow space for more important information. With MUL's move to version two of LibGuides in 2015, layout changes were made to the TS LibGuide to conform to library-wide standards implemented for all LibGuides. Layout changes were made based on usability studies conducted with students, and TS staff felt that these layout changes would also benefit staff. The changes primarily involved simplifying page layouts (three columns at 25/50/25 to two columns at 25/75), adding a standardized librarian profile box to the home page, and attempting to maintain shorter page lengths in order to avoid the need for multiple-page scrolls. Originally, a "Policies" page was placed as a top-level tab on the TS LibGuide, but because use of the page was extremely low, policies were moved to lower-level pages under their respective topics. For some time, the TS LibGuide hosted a page on open access (as part of Open Access Week celebrations) that was intended to educate staff internally on scholarly communication issues. As MUL became more comfortable with internal, private LibGuides over the years, this open access content was moved to its own internal guide and more fully developed. The pages that have undergone the most revision (but still remain part of the guide) are the "E-Book Platforms" pages. When the guide was started in 2009, MUL was providing e-book access to patrons on only a handful of platforms, all of which were provided by a consortium. Over the intervening years, e-book purchasing has grown exponentially on more than a dozen platforms, necessitating the growth of the e-book content provided on the TS LibGuide.

CONCLUSION

Communication within an academic library has long been a topic of interest because of its complexities and challenges. It is clear that technological advances have both hindered and helped the communication challenges within academic libraries. While the communication challenges faced by the public and technical services silos in academic libraries have been articulated and discussed at great length in the literature, few solutions have been found to overcome these barriers. Miami University Libraries' Technical Services Department has experimented with and found success using Springshare's LibGuides product as a successful method of reciprocal communication and collaboration between its public and technical services units. The flexibility, affordability, currency, and intuitive nature of the product allowed technical services staff to create a dynamic LibGuide that provides needed information about technical services functions and processes to public services staff in a centralized, self-service location.

NOTES

1. Gillian McCombs, "Public and Technical Services: The Hidden Dialectic," *RQ* 28, no. 2 (1988): 145.

2. Phillip G. Clampitt, *Communicating for Managerial Effectiveness,* 2nd ed. (Thousand Oaks, CA: Sage, 2001), 182–90.

3. M. Mautino and M. Lorenzen, "Interdepartmental Communication in Academic Libraries," in *Workplace Culture in Academic Libraries: The Early 21st Century,* ed. Kelly Blessinger and Paul Hrycaj, Chandos Information Professional Series (Oxford, UK: Chandos, 2013), 209.

4. Erin E. Boyd and Elyssa Gould, "Skills for the Future of Technical Services," in *Rethinking Library Technical Services: Redefining Our Profession for the Future,* ed. Mary Beth Weber (Lanham, MD: Rowman & Littlefield, 2015), 127.

5. Charles Martell and Michael Gorman, "QWL Strategies: Reorganization," *Journal of Academic Librarianship* 9, no. 4 (1983): 225.

6. Ibid., 224.

7. McCombs, "Public and Technical Services."

8. Maria Anna Jankowska and Linnea Marshall, "Why Social Interaction and Good Communication in Academic Libraries Matters," *Reference Librarian* 40, no. 83/84 (2003): 132.

9. Sarah C. Michalak, "This Changes Everything: Transforming the Academic Library," *Journal of Library Administration* 52, no. 5 (2012): 417.

10. Eleanor Gossen, Frances Reynolds, Karina Ricker, and Helen Smirensky, "Forging New Communication Links in an Academic Library: A Cross-Training Experiment," *Journal of Academic Librarianship* 16, no. 1 (1990): 19.

11. Ibid., 19–20.

12. H. Mphidi and R. Snyman, "The Utilisation of an Intranet as a Knowledge Management Tool in Academic Libraries," *Electronic Library* 22, no. 5 (2004): 395–96.

13. Kristen Costello and Darcy Del Bosque, "For Better or Worse: Using Wikis and Blogs for Staff Communication in an Academic Library," *Journal of Web Librarianship* 4, no. 2/3 (2010): 147.

14. Ibid.

15. Lenore England and Jennifer Diffin, "ERM Ideas and Innovations," *Journal of Electronic Resources Librarianship* 26, no. 3 (2014).

16. Bohyun Kim, "Organizational and Social Factors in the Adoption of Intranet 2.0: A Case Study," *Journal of Web Librarianship* 4, no. 2/3 (2010).

17. Karen Jensen, "Managing Library Electronic Resources Using Google Sites," *Journal of Electronic Resources Librarianship* 25, no. 2 (2013): 119–20.

18. Laura Harris, Julie Garrison, and Emily Frigo, "At the Crossroads: Bringing the Tenure and Promotion Process into the Digital Age," *College & Research Libraries News* 70, no. 8 (2009).

19. Jeremy Bullian and Alicia Ellison, "Building a Low-Cost, Low-Labor Library Web Site at Hillsborough Community College," *Journal of Web Librarianship* 7, no. 3 (2013).

20. Dave Hodgins, "Dynamic Space for Rent: Using Commercial Web Hosting to Develop a Web 2.0 Intranet," *Journal of Web Librarianship* 4, no. 2/3 (2010).

21. L. C. Osterhaus Trzasko, A. M. Farrell, and M. L. Rethlefsen, "Converting an Intranet Site to the Cloud: Using CampusGuides to Refresh a Library Portal," *Medical Reference Services Quarterly* 31, no. 3 (2012).

22. M. Griffin and B. Lewis, "Transforming Special Collections through Innovative Uses for LibGuides," *Collection Building* 30, no. 1 (2011); B. Lewis and M. Griffin, "Special Collections and the New Web: Using LibGuides to Provide Meaningful Access," *Journal of Electronic Resources Librarianship* 23, no. 1 (2011); Sharon Farnel et al., "Chapter 8: Where There's a Will There's a Way: Using LibGuides to Rescue Paper Ephemera from the Bibliographic Underbrush," in *Description: Innovative Practices for Archives and Special Collections,* ed. Kate Theimer, Innovative Practices for Archives and Special Collections (Rowman & Littlefield, 2014).

23. Elizabeth Kiscaden, "Creating a Current Awareness Service Using Yahoo! Pipes and LibGuides," *Information Technology & Libraries* 33, no. 4 (2014).

24. Christopher Guder, "The ePortfolio: A Tool for Professional Development, Engagement, and Lifelong Learning," *Public Services Quarterly* 9, no. 3 (2013).

25. J. J. Little et al., "Interdisciplinary Collaboration: A Faculty Learning Community Creates a Comprehensive LibGuide," *Reference Services Review* 38, no. 3 (2010).

26. Sara Roberts and Dwight Hunter, "New Library, New Librarian, New Student: Using LibGuides to Reach the Virtual Student," *Journal of Library & Information Services in Distance Learning* 5, no. 1/2 (2011).

27. N. Han and S. L. Hall, "Think Globally! Enhancing the International Student Experience with LibGuides," *Journal of Electronic Resources Librarianship* 24, no. 4 (2012).

28. Amy M. Suiter and Heather Lea Moulaison, "Supporting Scholars: An Analysis of Academic Library Websites' Documentation on Metrics and Impact," *The Journal of Academic Librarianship* 41 (2015).

29. Benjamin Turner, "Using LibGuides as a Platform for Student Research," *College & Research Libraries News* 71, no. 8 (2010).

30. Lenore England and Fu Li, "Electronic Resources Evaluation Central: Using Off-the-Shelf Software, Web 2.0 Tools, and LibGuides to Manage an Electronic Resources Evaluation Process," *Journal of Electronic Resources Librarianship* 23, no. 1 (2011).

31. England and Diffin, "ERM Ideas and Innovations."

32. R. A. Erb and B. Erb, "Leveraging the LibGuides Platform for Electronic Resources Access Assistance," *Journal of Electronic Resources Librarianship* 26, no. 3 (2014).

33. "An Investigation into the Use of LibGuides for Electronic Resources Troubleshooting in Academic Libraries," *Electronic Library* 33, no. 3 (2015).

34. J. W. Bazeley and B. Yoose, "Technical Services Transparency Using a LibGuide to Expose the Mysteries of Technical Services," *Library Resources and Technical Services* 57, no. 2 (2013).

35. Martha Fallahay Loesch, "Tech Services on the Web: Vale RDA LibGuide," *Technical Services Quarterly* 31, no. 1 (2014).

36. Kat Landry Mueller and Molly Thompson, "Biz of Acq—LibGuides: Changing the Game for Technical Services Procedures & Policies," *Against the Grain* 27, no. 4 (2015).

37. Bazeley and Yoose, "Technical Services Transparency."

38. Loesch, "Tech Services on the Web."

39. Mueller and Thompson, "Biz of Acq."

40. Mary Beth Weber, "The State of Technical Services," in *Rethinking Library Technical Services : Redefining Our Profession for the Future,* ed. Mary Beth Weber (Lanham, MD: Rowman & Littlefield, 2015), 25.

41. Ibid., 27.

42. S. Bordeianu and R. Lubas, "Interaction between Departments: Strategies for Improving Interdepartmental Collaboration through Communication," in *Workplace Culture in Academic Libraries,* ed. Kelly Blessinger and Paul Hrycaj, Chandos Information Professional Series (Oxford, UK: Chandos, 2013), 224.

43. Ibid.

44. Wendy Chu, "Implementation as Ongoing and Incremental: Case Study of Web 2.0 Use for Staff Communication," *Journal of Access Services* 9, no. 3 (2012): 149.

45. Adam Murray, "Electronic Resource Management 2.0: Using Web 2.0 Technologies as Cost-Effective Alternatives to an Electronic Resource Management System," *Journal of Electronic Resources Librarianship* 20, no. 3 (2008).

46. R. A. Erb and B. Erb, "Leveraging the LibGuides Platform."

47. Jeanette Ho, "Enhancing Access to Resources through the Online Catalog and the Library Web Site: A Collaboration between Public and Technical Services at Texas A&M University Libraries," *Technical Services Quarterly* 22, no. 4 (2005).

48. Kim, "Organizational and Social Factors," 200.

Core Competencies for Electronic Resources Librarianship

Sarah W. Sutton

BACKGROUND AND HISTORY

Electronic resources librarianship developed as a professional specialty during the 1990s as libraries embraced the advantages afforded by advances in information technology to deliver library resources quickly and easily to patrons in electronic format at any time, day or night. Academic libraries in particular first began to make electronic indexes available to patrons. This was quickly followed by a growing corpus of full-text digital content. Both serials librarians and systems librarians were often handed the responsibility for managing these new resources[1] and, as a result, saw their overall job responsibilities change. Although the first job ad for an electronic resources librarian appeared in 1990,[2] until 2013, when "Core Competencies for E-Resources Librarianship" was published, there existed no universal description of the duties and responsibilities of electronic resources librarians.

In 2008 the American Library Association (ALA) Executive Board approved a set of core competencies for librarianship. These had their origin in response to the first Congress on Professional Education and subsequent work by the ALA Presidential Task Force on Library Education.[3] The "Core Competences of Librarianship" was approved by the ALA Executive Board and published by the ALA in 2009. They define "the basic knowledge to be possessed by all persons graduating from an ALA-accredited master's program in library and information studies."[4] They also state that "librarians working in school, academic, public, special, and governmental libraries, and in other contexts will need to possess specialized knowledge beyond that specified here."[5]

The ALA maintains a list of "Knowledge and Competencies Statements Developed by Relevant Professional Organizations,"[6] but prior to 2013, no professional organization or other entity had developed a statement of competencies for electronic resources librarians. As a result, in 2010 Sutton[7] undertook research to identify such competencies. This research involved content analysis of the qualifications, for example, competencies, sought by employers of electronic resources librarians between 2005 and 2009 as they were described in job ads for electronic resources librarians. In 2011, upon the completion of this research, Sutton accepted an invitation to chair a North America Serials Interest Group (NASIG) task force that was charged with creating a list of competencies for electronic resources librarians that would be an appropriate expression of the specialized knowledge, beyond that expressed in the ALA's competences, required of electronic resources librarians. The overarching intention was for the competencies to assist electronic resources librarians and their employers to clarify the work of electronic resources librarians and thus provide a uniform basis for evaluating that work, as well as to inform the development of library and information science (LIS) curriculum development so as to prepare new librarians for work with electronic resources.

The NASIG Core Competencies Task Force extended Sutton's[8] research by seeking to learn what duties and responsibilities electronic resources librarians were performing in their daily work through an examination of job descriptions. The task force put out a call to the NASIG membership and others on several discussion lists specific to the work of electronic resources librarians (e.g., NASIG-L, SERIALST, and ERIL-L) asking for electronic resources librarians to share their job descriptions with the task force. The task force used the job descriptions they received to further identify what regular duties were being performed by electronic resources librarians and what their responsibilities were. The results of their content analysis of job descriptions, along with Sutton's results describing the qualifications that employers sought for electronic resources librarian positions, informed the task force's work on the "Core Competencies for E-Resources Librarians."

The task force shared their draft of the "Core Competencies for E-Resources Librarians" with the NASIG membership at the 2012 NASIG Annual Conference in order to obtain input on the competencies from experts in electronic resources librarianship and, in some cases, from those librarians whose job descriptions had informed the writing of the draft competencies. The task force learned at this event that there was a great deal of variance in the focus of the work of electronic resources librarians. Specifically, in many cases, librarians were performing a subset of the duties and responsibilities set out in the draft document, but, depending on the library, some of the duties and responsibilities were being performed by other library staff or by teams. The overwhelming sentiment of the attendees was that no single librarian could be expert in every single competency included in the draft document.

The task force had struggled particularly with prioritizing or otherwise organizing the competencies they had identified. The sentiments expressed by the NASIG membership confirmed that

> the competencies required for ERL positions vary greatly based on the type of institution in which the work is done and on the workflows within the organization. For example, an ERL in a small academic library might be responsible for the entire life cycle of electronic resources in that institution, while in a large research library, an ERL might be responsible for ER acquisitions alone, while others are responsible for access, administration, support, and evaluation.[9]

As a result, the introduction to the final "Core Competencies for E-Resources Librarians" suggests that "the competencies required of an ERL will encompass a subset of" the full list of competencies identified in the document.[10]

Subsequent to the 2012 NASIG Annual Conference, the task force revised the competencies based on the input received at the conference and from the NASIG Executive Board. They also revised the introduction to the document. The final version of "Core Competencies for E-Resources Librarians" was submitted to the NASIG Executive Board in spring 2013. The board approved them by unanimous vote and the document was published on the NASIG website in July 2013.

THE COMPETENCIES

The final set of "Core Competencies for E-Resources Librarians" includes seven broad areas of competence, many of which expand on competences identified in

ALA's "Core Competences of Librarianship." This was purposeful on the part of the task force, since the original intention of both NASIG and Sutton's original research was for the competencies to both assist electronic resources librarians and their employers to clarify the work of electronic resources librarians and thus provide a uniform basis for evaluating that work, and also to inform the development of the LIS curriculum so as to prepare new librarians for work with electronic resources.

The first core competency requires the electronic resources librarian to have knowledge beyond that of a generalist librarian of the life cycle of electronic resources. This includes electronic resources budgeting and acquisitions, specifically the complicated and complex work of "licensing [electronic resources] and the legal framework in which it takes place."[11] It also covers the application of general principles and theories of information organization to work with electronic resources as well as work with bibliographic utilities for that purpose, "a thorough understanding of records management," and a commitment to keeping up to date with trends related to all of these things.[12]

"Theoretical and practical knowledge of the structures, hardware, and software underlying the provision of access to electronic resources"[13] is the topic of the second core competency. Hardware particularly includes mobile and other devices through which electronic content is delivered. Also included are networks, and related standards, protocols, and software for communicating electronic content and for authenticating authorized users. This competency also covers digital scholarship as well as the "complex range of data generated by and related to electronic resources."[14] It is worth noting that, in the time since the "Core Competencies for E-Resources Librarians" was published, NASIG has also begun work on a set of core competencies for scholarly communications librarians that specifically addresses work with digital scholarship.

The third competency is closely related to the second; it covers knowledge of research and assessment specifically with regard to work with electronic resources. It speaks to the need for electronic resources librarians to manage the "complex range of data generated by and related to electronic resources."[15] This is another competency that mirrors one of the ALA's core competences but requires deeper, more specialized knowledge. Specifically, it covers not only knowledge and understanding of research methods and an understanding of the data itself and how it is generated, but also being able to "identify the principles and techniques necessary to identify and analyze emerging technologies and innovations" and to "apply principles of data collection, analysis, and reporting"[16] to this specific and complex data.

The fourth and fifth competencies also specify the application of general librarian competencies deeply and thoroughly to work with electronic resources. All librarians must be good communicators, but the fourth competency for electronic resources librarians is the ability to communicate with an unusually broad range of constituents.[17] This ranges from patrons with very little technological knowledge to information technology experts and computer scientists who may use the same terminology as librarians but apply very different meanings to that terminology. The fifth competency relates to supervision and management, specifically to the application of skills in project management, workflow, policy, systems administration, and technical support, which go beyond the skills required of a generalist.

Given that electronic resources are made possible by advances in communication and computer technology, it is not surprising that the sixth competency for electronic resources librarians requires them to keep up to date with trends and current issues not only in librarianship but also in technology, scholarly communication, licensing, and the legal framework in which electronic resources are obtained and used,[18] and standards including but not limited to resource usage and metadata.

The seventh and final competency, somewhat surprisingly, is related to the personal qualities that are desirable in an electronic resources librarian. Although surprising, the qualifications and characteristics covered in this competency were clearly sought by employers in job ads for electronic resources librarians.[19] Successful electronic resources librarians are flexible and open-minded as well as able to "function in a dynamic, rapidly changing environment."[20] They also have a high tolerance for complexity and ambiguity and are able "to recognize familiar patterns and also identify exceptions to the pattern[21] (e.g., selecting the correct holding in an e-resource knowledge base or troubleshooting an access outage)."[22]

APPLICATION OF THE CORE COMPETENCIES FOR E-RESOURCES LIBRARIANSHIP

There is evidence in the e-resources literature that the "Core Competencies for E-Resources Librarianship" are being used in a variety of ways in libraries. Much of it takes the form of presentations at conferences of professional organizations dedicated to electronic resources librarianship such as Electronic Resources & Libraries (ER&L) and NASIG, as well as conferences on the topic of other librarian specialties such as the Charleston Conference, which is dedicated to library acquisitions. The NASIG conference in particular has encouraged conference proposals related to the "Core Competencies for E-Resources Librarianship" in their calls for proposals beginning in 2014. Although in contrast to other, more established topics, this body of literature is relatively small, it appears to be continuing to grow and to garner the attention of librarians working in this specialty.

Several of the themes that are apparent in this body of literature are those conceived of by the authors of the "Core Competencies for E-Resources Librarianship" and reflect their overarching intention for the competencies to assist electronic resources librarians and their employers to clarify the work of electronic resources librarians, provide a uniform basis for evaluating that work, and inform the development of LIS curriculum development so as to prepare new librarians for work with electronic resources. But there are also some less expected themes apparent, specifically the use of the "Core Competencies for E-Resources Librarianship" as a basis for reorganizing library departments and workflows and comparisons of the competencies to practitioner experiences.

Librarian Education

Two views of librarian education appear in the literature, that of practicing electronic resources librarians on the preparation for electronic resources work that they received in their MLIS program and that of an educator on the level of electronic resources topics and courses in accredited MLIS programs. Both Lawson and Janyk[23] and Chilton[24] bemoan the lack of focus on electronic resources in MLIS education. As of 2014, only 19 percent of ALA-accredited MLIS programs included a course dedicated to electronic resources as part of their curriculum.[25] Lawson and Janyk[26] recommend additional focus on electronic resources in core courses covering such topics as collection development and technology.

Reorganization

The "Core Competencies for E-Resources Librarianship" have also been used in several cases as a basis for library or interlibrary departmental reorganization. Although this was not a use specifically envisioned by the task force authors of the competencies, given the impact that electronic resources have had on library collections and acquisitions, this should not come as a surprise. One such case took place at the University of Texas (UT) at Arlington Libraries beginning in fall 2012 as they planned for a library-wide reorganization of library staff and services in order to better meet user needs.[27] In the information resources unit in particular, the goals for reorganization included expanding the number of staff within the unit to meet the increased number of resources to be managed, and improving communications with other units that had some level of responsibility for e-resources acquisitions. Ensuring that new staff in the unit had the necessary competencies to accomplish the work was critical.[28]

Another reorganization took place within the Colorado State University Collections and Contracts Division as they worked to address "the gradual attrition due to retirements and the subsequent elimination of many of these positions."[29] Of particular interest is the observation that at Colorado State University "it also became apparent that one or two people could not handle the entire workload,"[30] since this supports the task force's finding that there is often more than one single librarian or library staff member contributing to the management of a library's electronic resources. In this case, as at UT Arlington, the goals for reorganization were to rebalance staff assignments in light of increasing e-resource subscriptions and purchases and decreasing purchases of print materials, as well as to improve communications among those responsible for work with e-resources.[31]

Staff Development and Skills Assessment

Another aspect of this idea that e-resources management extends beyond normal duties and responsibilities is reflected in the use of the "Core Competencies for E-Resources Librarianship" as a basis for library staff development and/or skills assessment. This is often one phase of library or department reorganization, and the literature demonstrates several instances of the use of the "Core Competencies for E-Resources Librarianship" for this purpose. Chilton[32] expresses this in her discussion of the need to share electronic resources expertise, as do Chamberlain and Reece.[33]

What is interesting in these and other cases is that the "Core Competencies for E-Resources Librarianship" are being used not only to train and evaluate the skills of professional librarians, but also to train and evaluate the skills and knowledge of paraprofessional staff. At Colorado State University, the "Core Competencies" influenced the upward reclassification training of a paraprofessional position that included "Core Competencies"–based learning outcomes such as obtaining a general understanding of the electronic resources life cycle, attaining mastery of the fiscal cycle, and understanding the purpose and function of an ERMS (electronic resources management system) and how it relates to workflows.[34] There is also evidence that the "Core Competencies" are being used as the basis of professional development activities at Shenandoah University.[35] At Auburn University, the "Core Competencies" were used first in a self-assessment of library staff's skills related to electronic resources and subsequently as a means of identifying and categorizing competencies where staff were lacking proficiency. These tasks also served as the starting point for staff training that was specifically focused on alleviating, as much as possible, the loss of staff and institutional knowledge.[36]

Professional Practice

Several scholars have voiced an interest in practitioner perspectives on the "Core Competencies for E-Resources Librarianship." The NASIG task force sought practitioners' input during the development phase of the competencies, and other researchers have also approached this theme. Lesher, Fowler, and Tovstiadi[37] explored the application of the "Core Competencies for E-Resources Librarianship" to work with physical libraries' collections in a small library. At the same time, NASIG formed a new task force that was charged with creating an addendum to the "Core Competencies for E-Resources Librarianship" that incorporated competencies for work with print serials collections. This addendum was published in 2016.

Through a series of interviews designed to complement Sutton's (2011) work by identifying practitioner perspectives on the "Core Competencies for E-Resources Librarianship," Ross[38] asked interviewees about four broad categories of work with electronic resources: technical, legal, analytical, and interpersonal. The respondents in this study ranked interpersonal competency, that is, "effective communication with everyone who uses or interacts with electronic resources," as being the most important competency required for electronic resources librarians. At about the same time, Fleming-May and Grogg[39] compared the "Core Competencies for E-Resources Librarianship" to the results of a survey of electronic resources librarians about the job duties and responsibilities they performed and where they obtained the training that qualified them to complete those duties.

Similarly, Baggett sought to use the "Core Competencies for E-Resources Librarianship" for "empowering staff and improving patron service." Specifically, she used them to create professional development activities for library staff in order to accomplish this.[40]

FUTURE IMPACT

It is clear that the "Core Competencies for E-Resources Librarianship" are impacting electronic resources librarianship in a variety of ways, not least of which are those identified here. Scholars and practitioners are reporting their impact on training and professional development for both professionals and paraprofessionals who work with electronic resources. There is also evidence that the "Core Competencies for E-Resources Librarianship" have influenced workflows and the practice of electronic resources librarianship.[41]

This presents a growing dilemma for those, like this author, wishing to identify and measure the impact of the "Core Competencies for E-Resources Librarianship," as well as those wishing to ensure their continuing positive impact. Like the chicken and the egg, the more that the "Core Competencies for E-Resources Librarianship" influence education, workflows, hiring, and evaluation, and organizing library personnel for work with electronic resources, the more difficult it will be to identify whether the sources of those changes was the "Core Competencies for E-Resources Librarianship" or whether the sources influenced the "Core Competencies." In other words, the original "Core Competencies for E-Resources Librarianship" were based on qualifications sought in job ads and responsibilities identified in job descriptions. Now job ads and job descriptions are being written based on the "Core Competencies for E-Resources Librarianship." If this is allowed to become a closed system of influence, there is the risk that the "Core Competencies for E-Resources Librarianship" will become stagnant and of less use.

There currently exists a window of opportunity for examining this impact through the comparison of current job ads and descriptions for electronic resources positions to those that influenced the development of the "Core Competencies for E-Resources Librarianship." But this opportunity will not last long, both because of the ephemeral nature of job ads and because of the increasing potential that the cycle of influence may become a closed system. Soon, researchers and scholars interested in maintaining the relevance of and advancing the usefulness of the "Core Competencies for E-Resources Librarianship" will need to find additional measures of the work of electronic resources librarians.

NOTES

1. Ross and Sutton, *Guide to Electronic Resource Management*.
2. Dewald, "Anticipating Library Use by Business Students."

3. Hayden, "American Library Association President's Task Force on Library Education Final Report."
4. American Library Association, "ALA's Core Competences of Librarianship."
5. Ibid.
6. American Library Association, "ALA | Knowledge and Competencies Statements."
7. Sutton, "Identifying Core Competencies for Electronic Resources Librarians in the Twenty-First Century Library."
8. Ibid.
9. NASIG Core Competencies Task Force, "Core Competencies for Electronic Resources Librarians," 1.
10. Ibid.
11. Ibid., 2.
12. Ibid., 3.
13. Ibid., 4–5.
14. Ibid., 6.
15. Ibid.
16. Ibid., 7.
17. Ibid., 8.
18. Ibid., 9–10.
19. Sutton, "Identifying Core Competencies for Electronic Resources Librarians in the Twenty-First Century Library."
20. NASIG Core Competencies Task Force, "Core Competencies for Electronic Resources Librarians," 10.
21. Ibid.
22. Ibid.
23. Lawson and Janyk, "Getting to the Core of the Matter: Competencies for New E-Resources Librarians."
24. Chilton, "Human TERMS of Engagement."
25. Ibid.
26. Lawson and Janyk, "Getting to the Core of the Matter."
27. Chamberlain and Reece, "Library Reorganization, Chaos, and Using the Core Competencies as a Guide."
28. Ibid.
29. Erb, "The Impact of Reorganization of Staff Using the Core Competencies as a Framework for Staff Training and Development."
30. Ibid.
31. Ibid.
32. Chilton, "Human TERMS of Engagement."
33. Chamberlain and Reece, "Library Reorganization, Chaos, and Using the Core Competencies as a Guide."
34. Erb, "The Impact of Reorganization of Staff Using the Core Competencies as a Framework for Staff Training and Development."

35. Baggett, "Take the NASIG Core Competencies Out for a Joy Ride."
36. Sullenger et al., "Core Competencies to the Rescue."
37. Lesher, Fowler, and Tovstiadi, "'And Other Duties as Assigned.'"
38. Ross, "Practitioner Perspectives on the Core Competencies for Electronic Resources Librarians: Preliminary Results of a Qualitative Study."
39. Fleming-May and Grogg, "Earnest Expectations: How Closely Do the . . ."
40. Baggett, "Deconstructing the Core Competencies to Build the Digital Future."
41. Baggett, "Take the NASIG Core Competencies Out for a Joy Ride."

REFERENCES

American Library Association. "ALA | Knowledge and Competencies Statements," 2010. www.ala.org/ala/educationcareers/careers/corecomp/corecompspecial/knowledgecompetencies.cfm.

———. "ALA's Core Competences of Librarianship." Chicago: American Library Association, 2008. www.ala.org/ala/educationcareers/careers/corecomp/corecompetences/finalcorecompstat09.pdf.

Baggett, Stacy B. "Deconstructing the Core Competencies to Build the Digital Future." Poster presentation at the NASIG 30th Annual Conference, Washington, DC, May 28, 2015.

———. "Take the NASIG Core Competencies Out for . . ." Presented at the Charleston Library Conference, Charleston, SC, November 4, 2015. https://2015charlestonconference.sched.org/event/4CXS/take-the-nasig-core-competencies-out-for-a-joy-ride.

Chamberlain, Clint, and Derek Reece. "Library Reorganization, Chaos, and Using the Core Competencies as a Guide." Presented at the NASIG 2013 Annual Conference, Buffalo, NY, June 8, 2013.

Chilton, Galadriel. "Human TERMS of Engagement." Presented at the Electronic Resources & Libraries Conference, Austin, TX, March 18, 2014. https://er12014.sched.org/event/1hGUaLk/human-terms-of-engagement.

Dewald, Nancy H. "Anticipating Library Use by Business Students: The Uses of a Syllabus Study." *Research Strategies* 19, no. 1 (2003): 33–45. doi:10.1016/j.resstr.2003.09.003.

Erb, Rachel A. "The Impact of Reorganization of Staff Using the Core Competencies as a Framework for Staff Training and Development." *The Serials Librarian* 68, no. 1–4 (May 19, 2015): 92–105. doi:10.1080/0361526X.2015.1017417.

Fleming-May, Rachel, and Jill Grogg. "2014 Charleston Library Conference: Earnest Expectations: How Closely Do the . . ." Presented at the Charleston Library Conference, Charleston, SC, November 6, 2014. https://2014charlestonconference.sched.org/event/1txnhr3/earnest-expectations-how-closely-do-the-nasig-core-competencies-for-electronic-resources-librarians-reflect-their-daily-experience.

Hayden, Carla. "American Library Association President's Task Force on Library Education Final Report," January 2009. www.ala.org/ala/aboutala/governance/officers/ebdocuments/2008_2009ebdocuments/ebd12_30.pdf.

Lawson, Emma, and Roen Janyk. "Getting to the Core of the Matter: Competencies for New E-Resources Librarians." Presented at the NASIG 2013 Annual Conference, Buffalo, NY, June 7, 2013. www.slideshare.net/NASIG/getting-to-the-core-of-the-matter-competencies-for-new-eresources-librarians.

Lesher, Marcella, Stacy Fowler, and Esta Tovstiadi. "'And Other Duties as Assigned': Expanding the Boundaries of the E- Resource Lifecycle to Get Things Done." *The Serials Librarian* 70, no. 1–4 (May 18, 2016): 272–76. doi:10.1080/036152 6X.2016.1153334.

NASIG Core Competencies Task Force. "Core Competencies for Electronic Resources Librarians." NASIG, 2013. www.nasig.org/uploaded_files/92/files/CoreComp/CompetenciesforERLibrarians_final_ver_2013-7-22.docx.

Ross, Sheri. "Practitioner Perspectives on the Core Competencies for Electronic Resources Librarians: Preliminary Results of a Qualitative Study." Presented at the Electronic Resources in Libraries conference, Austin, TX, 2014.

Ross, Sheri, and Sarah W. Sutton. *Guide to Electronic Resource Management.* Libraries Unlimited, 2016.

Sullenger, Paula, Shade Aladebumoye, Nadine Ellero, and Susan Wishnetsky. "Core Competencies to the Rescue: Taking Stock and Protecting Institutional Knowledge." *The Serials Librarian* 68, no. 1–4 (May 19, 2015): 223–29. doi:10.1080/036152 6X.2015.1017708.

Sutton, Sarah. "Identifying Core Competencies for Electronic Resources Librarians in the Twenty-First Century Library." Texas Woman's University, 2011.

10

Using the Core Competencies for E-Resource Librarians to Reengineer Technical Services

Christine Korytnyk Dulaney and Kari Schmidt

INTRODUCTION
From Print to Online Revisited

In 2013 the authors presented "From Print to Online: Revamping Technical Services with Distributed and Centralized Workflow Models"[1] at the NASIG Annual Conference in Buffalo, New York, where they described how each of their libraries reorganized electronic resource management (ERM) functions within traditional technical services settings. The Bender Library (Washington, DC) used a centralized model, while the Pence Law Library (Washington, DC) used a distributed workflow model to revamp and realign work. Within the centralized model, a stand-alone ERM unit was formed and worked alongside existing acquisitions and cataloging units, which provided for an intense focus on building ERM expertise, rapidly expanding the e-resource collection, shifting material types to electronic-only, implementing ERM and discovery service systems, and e-resource assessment. Likewise, within the distributed model, positions and workflows were realigned to assume ERM work which allowed for shared knowledge and responsibility for the electronic resource collection throughout technical services, a shift in culture from efficiency to a learning organization, and the creation of a team-based environment.

Although both paths were successful in their own right, both transition models within technical services did not upend or transform the linear-based traditional acquisition and cataloging paradigm that is the hallmark of technical services operations. The library employing the centralized ERM model experienced a siloing of ERM expertise and a continued lopsided distribution of staff that favored print-based acquisitions and cataloging work, even with workflow advances that embraced automation and with more than 80 percent of the materials budget going to e-resources. The library utilizing a distributed ERM model retained the traditional units of acquisitions and cataloging, as well as the rigidity and lack of collaboration which typify this type of functional organization.

The unsatisfactory results of these reorganizations highlight the ongoing transitional state of technical services. To get beyond this transitional state, however, requires a radical overhaul since different models of more fully "embracing" ERM work may only end up begging for a fuller transformation of the traditional technical services paradigm. Using the "Core Competencies for Electronic Resources Librarians"[2] as a tool during this fuller transformation will break the existing paradigm and open up new opportunities for technical services to embrace a library's larger mission within a host organization.

CHANGING LIBRARY MISSION

In order to understand the transitional state of technical services and why the centrality of electronic resources in our libraries calls forth a paradigm shift in technical services, we need to understand the transformational nature of the Internet and its ability to create systems of interconnected networks. As a catalyst for change and innovation, the computer network has affected every aspect of users' lives—cultural, social, and interpersonal. The network has changed how we teach, how we learn, and how we conduct research. This integration of networks has created new opportunities for communication, knowledge exchange, relationships across all types of borders and boundaries, and innovation. Consequently, the changes brought about by the network have transformed our libraries.

Jeehyun Yun Davis has identified four major sources that are driving change: economy, social behaviors, technology, and academia.[3] As these "change drivers" transform budgets, user behavior and expectations, workflows, and the process of scholarly research and communication, libraries have had to respond to these challenges. In the networked world, the library is being reimagined from a warehouse of artifacts into a space for learning and creativity. The library further serves as the platform that leverages these changes in order to create new knowledge.[4] In response to changes in user behavior and expectations, a re-conceptualization of the library mission is occurring. Where the library's role has traditionally been one of preserver of knowledge and culture, this role is shifting to one of an active agent in the learning process. As David Lankes states, "The mission of libraries is to improve society through facilitating knowledge creation in their communities."[5]

In fulfilling this mission, libraries have had to respond to changes in collections and in the infrastructure that supports those collections. As libraries transform from warehouses of artifacts to collaborative spaces for learning and innovating, users expect customized and intuitive systems for research and resource discovery. The success of the library is increasingly based on its ability to meet changing user needs, which in turn is based on the flexibility of library staff to create and offer user-centric, web-based collections and delivery systems.

EXPANDING E-RESOURCES, NEW OPPORTUNITIES, AND TRANSITION

Traditionally, the library has been defined by the size and the quality of its print-based collection of books and journals. For technical services staff, the management and maintenance of this print collection involved a piece-by-piece, linear process through the functional areas of acquisitions and cataloging. All services revolved around maintaining, growing, and providing access to these tangible materials.

As content migrated from print to electronic format, collections have become increasingly complex, with users demanding content in whichever format is most convenient for their use. To handle these increasingly complex and expensive resources with declining or stagnant budgets, new acquisitions vehicles are emerging, many based on a "just-in-time" model of selection. These new purchasing models include demand-driven acquisitions (DDA) and evidence-based acquisitions (EBA), bundled aggregated content, "big deals," new delivery platforms, and a variety of e-book access models. New technological changes, such as the adoption of next-generation library management systems, the discontinuation of the OPAC search, and shelf-ready services create additional challenges to the status quo. As electronic resources and digital collections continue to increase in their size and complexity, print collections decrease and other tangible formats are discontinued wholesale.

Yet these changes create opportunities to expand technical services operations into new areas, such as metadata creation for digital collections, metadata management of locally created data sets and open educational resources, discovery service optimization, and bringing local bibliographic environments into the world of linked data. Libraries no longer consist of owned collections, but are now hybrid collections of owned, leased, and, increasingly, locally created digital objects and artifacts.

The management of this complex and changing collection profile, however, challenges the traditional technical services paradigm of a linear, piece-by-piece acquisitions and cataloging process. In addition, the effectiveness of the traditional print-based workflows diminishes when faced with the complexities of managing electronic and digital resources. Based on the needs of print collections, staff skill sets prove inadequate to handle electronic and digital resources as well. These challenges push technical services departments into a transitional state of handling electronic resources with print-based skills, workflows, and mindsets. Only a comprehensive overhaul of the traditional technical services paradigm can overcome these challenges.

Recognition of the need to reengineer the technical services paradigm has been articulated for many years. Thought-provoking leaders like Bradford Eden point out that the desire for change has actually been with the profession since the 1980s. In charting a way forward, Eden outlines an administrative approach that includes deep workflow reviews, standardization of bibliographic processes, outsourcing and contracting with vendors, and staff training and reclassification to support work with electronic and digital content.[6]

Tweaked workflows and modified organizational structures, however, are not significant enough to pull technical services out of its transitional state. The need for a more significant transformational response can be inferred from the study completed by Jeehyun Yun Davis. In this study, Davis describes the empirical data drawn from interviews with nineteen technical services directors at large research university libraries. Davis uses an organizational modeling exercise to understand current patterns, with a focus on the traditional acquisitions and cataloging functions of technical services.[7]

The responses highlight the underlying forces that require a reengineering of technical services, including identifying current and future functions and needed skill sets. This work defines how the current transitional state of technical services drives the trend toward the centralization and consolidation of technical services functions, the re-conceptualization of positions to accommodate emerging work, the gradual reassignment of staff to work on growing e-resource collections, new work emerging because of electronic and digital collections, and traditional features of technical services work occurring outside of the functional area.[8] A striking feature of the data is the number of times participating libraries have reorganized technical services or are planning to in the future, with thirteen of the respondents reorganizing within the last five years and fourteen planning for a reorganization within the next five years.[9]

In addition, Davis's findings identify a higher level of desired technology hard skill sets, which were well beyond traditional cataloging standards. This knowledge includes more complex and future-focused skills in programming, the semantic web, linked data, and non-MARC metadata schema.[10] Davis also draws attention to the participants' desire for a greater quantity of soft skills in technical services staff, such as the "ability to collaborate," "communication skills," "flexibility," "proactivity," and "willingness to take a risk."[11] The emerging hard and soft skills identified by participants lead Davis to recognize that there is a "gap between the skills that are held by current technical services personnel and the skills that are needed for new and emerging technical services functions."[12]

Likewise, Pastva et al. define a new normal in acquisitions and cataloging work where electronic resources are the engine propelling new challenges. Acquisitions departments continue to grapple with new models ranging from DDA to EBA, alongside the management of e-book aggregator packages, diminished print approval plans, expanded consortium purchases of e-books, changing big deal models, proprietary data sets, streaming media, and database models for e-journal packages. Similarly, cataloging must adjust to new standards and processes, including RDA (Resource Description and Access), batch-loading vendor-created records, learning emerging metadata schema, defining legacy database cleanup because of wide-scale weeding, identifying data quality issues, and planning for the emerging linked data environment, as well as the deeper automation of database management.[13]

The new purchasing vehicles and cataloging workflows which arise from the need to manage growing collections of electronic resources defy the practices and standards defined by the traditional technical services print-based paradigm. Where print resources have well-defined standards for description and management, electronic resources tend to be changeable and require technical proficiency to manage. Furthermore, electronic resources, particularly databases, are increasingly expensive. The problem facing libraries is exemplified by the findings of Stachokas, who documents that in many libraries "60% of the budget is devoted to electronic resources on average, but only 25% of technical services staff are assigned to work with these resources."[14] This asymmetrical structure is typical in libraries that have created segregated electronic and print ghettos.

The need for radical transformation to break out of this transitional state is underscored by Sally Gibson. She advocates for a redesign of technical services' staffing models and skills. Transactional functions, where independence and clearly defined roles support linear, case-by-case problem-solvers, must be transformed into collaborative operations where technical services personnel are regarded as solution creators. Ultimately, technical services staff must transform their skills and workflows so that they can contribute to a library's emerging role as a "content creator."[15] Gibson supports greater innovation and creativity within a flexible environment where new processes may be adjusted and readjusted as needed.[16] Gibson's vision, the empirical data that Davis and Stachokas present, Pastva et al.'s observations, and Eden's rallying cry for change emphasize the disruptive forces underlying the transitional state of technical services and the changing mission imperatives of libraries.

APPLYING THE CORE COMPETENCIES

A useful tool when realigning traditional work to accommodate electronic resources management, the "Core Competencies for E-Resources Librarianship"[17] define specialized competencies which can be used in conjunction with the American Library Association's "Core Competences for Librarianship."[18]

While the intention of the "Core Competencies for E-Resources Librarianship" is to supplement and build upon the more generalist competencies which the ALA defined, the e-resources librarian (ERL) competencies also provide a blueprint for updating existing position descriptions or crafting new ones in the face of staff attrition due to retirements, organizational redesign, loss of positions, or due to the implementation of print-to-electronic transition projects. The "Core Competencies" for ERLs are flexible enough to accommodate this type of application regardless of the size or the type of library involved. As stated in the introduction, the competencies themselves are designed for flexible adaptation:

> An ERL in a small academic library might be responsible for the entire life cycle of electronic resources in that institution, while in a large research library, an ERL might be responsible for ER acquisitions alone, while others are responsible for access, administration, support, and evaluation.[19]

The "Core Competencies" focus on seven areas: (1) a deep knowledge of the life cycle of electronic resources, including ER acquisitions processes, licensing, and principles of information organization and bibliographic management, particularly metadata management and schema; (2) technological capabilities, involving both a practical knowledge of hardware, software, networking, programming, and standards, as well as the theoretical concepts underlying the electronic environment; (3) research and assessment knowledge, not only about what and how to collect, and how to manipulate and analyze data, but also the ability to assess technology and its use strategically; (4) holistic communication skills, including interpersonal communications that enable effective interaction with a variety of stakeholders and the ability to communicate empathetically in order to provide efficient and excellent service; (5) capabilities to supervise and manage personnel, projects, workflows, and policies to ensure both solid relationships and effective systems management; (6) a commitment to understanding trends and continued professional development; and (7) the demonstration of personal qualities such as flexibility, ease with complexity, ability to synthesize ambiguous information, and a commitment to service.[20]

Since their adoption, the "Core Competencies" have been embraced and integrated in various libraries in innovative and constructive ways. Libraries have used the competencies to assess both staff skills and to reorganize entire departments.

At Auburn University Library, the Serials Services Department used the "Core Competencies" to perform individual self-assessments. Each staff member was evaluated for his or her proficiency with each competency in order to assess the strengths and weaknesses of the department.[21] The results led to an action plan that included delegation of duties performed by the manager in the unit, an identification of further professional development in the area of licensing, the desire to learn and take on troubleshooting work by support staff, and ongoing training on the library's link resolver software.[22]

As part of a larger reorganization of the serials and electronic resources unit of the University of Texas at Arlington, library managers employed the "Core Competencies" as a means to recruit additional staff within the organization who possessed demonstrated capabilities outlined in the competencies. They built a self-assessment instrument, "Knowledge, Skills, Abilities, and Preference/Passions" (KSAP), which they used to evaluate candidates.[23] The unit, which was comprised of four staff, worked within a decentralized electronic resources management staffing model. In this organizational model, the majority of the acquisition work was handled inside the unit, while link resolver, cataloging, proxy server, and A-to-Z list management were the responsibilities of other units.[24] The goal of the project was both the centralization of electronic resources management and adding staff to the unit. Building the KSAP based on the

"Core Competencies" helped ensure that staff with the appropriate skill sets joined the unit. Although the authors stated limitations to their application of the "Core Competencies," particularly in how staff rated themselves on the KSAP instrument, they ultimately concluded:

> The Core Competencies were helpful not only in defining the qualities needed by staff in working with e-resources, but also as a guide for training new and existing staff by identifying areas for growth . . . [and] served as a means to educate others through the library about the many specialized skills and abilities required to work successfully with electronic resources, as well as the personal qualities needed to be effective.[25]

Similarly, Colorado State University's (CSU's) library applied the "Core Competencies" to improve upon electronic resources management as part of a concentrated reorganization of the Collections and Contracts Division. This group managed the bulk of e-resource work but shared responsibility with the Metadata and Preservation Services Division for bulk MARC loads, copy cataloging, and metadata creation for databases in the metasearch system.[26] The impetus for reorganization came from an analysis of the library's collections strategy, which concluded that "operations still needed further refinement as many processes were still vestiges of a print-dominant collection [and] . . . the sharp increase in electronic resources indicated staff roles were not aligned with this unwavering trend."[27] Out of this analysis a reorganization committee was formed from members of the two divisions to "ensure operations were aligned with current expenditures, but to also increase efficiency and flexibility in collection development, determine the optimal utilization of staff, and identify functions or tasks that can be discontinued, combined, or automated."[28] As a result, collection development remained with the Collections and Contracts Division and a new unit was formed, called Acquisitions and Metadata Services, and placed organizationally within the Digital Library and e-Publishing Services Division.

With all electronic resources management work under one roof at the CSU library, the ERM librarian used the "Core Competencies" to retool, expand, and upgrade a support staff position where a sizable proportion of the job was spent on print serials acquisitions processes that edged out any focus on e-journal management processes and issues. Each competency was analyzed alongside the support staff's position description in order to integrate appropriate work into the position, such as expanded troubleshooting responsibilities, participation in the Materials Budget Group, evaluation of workflows, and expectations of ongoing professional development.[29] In addition, the "Core Competencies" were utilized to analyze another staff position where responsibilities for link resolver maintenance expanded to include batch loading of MARC records, proxy server configurations, and expanded troubleshooting work.[30] The reorganization was deemed a success, and applying the "Core Competencies" aided in establishing "a better balance between managing print and electronic resources."[31]

Kimberly Abrams's survey of ERM models in libraries summarizes some of the outcomes that resulted when organizing work based on technical services. Centralized models integrate all e-resource activities into a single unit, which is often headed by one ER librarian. In contrast, a second or decentralized model integrates e-resource duties alongside print duties and spreads work among existing library staff.[32] This decentralized model is highly favored in hybrid libraries, which support both print and electronic resources.[33] Abrams outlines a third or distributed model, where electronic resources management duties are distributed among various library staff who meet regularly to discuss workflows and problems and share information.[34] This model as implemented at the University of Maryland of Baltimore County (UMBC) emphasizes teamwork, flexibility, and the customization of workflows to meet local needs based on a modularized flow within the ERM process.[35] At UMBC

> the flexibility of thinking about each resource workflow as a separate system enables the ability to grow or shrink the resources associated with that resource based on need. Having a clear idea of the process needed to accomplish each area of the electronic resource plan allows for the flexibility that 1 staff member, or even 20, can work through that process.[36]

Yet even in these three models—centralized, decentralized, and distributed—electronic resources work typically remains set apart and not fully integrated into the technical services paradigm. The examples of how libraries apply the "Core Competencies" focus on addressing organizational vacuums and creating capacity in order to complete electronic resources management work that was either not being done or for which the necessary skill sets were lacking among traditional technical services staff. A common feature of these examples is that application of the "Core Competencies" was part of larger organizational mission imperatives which featured an intentional focus on the management of the e-resources collection because of user demand and use, budget trends where e-resource expenditures outpaced print, and the desire to tighten processes and realign work. In this departmentalized model, the barriers to collaboration and innovation are high, because the linear-based workflows remain at odds with cyclically based ERM workflows.

Applying the "Core Competencies" as a method for reengineering technical services places the electronic resources life cycle[37] at the center of operations and highlights the need for a new organizational approach based on process. The traditional print-based technical services department is a functional organization based on a clustering of common job duties. This functional hierarchy allows for a high degree of specialization and scalability. As staff concentrate on perfecting their work based on their particular specialization, however, barriers and silos build between the various functions.[38]

In contrast, the central feature of the "Core Competencies," which makes them such a useful tool for reengineering technical services, is their foundation in the nonlinear, electronic resources life cycle. The cyclical, process-based nature of this life cycle recalibrates workflows away from the linear-based acquisitions and cataloging paradigm of print-based workflows and towards collaboration and a user-based outcome. In a process-based organization, work is designed around an "end-to-end flow of different processes" and considers not only the activities that staff perform, but also how those activities interact with one another as well as how they improve speed, collaboration, and efficiency. The process-based organization values customization, flexibility, and adaptability.[39] Consequently, the focus shifts from the completion of discrete tasks to how the work will impact the user. Applying the "Core Competencies" as part of an overhaul or redesign of a technical services department means asking hard questions related to the appropriate number of people to do certain tasks, the efficacy and efficiency of legacy tasks, and whether or not staff trained in traditional processes have the skill set to work within a new paradigm.

The importance of creating a radical, transformational change in library technical services departments is clear. Incremental staff training, cumulating in new workflows without a holistic integration into all aspects of the work, and revising outdated, functional organizational structures are only the beginning. In a networked world, the vision of the library's role in a community has been reimagined and articulated with a new mission that emphasizes learning outcomes and community change. To meet this change, library technical services' work must be transformed. Because electronic resources are central to this mission, to our collections and to our users, the new strategic emphasis must shift to acknowledge this reality. The "Core Competencies" provide the blueprint for re-imaging staff skills and refocusing workflows that are in sync with the cyclical life cycle of the electronic resource and that move away from the traditional, linear, print-based technical services paradigm. Without integrating these competencies into all phases of the work and organizing the work around a process with a user-centric outcome, technical services will not achieve success in providing a responsive, intuitive infrastructure to support access to resources so users may create and contribute new knowledge within the communities where they work and learn.

NOTES

1. Kari Schmidt and Christine Korytnyk Dulaney, "From Print to Online: Revamping Technical Services with Distributed and Centralized Workflow Models," *The Serials Librarian* 66 (2014): 65–75, http://dx.doi.org/10.1080/0361526X.2014.879033.

2. NASIG, "Core Competencies for E-Resource Librarians," approved and adopted by the ASIG Executive Board, July 22, 2013, revised with minor edits by CEC, January 26, 2016, www.nasig.org/site_page.cfm?pk_association_webpage_menu=310&pk _association_webpage=7802.

3. Jeehyun Yun Davis, "Transforming Technical Services: Evolving Functions in Large Research University Libraries," *Library Resources & Technical Services* 60, no. 1 (January 2016): 52–65.

4. David Weinberger, "Library as Platform," *Library Journal*, 137, no. 18 (September 4, 2012): 34–36, http://lj.libraryjournal.com/2012/09/future-of-libraries/by-david -weinberger/#_.

5. David R. Lankes, *The Atlas of New Librarianship* (Cambridge, MA: MIT Press, 2011), 15.

6. Bradford Lee Eden, "The New User Environment: The End of Technical Services," *Information and Technology and Libraries* 28, no. 2 (June 2010): 93–100.

7. Davis, "Transforming Technical Services," 59–61.

8. Ibid., 57–59.

9. Ibid., 61.

10. Ibid., 61–62.

11. Ibid., 62.

12. Ibid.

13. Joelen Pastva, Gwen Gregory, and Violet Fox, "Keep Calm and Carry On: The New Technical Services," in *Rethinking Technical Services: New Frameworks, New Skill Sets, New Tools, New Roles*, ed. Bradford Lee Eden (Lanham, MD.: Rowman & Littlefield, 2016), 30–38.

14. George Stachokas, "Electronic Resources and Mission Creep: Reorganizing the Library for the Twenty-First Century," *Journal of Electronic Resources Librarianship* 21, no. 3-4 (2009): 207.

15. Sally Gibson, "Creating Solutions Instead of Solving Problems: Emerging Roles for Technical Services Departments," *Technical Services Quarterly* 33, no. 2 (2016): 145–53, http://dx.doi.org/10.1080/07317131.2016.1134998.

16. Ibid., 152.

17. NASIG, "Core Competencies for E-Resource Librarians."
18. American Library Association, "Core Competences for Librarianship," approved by the ALA Executive Board, October 25, 2008, www.ala.org/educationcareers/sites/ala.org.educationcareers/files/content/careers/corecomp/corecompetences/finalcorecompstat09.pdf.
19. NASIG, "Core Competencies for E-Resource Librarians."
20. Ibid.
21. Paula Sullenger, "A Departmental Assessment Using the Core Competencies for Electronic Resource Librarians," *Serials Review* 40 (2014): 88–96, http://dx.doi.org/10.1080/00987913.2014.922377.
22. Ibid., 91–92.
23. Clint Chamberlain and Derek Reece, "Library Reorganization, Chaos, and Using the Core Competencies as a Guide," *The Serials Librarian,* 66, no. 1–4 (2014): 248–52, http://dx.doi.org/10.1080/0361526X.2014.881162.
24. Ibid., 250.
25. Ibid., 251.
26. Rachel A. Erb, "The Impact of Reorganization of Staff Using the Core Competencies as a Framework for Staff Training and Development," *The Serials Librarian* 68, no. 1–4 (2015): 92–105, http://dx.doi.org/10.1080/0361526X.2015.1017417.
27. Ibid., 94.
28. Ibid., 95.
29. Ibid., 97–99.
30. Ibid., 104.
31. Ibid.
32. Kimberly R. Abrams, "Electronic Resource Management and Design," *Journal of Electronic Resources Librarianship* 27, no. 3 (2015): 151–64, http://dx.doi.org/10.1080/1941126X.2015.1059642.
33. Lai-Ying Hsiung, "Expanding the Role of the Electronic Resources (ER) Librarian in the Hybrid Library," *Collection Management* 32, no. 1–2 (2007): 31–47, http://dx.doi.org/10.1300/J105v32n01_04.
34. Abrams, "Electronic Resource Management and Design," 152.
35. Lenore England and Kelly Shipp, "ERM Ideas and Innovations: Flexible Workflows for Constantly Changing ERM Environments," *Journal of Electronic Resources Librarianship* 25, no. 3 (2013): 218–25, http://dx.doi.org/10.1080/1941126X.2013.813312.
36. Ibid., 220.
37. Oliver Pesch, "ALCTS Serials Standards Forum," American Library Association Conference, 2004, www.ala.org/alcts/sites/ala.org.alcts/files/content/events/pastala/annual/04/Pesch.pdf.
38. Erik Devaney, "The Pros and Cons of Seven Popular Organizational Structures," http://blog.hubspot.com/marketing/team-structure-diagrams#sm.00001xkwswjirjcotw144kh72ru90.
39. Ibid.

11

Is "E" for Everybody?

Reorganizing to Fit E-Resources across Acquisitions and Resource Sharing

Judith Emde and Angela Rathmel

During the summer of 2014, two departments at the University of Kansas Libraries (KU Libraries) were charged by the libraries' interim co-deans to blend into one department: Acquisitions and Resource Sharing. The Acquisitions Department was responsible for acquiring all types of content for the library collection, and the Resource Sharing Department was responsible for interlibrary lending and borrowing. Each had been in place organizationally since 2005. The structure was still organized predominantly to support the management of print resources, even though nearly 75 percent of the collections budget was now devoted to e-resources. With the ever-increasing complexity of e-resource coordination and management, additional staff needed to be trained to enhance the libraries' investment in e-resources by improving their discovery to users and to efficiently assist in stewarding the limited collections budget. At the KU Libraries, there was a recognition of transferable skills between the two departments. Acquiring materials in either department required strong attention to detail and advanced searching skills in bibliographic databases. A goal was to organize the two departments consisting of twenty-two staff combined as evenly as possible into three units, each with a manager who would have the opportunity to develop administrative skills.

This chapter will describe the review and study process that assisted in developing a proposal on how to reorganize the departments. The acquisitions and resource-sharing trends faced by KU Libraries, along with vendor and technical systems in place, contributed to the discussions. The formats and context of the numerous meetings involving the staff indicated the desire and need to have broad participation in the brainstorming process. The reasoning and description of several proposed models will be described. The final model and implementation process resulted in a complete physical space reorganization.

LITERATURE REVIEW

There is no question that widespread library restructuring is occurring in response to the changing scholarly landscape and its effect on libraries, particularly as budgets are increasingly devoted to e-resources. A review of the acquisitions literature is appropriate to this study because the most tangible change had to do with the transition from print to electronic materials acquired by libraries, whether they were borrowed, lent, or purchased for the library collection.

The impact of e-resources on reorganizational efforts can be seen as a quantitative reaction to declining print-based workflows in both acquisitions and resource sharing. However, the acquisitions and e-resource management literature suggests the qualitative effect of e-resources on workflow as the greater influencing factor on staffing and organizational responses. Newton Miller refers to the "notoriously volatile" nature of e-resources, noting the movement of titles from package to package and access breakdowns among the many management details.[1] Han refers to e-resources as a "totally different species compared to physical materials."[2] Stachokas addresses the "sheer amount of information tracked for e-resources" which "far exceeds that of library print acquisitions," including "license agreements with amendments, unique login information for administration Web sites, and multiple vendor contacts for technical support."[3]

Two interesting trends in the acquisitions literature reveal the impact of e-resources. First, the frequency with which acquisitions literature was reviewed began to increase, indicating the rapid change and expansion of scholarly content in this area. At the turn of the century, acquisitions literature reviews went from covering a span of eight years' worth of content from 1996 to 2003[4] to covering just four years in 2004–2007,[5] and subsequently to only two-year increments in the latter part of that decade.[6] Similarly telling, in 2008, the journal *The Acquisitions Librarian* changed its title and scope to become *The Journal of Electronic Resources Librarianship*.

The reviews of the acquisitions literature leading up to the early 2000s suggests that workflow restructuring may have resulted, on the one hand, from some technological efficiencies that e-resources allowed, and on the other, from challenging and more specialized staff responsibilities, like licensing negotiation.[7] Later reviews reveal the economic challenges that also may have driven staffing and workflow changes between 2008 and 2011, as a result of acquiring less and canceling more.[8] But the mentions of "big deal" packages, vendor consolidations, and new purchasing models in that same period reflect specific qualitative differences that would impact workflows and necessitate restructuring.

The development of the electronic resource management system (ERMS) may have resulted in greater efficiency in both staffing and the management of workflows. But serials, e-resources, and library organizational literature of the same period produced a number of influential models that would change the way workflows themselves were conceived as wholly different than print, and which would spark a rethinking of organizational structure beyond departments in technical services at the front lines of this format change.

The Digital Library Federation's Electronic Resources Management Initiative (DLF ERMI) report,[9] for example, describes the shift from a linear to a more dynamic process model for acquisitions and management. This different model suggested a more collaborative approach to the workflow and organizational structure of the library as a whole in response.[10] Fuller-Clendenning, Duggan, and Smith, while describing a restructuring in serials and e-resources staffing specifically, illustrate the coordinating role that e-resources workflow has between multiple areas of the libraries, including technical services, collections, library information technology, and public services.[11] Myriad sample cases of restructuring beyond acquisitions have been shared across libraries from the perspective of selection and collection management[12] and in public service.[13] New models of acquisitions continued to grow, as noted in the literature reviewed through 2013.[14] These models influenced workflows beyond continuing resources' transitions from print to electronic, and influenced organizational structures beyond acquisitions departments.

Unfortunately, ERM systems, which were built on the new dynamic workflow blueprint recommended by the DLF ERMI report, failed to adequately account for such far-reaching evolutions in workflow and organizational structure that spanned the library as a whole. As separate systems, ERMs created workflow redundancy, and their lack of interoperability with existing integrated library systems (ILS) resulted in inflexible and under-realized support for the kinds of communication and collaboration necessary across the e-resources life cycle.

The problem of one-stop versus connected-distributed systems in tools like ERM and ILS systems mirrors the dilemma facing e-resources staffing and changing organizational structures in response to e-resources workflow. Should e-resources be specialized into a single unit, or focused on individual personnel, like the e-resources librarian? Or, given the development of a more dynamic and interdependent life cycle, should the work be distributed across multiple parts of the organization and personnel? The answers to these questions vary depending on specific institutional contexts, especially with regard to staffing, communication structures, and systems. Answering this question organizationally requires viewing how individual staffing and group-based workflow functionality have evolved in response to e-resources.

While no study has produced a single ideal pattern for how departments should be structured to manage e-resources, almost all discussion of e-resource management workflows suggests process mapping as a key tool.[15] Not only does it help to visualize the ways in which traditional print functions do not easily map directly to e-resource workflows, but it reveals the interdependencies that would lead to the effective development of new centralized, distributed, or hybrid organizational models. Reorganizational case studies that address this specifically point to centralized approaches as best suited for smaller organizations or organizations with timely, project-driven initiatives for transitioning print to electronic (like an ERM implementation), or where such specialized staffing can be acquired.[16] Distributed case studies, in contrast, tend to reflect larger organizations that are developing existing staff- and team-based structures, and occur in reaction to an already expanded e-environment.[17] The case studies also appear to loosely follow a historical or developmental progression of a library's adoption of e-resources and workflows, from highly centralized to hybrid and distributed models accordingly. As Collins summarizes,[18] highly centralized models favor stricter format division (e.g., print to electronic), the e-resource librarian does all or most of the work and a perception of e-resources as an "add-on concept." Hybrid or distributed models, on the other hand, favor coordination (with the e-resource librarian or unit coordinating distributed functions) and the intentional and holistic development of staff and learning organizational structures.

The importance of developing a structure that supports a learning organization as opposed to the traditional process-based mindset typical of departments that are primarily responsible for e-resources is also noted throughout the e-resource management literature. Boss and Schmidt outlined the effect on the academic library as it evolved and observe that the "management of ER is a perfect laboratory to develop skill sets based on the concept of the learning organization."[19] Novak and Day, addressing the commonalities across organizational restructuring, note the influence of change management theories and find five common stages that libraries address in responding to such change: internal and external influencing factors, analysis and diagnosis, communicating the plan with openness and transparency, implementation that involves support for new skills and roles, and the need for continuous assessment.[20] England and Miller attempt to leverage both the benefits of a learning organization and process-based workflows with business process management, touting this approach as a more collaborative tool for defining processes than traditional change management approaches.[21]

The strategy for how to move from the larger theoretical models of change management to the practical realities of e-resource management and changing an organizational structure was helped by the development of two key models for understanding e-resources workflows and staffing: "Techniques of E-Resource Management" (TERMS) and NASIG's "Core Competencies for Electronic Resource Librarians."

Jill Emery and Graham Stone's TERMS project[22] outlines the life cycle of e-resources (figure 11.1) and shows not only the dynamic change in workflow, but how the workflow involves not just single e-resources units, but entire areas of the library. Developed as a crowd-sourced wiki project, TERMS collected

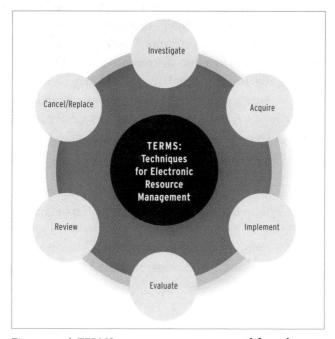

Figure 11.1 | **TERMS e-resources management life cycle**

very real and practical techniques, while its model raised important questions about the flow of work and communication channels across a given organization.

The "Core Competencies for E-Resources Librarians"[23] further emphasized the importance of understanding the e-resource life cycle as a skill set in addition to its significance for workflow. These competencies have been suggested as a resource for employers to develop job descriptions, and many have used them as justification for better aligning increased budgeted content allocations with e-resources and staffing. Criticisms of the "Core Competencies" reflect the fact that e-resource librarianship by its nature "will always exist in a constant state of flux."[24] The "Core Competencies" suggest a highly centralized approach that may misrepresent the e-resources life cycle to some degree. More distributed options may be necessary for developing staff skill sets and wider organizational implementation. Applications of the "Core Competencies" have been very useful for assessing each of these. For specialized approaches, they can help guide the refinement of recruitment advertisements and talent management.[25] For hybrid and distributed approaches, they can be useful pre- and post-test tools for assessing existing staff strengths and weaknesses,[26] or more specifically as a tool for mapping the competencies to knowledge, skills, abilities, and preferences assessments,[27] and for staff training and development.[28]

Both the centralized and distributed models together reveal key roles, or specializations, that can inform how e-resource duties might be arranged in organizations. It is useful to understand that specialization "signifies a trend towards standardization and stabilization," as Zhu notes in a study of the role of licensing.[29] This suggests that wherever such stability exists or is called for, a coordinating role or centralized approaches may be most appropriate. E-resources assessment and data analysis are an example, given the development of the COUNTER usage data standard, as well as the fact that continuous assessment is a key part of the learning organization and change management.[30] E-resource roles in user services and, by extension, troubleshooting are probably the most prolific examples and evolved "naturally out of the reference and access services environments."[31] Cataloging, with a solid history of standardization, maintains core e-resource specializations as well, particularly with systems implementation and linking and discovery.[32] However, the ERM environment for cataloging roles continues to be challenged by the "[lack of a] single set of rules to construct workflows."[33] This suggests a need for hybrid or distributed approaches to personnel.

The University of Kansas's motivation for restructuring its Acquisitions and Resource Sharing departments mirrors many experiences shared by others in the literature, including personnel changes, new technologies, and the reduction of hierarchy within the library, which are all common drivers of organizational restructuring.[34] KU Libraries had undergone a major restructuring in 2012, influencing the organization of special collections, area studies, collection development, reference, user services, and library instruction and tending toward a more user-focused organization while also placing greater emphasis on major initiatives such as scholarly communication, digital humanities, data management, and the digitization of unique resources. In the Acquisitions Department, the retirement of three long-standing employees, including one department head, contributed to the need to rethink the organization as it was faced with the loss of extensive legacy experience and knowledge.

The specific approach taken by the planning team was also similar to other studies in the literature, since it included a strong focus on continuous learning and change management, and process mapping of the current state of each of the departments involved. However, while the future state was highly informed by the e-resource life cycle and relevant competencies, developing new roles and the resulting organizational structure were uniquely built upon the existing skills, strengths, and abilities of KU's specific environment. These are detailed in the following section.

BACKGROUND

The University of Kansas is a public research university supporting more than 370 degree programs and is one of 34 members of the Association of American Universities. The main campus in Lawrence and the Edwards campus in Overland Park have a combined enrollment of approximately 25,000 undergraduate and graduate students and 1,650 faculty. Even though the libraries associated with the law and medical schools have different reporting and funding lines, all collaborate on licensing common e-resources together.

The Acquisitions staff work closely with the Content Development Department, with both departments reporting to the assistant dean of content and access services. Staff interact routinely in assessing usage, reviewing approval plans, monitoring the collections budget, implementing different methods in acquiring materials, and recognizing new formats to acquire. Distinctive Collections, which is composed of Special Collections, Kansas Collections, University Archives, and International Collections, is dependent on Acquisitions for purchasing and to some extent managing resources in those areas.

As for the fiscal environment, the budget for collections has been flat since 2009. Even though the collections budget has not received a percentage cut, with the annual inflation costs and the need to support new faculty and programs, stewardship of the collections requires a constant review of resources supported in order to discontinue low-use or irrelevant resources every year. In the past few years, content development librarians have canceled some medium- to high-usage materials and are continually identifying new purchasing models in order to curb expenses. New models include the 2008 implementation of demand-driven acquisitions, where records are loaded into the catalog for potential purchase by KU patrons. Consortial participation in the Greater Western Library Alliance and RapidILL allow for collaborative efforts in licensing resources, including some big deal packages and the sharing of resources through interlibrary loan at a reduced cost.

DETAILS OF PREVIOUS ORGANIZATION

The Resource Sharing Department, led by a faculty member, consisted of two separately supervised units, Borrowing and Lending, including support staff and student assistants. The terminology used to refer to print and electronic formats in this department is *loans* and *copies* respectively. Both units incorporated both formats within each unit. Although assigned to distinct staff within the units, cross-training across format was a well-established practice in each unit. The department also managed a satellite service desk.

The Acquisitions Department, led by a faculty member, consisted of three units of support staff: Continuing Resources, Payments and Accounting, and Firm Orders and Approval. A serials librarian (faculty) and a licensing and rights management specialist reported directly to the head of Acquisitions. The Firm Orders and Approval unit, while incorporating orders in all formats, had a distinct division of staff handling print or electronic orders. Staff from the International Collections Department assist with the ordering of primarily print-based materials in Spanish/Portuguese and Slavic languages. A member of the Acquisitions Department is responsible for East Asian purchasing in all formats.

The Continuing Resources unit had been recently reorganized from what was formerly two distinct units for serials receipts and serials ordering. Receipts were predominantly print, while ordering covered both formats. The unit was responsible for e-resource maintenance and monitored a troubleshooting service e-mail account. The bulk of e-resource management was handled by the Continuing Resources unit, including maintenance of an ERM, knowledge base upkeep, linking issues, e-resource troubleshooting, usage reports, vendor contacts, platform changes, log-in/URL information, record maintenance, e-package reconciliation, and more.

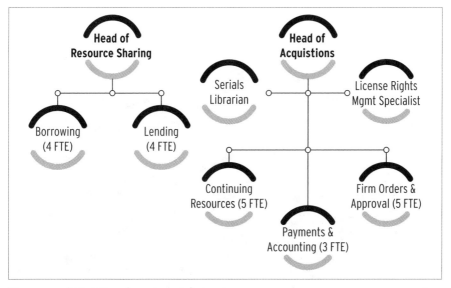

Figure 11.2 | **Previous departmental structures**

Over time as units and subdivisions shifted in number of employees, the supervisory lines didn't necessarily change, thus creating an uneven allocation of staff to supervisors (see figure 11.2). In some cases, only one or two employees reported to a supervisor. One small unit rotated supervisors annually. A year before beginning the organizational review, eight supervisors were in place within the two departments.

TRENDS WITHIN THE KU LIBRARIES ENVIRONMENT

Trends in borrowing and lending requests and print acquisitions within KU Libraries for the past five to ten years indicate a downward movement. The statistical evidence provided some justification to the staff for the need to shift staffing resources and workflows to support the increasing management demands of e-resources.

Interlibrary Loan (Resource Sharing)

Figure 11.3 shows an overall downward trend for filled loans (print) and copies (electronic) borrowed from other libraries, as well as filled loans and copies delivered. The most significant drop is reflected in both borrowing and lending copies. Borrowing copies dropped by 68 percent from FY06 to FY16, while lending copies dropped by 42 percent. In reviewing Association of Research

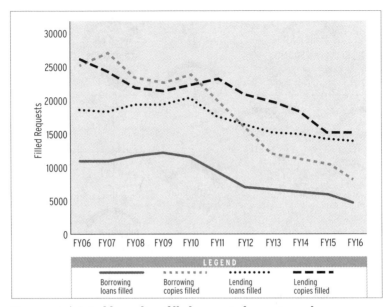

Figure 11.3 | **Interlibrary loan filled requests for copies and loans for KU Libraries**

Libraries statistics from 2011 to 2015 for four of KU's peer institutions,[35] similar decreases are represented: filled lending requests decreased by approximately 14 percent and borrowing by 11 percent, with up and down fluctuating numbers year after year. During that same time period, KU Libraries showed a steady decrease of filled lending of 28 percent and 42 percent for borrowing.

Some of the reasons accounting for this downward trend at KU Libraries include the licensing of "big deal" packages such as the ScienceDirect Freedom collection and e-book collections such as ebrary Academic Complete. The growing availability of open access articles in institutional repositories and archives such as PubMed Central influence interlibrary loan (ILL) submissions. Patrons are locating literature available through mass digitization projects such as HathiTrust or the Biodiversity Heritage Library. The increasing number of records loaded in the library catalog due to demand-driven acquisitions (DDA) improves the availability of monographs for researchers and decreases the number of ILL requests for books.

Acquisitions

Due to a flat budget since FY09, funding for monographs has either remained constant from year to year or has declined. Over the past few decades, scholarly monograph purchasing has plunged in order to support the serial packages and accompanying annual increases that are funded by stagnant or diminished collections budgets. With the transition to DDA in 2008 at KU Libraries, initially in the sciences for both print and electronic versions, the number of monographs purchased has dropped. The application of DDA has been extended across most disciplines.

Firm order funding is allocated annually across a number of subject areas to allow for the purchase mainly of monographs and other formats such as DVDs, new serials titles, back files of serials, and more. These funds allow for monograph purchases not available through the profiles established with approval plans. Figure 11.4 illustrates the decreasing number of monographic firm orders from FY12 to FY16. Figure 11.5 shows the steady decline of funding and the number of titles received on approval plans

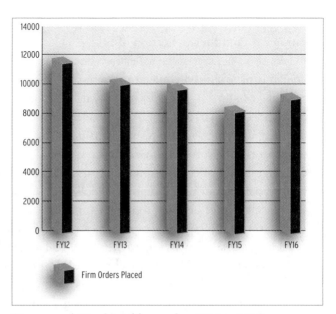

Figure 11.4 | **Number of firm orders FY12 to FY16**

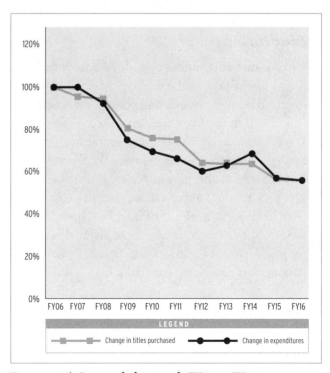

Figure 11.5 | **Approval plan trends FY06 to FY16**

through YBP (now Gobi Library Solutions) from FY06 to FY16 due to allocation cuts and the application of DDA.

With 75 percent of the collections budget devoted to e-resources, workflow demands have shifted while at the same time continuing to devote a smaller percentage of time to print. Accompanying the evolving nature of e-resources are new types of formats and purchasing models resulting in different challenges and licensing idiosyncrasies. E-resource management generates a massive amount of information from vendor data, licenses, and the nonstop flow of e-mail exchanges and notices. Accumulating and tracking usage statistics for assessment is paramount in the support of collection decisions. With a flat budget, the cancellation of ongoing resources annually has become a routine activity.

Methods of acquiring e-resources are ever-changing due to technical developments, along with innovative ways to offer content to libraries that have shrinking budgets. DDA continues to expand with more offerings of records in the library catalog. The purchasing models for streaming video are complex and differ from one vendor to another. Streaming video requires further licensing attention to archival and performance rights. Attention needs to be paid to new purchase models such as evidence-based acquisitions, which is developing in part due to the diminishing application of short-term loans by publishers.

External Influences

Environmental changes outside of academic libraries can have direct and indirect influences on the workings of acquisitions and resource sharing departments. Bankruptcies can potentially be devastating to a collections budget if substantial funds have been deposited. Therefore, it is of the utmost importance to remain vigilant in maintaining an awareness of the financial health of library service companies. Fortunately, KU Libraries was not severely affected by the Swets bankruptcy in 2014. Mergers can affect the costs of services and products, product organization, platform changes, and personnel reorganization. EBSCO acquiring YBP and ProQuest buying out the Ex Libris Group prompted changes in vendor reps, customer service, and developmental plans for products such as eIntota assessment. These external business actions change how work is conducted internally.

Library Systems in Place

KU Libraries remain with the Voyager ILS currently under the Ex Libris umbrella of products. Working with an ILS that was designed for the management of print resources creates challenges to adequately address the unique workflows for e-resources.

The Acquisitions Department uses Voyager for serials check-in, holdings, and fund management. OCLC is searched for brief records for monographic orders. ProQuest Workflow Solutions' (previously Serials Solutions) products—360 Resource Manager, 360 Link, and 360 Core—are used for creating and maintaining the libraries' e-journal knowledge base, link resolver, and management of licenses and vendor contacts. ProQuest's Intota assessment product had been licensed to assist in potentially aiding in an improved accumulation and tracking of e-resources, but with the ProQuest acquisition of Ex Libris, the Intota integrated solution will not be developed in deference to the Ex Libris Alma product. Gobi Library Solutions (previously YBP Library Services and now an EBSCO product) and Harrassowitz are KU Libraries' major monograph vendors. Several specialized vendors are also utilized for ordering foreign language materials, musical scores, and DVDs. EBSCO and Harrassowitz supply continuing resource support services.

The Resource Sharing Department accesses the Voyager catalog and circulation modules in its workflows. OCLC's Interlibrary Loan and ILLiad products are the tools used for the submission of borrowing and lending requests, fulfillment, and cost management. Two of the major resource-sharing collaborations are with the Greater Western Library Alliance (GWLA) and RapidILL. Resource Sharing utilizes the Relais D2D software through GWLA to streamline operations and establish efficient routing lists for interlibrary loan requests. Auto Graphics Share-It is applied for determining holdings in the state library of Kansas catalog/ILL system.

Any blending of the two departments and assimilating aspects of e-resource management into the roles of additional staff requires training on unfamiliar systems. Many of the staff's intrinsic skills demonstrate a potential for transferring such abilities and understanding to other aspects of content acquisition and management.

MOVING TO A FUTURE STATE

These identified environmental trends for KU Libraries and beyond indicated and informed the need to rethink the organization of the separate Acquisitions and Resource Sharing departments in order to develop and improve e-resource management. So in fall 2014, the University of Kansas began a project to identify a new, truly blended organizational structure for activities in the Acquisitions and Resource Sharing departments that would

1. address change in the immediate environment (emphasizing online content acquisition and delivery) and changes in the scholarly communication landscape (open access)

2. reduce the number of supervisors and multiple breakdowns of supervision (subordinate supervision) in order to move toward consolidating supervisors and producing a smaller cadre of management staff who have sufficient responsibility and time to develop management expertise

Addressing the project charge and outcomes included creating a process that reflected expertise and input from department staff with respect to workflow, and expertise from the members of a core planning team with respect also to workflow, the project charge, and process. While staff and units certainly have made ongoing changes to workflows in response to e-resources, not all workflows had changed as effectively as they could because of the limits of existing organizational structures and systems. Support for e-resources in this case meant rebalancing staff resources for activities like information management and assessment and a greater focus on user service as much as supporting acquisitions and the interlibrary loan of e-resources and newly emerging formats. The next section will describe how the staff and the planning team took the information above, and using project management and process-mapping techniques, analyzed the current state of the individual departments and created a new organizational model and future state for a combined department.

PROCESS AND TIME LINE

With the heads of each department serving as project leads, the core planning team also included the assistant dean for the division in which the department would report and an external facilitator provided by the library administration. Over the course of the planning process, the team would grow to include three new unit managers hired into the blended Acquisitions and Resource Sharing Department. The planning team would form the basis for a departmental leadership team that included the new department head, the three unit managers, and two faculty librarians as the new combined departmental structure took effect.

The planning team was committed to involving all staff in gathering information and feedback on nearly every decision point, and designed the process accordingly. Following project management principles, a project scope statement was developed through interviews with the library administration (as project sponsors) and the key stakeholders of the project. The scope statement included the purpose, or project charge, as previously stated; a fuller description of the purpose; the desired, tangible results (aka deliverables); a communication plan; acceptance criteria (or decision-making approach); and a time line, including anticipated constraints and influencing factors. The scope statement was approved by the key stakeholders when it was first developed, and when it was later reviewed and revised.

One of the first steps, after creating the scope statement for this project, was establishing ground rules for how we would communicate, participate, and function throughout the course of the project. These ground rules were developed by staff, and were posted throughout the project's duration in departmental meetings and stored in a shared location. Determining the time line involved breaking down each of the desired results of the project into components and actionable parts, also known in project management terminology as the "work breakdown structure" or "WBS." A high-level time line based on the work breakdown structure for this project was also included with more detail within the project scope statement.

The project essentially was structured in two parts: an analysis of the current state, and the development of a future state. In the first year of the project, the two departments reviewed the literature, interviewed peer institutions based on their participation in similar analyses, met with library stakeholders to understand their needs, mapped current workflows, identified future workflow efficiencies, and developed and analyzed six potential models to arrive at a new organizational structure for the department. The mapping of workflows was a time-intensive endeavor led by the external facilitator. Each staff member was interviewed to outline his or her work performed and systems used. One of the most worthwhile activities held after the mapping project was having staff members speak about their own individual workflows to members of both departments in small groups. As a result of these interactions, respect and acknowledgment of the complexity of work done across the departments developed among the staff. Another introspective activity was an invitation extended to each staff member to meet one on one with the libraries' organizational development coordinator to discuss his or her personal and professional strengths, which could potentially lead to a better understanding of how those talents could be applied differently within a reorganized department. These interviews were summarized and shared with the planning team to assist in shaping units within the new department. Since a major reorganization would result from this review project, it was logical to devote several meetings to brainstorming potential efficiencies in workflows, tasks, and application of systems. Each suggestion was rated based on its low or high impact and its difficulty in implementation. Ideas ranged from stop processing post-cancellation print serial issues to identifying how ILLiad is used overall. Was ILLiad being used to its full capacity? Before any model with assigned staff could be proposed, the leadership team determined the full-time equivalents (FTEs) needed to complete an extensive list of functions within a blended department.

The time line for this project, which began officially at the start of the 2015 fiscal year (July 1, 2014), was originally estimated to be completed within six months. In January 2015, that end date was revised to conclude by the end of the spring 2015 semester, and not to exceed the summer 2015. The final organizational model was complete as of June 2015, just beyond the expected time line. However, the executive summary report to the administration and the official close of the project did not occur until the beginning of July 2015. This unfortunately did not allow much time to take advantage of the slower acquisitions and resource-sharing activity during the summer months to begin implementation.

ORGANIZATIONAL MODELS

By comparing the environment and staff at KU to other institutions considering similar workflows, the organizational structures and trends influencing the need for reorganization, and the potential identified efficiencies, the planning team developed four potential organizational models for staff to consider, following a basic three-piece format that intentionally limited the division of staff among three units while considering the functional life cycle of e-resource management. In this way, the "Core Competencies" and TERMS were integrated and considered in the design of the proposed models that staff would review as well. The models were described accordingly as (1) supply chain model, (2) service points model, (3) format model, and (4) functional model.

The models aimed to challenge the notion that the workflows and organization supporting e-resources must necessarily be format-driven or -structured, even though format was the primary initial mindset. The format division model was presented with others that focused on changing service expectations, communication and information management, and entirely new concepts for work than previously imagined. Involving staff to think creatively while also seeing themselves and their current work in each of the models required presenting the work using language they already knew. Each model also represented necessary functions either within a specific unit or centralized to represent functions that cross all units—everyone is responsible in some way for these things.

The *supply chain model* (figure 11.6) views work in an assembly-line fashion, dividing functions linearly across the department, while also blending inter-library borrowing, lending, and acquisitions activities, as well as print and electronic formats within each unit. In this model, no one person or unit

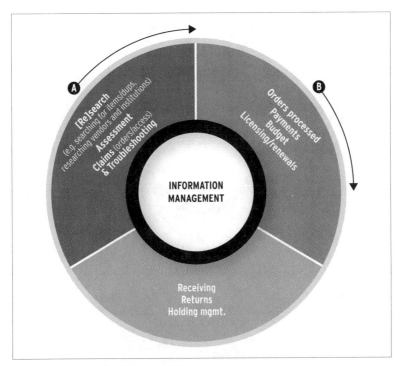

Figure 11.6 | **Supply chain model**

follows the process from start to finish. This model may not make sense in a system where some activities occur simultaneously with others. For example, searching and ordering are nearly simultaneous in the interlibrary loan system, ILLiad, but for acquisitions systems these activities are mostly separate. This particular model would also require strong cross-communication to function, more so than any other model. However, the model did represent the ability to maximize existing staff skills and develop specializations. Information management would be everyone's responsibility.

The *service points model* (figure 11.7) blends some ILL and acquisition activities, as well as print and electronic formats, while aiming to group similar activities within units. Each unit piece functions as a service, and in different ways, each unit can see the entire life cycle. This model was the most clearly user-focused model, offering the potential for a single service point for the entire department, something that was desired by external stakeholders. The other benefit of the model was its centralization of support for e-resources. This model, however, would require a greater need for cross-training, and assessment would be everyone's responsibility.

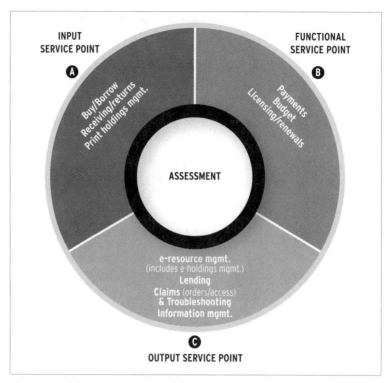

Figure 11.7 | **Service points model**

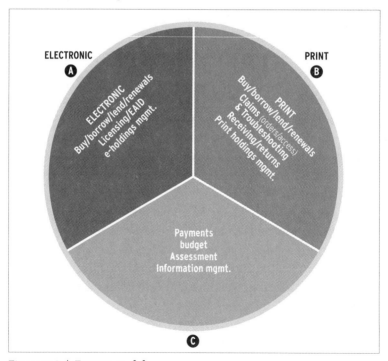

Figure 11.8 | **Format model**

The *format model* (figure 11.8), as its title indicates, divides function by format into two units, though blending p/e (print and electronic) formats and claims functions of A and B into a third unit. The downside to this model is that units divided by format may experience some marginalization and/or a lack of development as change continues. It can also mean that some work-flows result in a duplication of effort and more frequent handoffs. For example, determining format (e versus p) may require research and investigation that are duplicated by the research and investigation of another unit. This model was not seen as ideal, but because it was the most conceptually understood from the perspective of what was driving the change (e-resources), it was useful to see the problems of applying traditional models and workflows to e-resources, and revealed the necessary interdependencies that existed between both formats.

Finally, the *functional model* (figure 11.9) groups activities by function into two units, blending print and electronic formats throughout, and concentrating ILL activities in a single unit. This model was most similar to the existing organizational arrangement. As in the service points model, each unit can see the entire life cycle in different ways. Claims and troubleshooting, including the EAID e-mail account, would be everyone's responsibility. To meet the change,

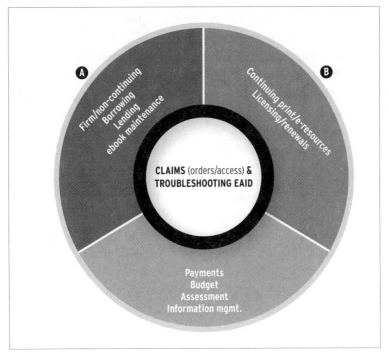

Figure 11.9 | **Functional model**

staff would need to be shifted from Unit A activities in support of those in Units B and C. This would mean learning entirely different skills.

The four models were shared with staff, who, through a series of brainstorming sessions, provided feedback. Two additional models were also posed by staff for further consideration, but these were very similar to each other and similar to existing proposed models. However, they did explore new conceptual language for existing structures. For example, using language defined in terms of temporary versus permanent was new but similar to the functional model's (figure 11.9) reference to *firm/non-continuing* versus *continuing print/e-resources*. On the other hand, temporary could also be interpreted to represent ILL and permanent to represent acquisitions. While seeing traditional workflows and structure in these new terms showed progress, the additional models themselves would have represented more of the status quo, or of blending "in name only."

Having reviewed all six of the models, the original evaluation template, and staff feedback, the planning team prioritized a smaller set of evaluative criteria that were most directly tied to the project outcomes to guide decision-making. Those criteria ask whether the ultimate recommended model

- Supports e-resources and the changing scholarly landscape (open access), including new roles identified through this process
- Supports user (patron and external stakeholder) needs, which includes seeing the life cycle inasmuch as it allows us to (1) minimize gaps for efficient workflow, and (2) most efficiently meet user needs through a clear awareness of where their request is in the process
- Positions library and departments to address efficiencies (identified by staff through this process, as well as future opportunities) and the new roles/expertise identified
- Allows for enough flexibility to transition to new models, systems, and continually changing workflow needs

The ultimate model chosen for the newly combined Acquisitions and Resource Sharing Department (figure 11.10) took most aspects of the service points model for its focus on service and the life cycle of acquisitions and resource sharing, but the model was adapted to include elements of the functional model, keeping interlibrary lending with its traditional ILL structure. In this way lending is considered another type of "request," rather than functioning as a holdings management or unique service to other libraries as the service points model had originally proposed. The close relationship described in the service points model between the functions of accounting, licensing, and the renewal of continuing resources made more sense to combine than

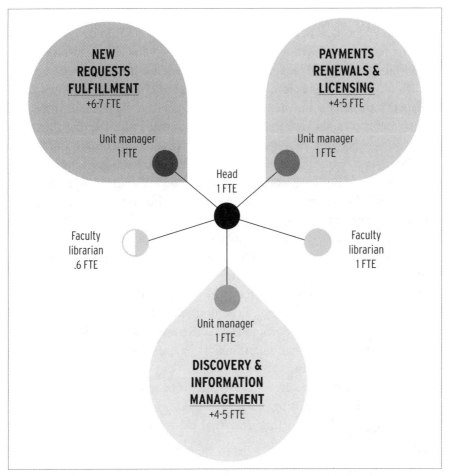

Figure 11.10 | **Acquisitions and Resource Sharing organizational chart**

the functional model, and better matched KU's staffing strengths. Assessment and service functions were centralized within a unit called Discovery and Information Management since these functions would inform both service and information and the entire department needed to function as a single service point. This also allowed faculty librarians to develop their role more evenly across all three units and develop new expertise, while providing traditional specialty where necessary in each distinct unit.

Unit names identified through the process reflect new realms of work over traditional functional terminology, although, by remaining as service points in both acquisitions and resource sharing, these functional identities remain intact. The New Requests Fulfillment Unit (6–7 FTE plus a unit manager) includes the processing and fulfilling of new requests for any materials or online access to materials regardless of types (continuing and non-continuing resources) or how that fulfillment functions (borrowing, lending, acquiring). The unit is also responsible for day-to-day claims and troubleshooting associated with request fulfillment. The Payments, Renewals and Licensing Unit (4–5 FTE plus a unit manager) includes realms of work related to invoices, payments, and budget management; complex order placement (e.g., credit cards, memberships and packages, new licenses, etc.); renewal and cancellation processing; and license negotiation and rights management. License negotiation remains the responsibility of one staff member working interdependently with other members of the unit and the department head. Finally, the Information Management and Discovery Unit (4–5 FTE plus a unit manager) was designed to serve as the single service point for the combined department. Its realm of work includes print, electronic, and open-access holdings management (includes serials check-in) and departmental information management (including the documentation of policies and procedures). This unit is also responsible for systems management of Voyager, ProQuest Workflow Solutions (aka Serials Solutions), eIntota assessment, and ILLiad; assessment (including circulation and e-resource usage collection and reporting); and proactive, project-based claims and troubleshooting.

The assignment of positions across the three units was designed so that each manager was supervising between four and eight staff. This model eliminated many complex reporting lines that existed previously. The following exceptions remain:

- Two tenured faculty (1.6 FTE) report directly to the head of the department, advising the units as members of the new departmental leadership team.
- The remaining .4 FTE of one of these tenured faculty has an additional reporting line to another department (Organizational Development).
- One .5 FTE staff reports directly to another department (Reference) while remaining a member of the assigned unit in Acquisitions and Resource Sharing.

Reducing the number of supervisors and flattening the hierarchy of the organization allowed for the development of more cohesiveness within the three units and departmental leadership team.

A number of new roles needed to address support for e-resources and to accommodate yet unfilled vacant positions. Outlining these roles included considering the specific needs that each role addressed, the increase or reduced FTE associated with various work, and the skills necessary to perform the work. It was reiterated throughout the process that reductions in FTE associated with various work would not result in layoffs, but rather would provide the opportunity to develop staff in new areas necessary to meet the project outcomes. The ability to quantify the overall staffing needs and map these to each proposed organizational model gave staff an additional opportunity to begin seeing themselves and their work in new ways.

IMPLEMENTATION AND ASSESSMENT

The scope for implementation involved creating five of the original planning project's deliverables or desired results: a functional chart of workflow in the new model, the development of a single service point, a space plan, an assessment of success, and documented position descriptions.

The most important part of implementation was answering for staff the question: "What does this mean for me?" This involved creating individual "new role" documents that addressed for each staff member what they would keep doing, stop doing, and start doing and discussing in individual conversations with them about how this would build on their existing skills, experience, and strengths while allowing them to grow in new areas. Those documents made it much easier to update everyone's position descriptions more fully so that we could begin to set goals for 2016 related to transitioning and training in those new roles.

Next, assessment of the planning process from the perspective of both staff and the planning team was conducted at the close of the project. Most felt the process was inclusive, sometimes too much at the expense of time. The implementation stage was adjusted accordingly in order to streamline communication to concrete decision points.

Implementing a reorganized departmental space was prioritized next in order to get staff together in their new units and with their managers. The approach to this task was informed by the advice of a peer institution analysis recommendation to mirror the functional life cycle of the model within the space. This assessment involved looking at noise, lighting, and space design. Ultimately every single staff workstation was moved to a new location, a small meeting room was constructed, and sink and coffee areas were enclosed into a partitioned break room and centralized supply storage. At the time of writing, a post-assessment of the space as it relates to improved team structures, communication, and function was forthcoming.

In the second year of implementation, and in advance of the fall semester, a single service point was launched and an open house for all library staff was planned.

Assessing the function of the model is perhaps the largest-scale assessment still to be developed and will likely be ongoing. The final organizational chart in conjunction with this report represents how the organization model functions with respect to direct reporting lines, dotted lines, and the leadership structure. Now the department must look at how work and efficiencies are functioning through the lens of the new organizational model and adjust it accordingly. The ultimate functional chart resulting from implementation will reflect how the work of the department flows from unit to unit, with a particular focus on handoffs and communication. This may be in the form of new workflow maps, procedure documentation, or other methods that reflect how the work gets done, how information flows, and how a multitude of decisions are made (and not just performance evaluation decisions).

CONCLUSION

While each institution may come to a different conclusion about whether e-resource management is suitable for everybody, this study summarizes and reflects similar processes and conclusions for getting there. The question of responding to change is more than just a matter of numbers and data. Electronic resources represent the majority of libraries' current collection budgets, but simply hiring more e-focused staff or adding e-functions to existing staff are not necessarily the answer. Just as usage statistics are one consideration in evaluating a library's electronic resources, likewise, careful consideration is needed for how people and environment work in new and constantly changing ways.

The qualitative nature of this question is reflected in the fact that workflows have changed drastically in response to the growth of e-resources and other changes in the scholarly publishing landscape, requiring changes in how staff work and how organizations are structured. This is true across the library—and not just in the department responsible for acquiring e-resources. The literature and numerous case studies have reinforced the fact that resources of time and thought are necessary to understand the "how" of this problem. Process mapping, taken together with modeling the life cycle of e-resources management and the specialized skills and competencies needed, help make new organizational possibilities more transparent and attainable.

The ubiquitous concept that information services environments are constantly changing becomes more concrete with regard to the people responding and operating within that change. The changes prompted by the transition from print to electronic formats have already been surpassed by issues of open access, and it would be a disservice to our organizations, staffing, and workflows to consider such responses to change as a "one and done" endeavor. It is neither a one-person or one-library-department issue, nor is it a unique event in the history of library organizational management.

It can be challenging to replicate another organization's approach, given the circumstances and cultures unique to each institution. While at the very least such case studies bring reassurance that we are not alone in this endeavor, less asynchronous approaches may be required to respond as quickly as our users expect. Libraries, as learning organizations, and the people that work in them must always be growing and adapting in order to anticipate and respond more flexibly to users' current and future needs.

NOTES

1. Laura Newton Miller, David Sharp, and Wayne Jones, "70% and Climbing: E-Resources, Books, and Library Restructuring," *Collection Management* 39, no. 2–3 (2014): 110–26, doi:10.080/01462679.2014.901200.
2. Ning Han, "Managing a 21st-Century Library Collection," *The Serials Librarian* 63, no. 2 (2012):158–69, doi:10.1080/0361526X.2012.700781.
3. George Stachokas, "Electronic Resources and Mission Creep: Reorganizing the Library for the Twenty-First Century," *Journal of Electronic Resources Librarianship* 21, no. 3–4 (2009): 206–12, doi:10.1080/19411260903446170.
4. Barbara S. Dunham and Trisha L. Davis, "Literature of Acquisitions in Review, 1996–2003," *Library Resources & Technical Services* 52, no. 4 (2008): 238–53.
5. Barbara S. Dunham and Trisha L. Davis, "Literature of Acquisitions in Review, 2004–7," *Library Resources & Technical Services* 53, no. 4 (2009): 231–42.
6. Jeanne Harrell, "Literature of Acquisitions in Review, 2008–9," *Library Resources & Technical Services* 56, no. 1 (2012): 4–13.
7. Dunham and Davis, "Literature of Acquisitions in Review, 1996–2003."
8. Harrell, "Literature of Acquisitions in Review, 2008–9"; Paul D. Moeller, "Literature of Acquisitions in Review, 2010–11," *Library Resources & Technical Services* 57, no. 2 (2013): 87–99.
9. Timothy D. Jewell et al., *Electronic Resource Management: Report of the DLF ERM Initiative* (Washington, DC: Digital Library Federation, 2004), http://old.diglib.org/pubs/dlf102.
10. Joan E. Conger, *Collaborative Electronic Resource Management: From Acquisitions to Assessment* (Westport, CT: Libraries Unlimited, 2004); Joan Conger and Bonnie Tijerina, "Collaborative Library-Wide Partnerships: Managing E-Resources through Learning and Adaptation," in *Managing the Transition from Print to Electronic Journals and*

Resources: A Guide for Library and Information Professionals, ed. Maria Collins and Patrick Carr (New York: Routledge, 2008).

11. Lynda Fuller-Clendenning, Lori Duggan, and Kelly Smith, "Navigating a Course for Serials Staffing in the New Millennium," *Serials Librarian* 58, no. 1–4 (2010): 227, figure 3.

12. Newton Miller, Sharp, and Jones, "70% and Climbing"; Jim Vickery, "Reorganization in the British Library to Acquire Electronic Resources," *Library Collections and Technical Services* 23, no. 3 (2001): 299–305.

13. Cyril Oberlander, "Challenges of Sharing Online Information through Traditional and Non-Traditional ILL," *Collection Management* 31, no. 1–2 (2007): 205–23, doi:10.1300/J105v32n01_14; Dawn McKinnon, "Notes on Operations: Using Perceptions and Preferences from Public Services Staff to Improve Error Reporting and Workflows," *Library Resources & Technical Services* 60, no. 2 (2016): 115–29.

14. Angela Dresselhaus, "Literature of Acquisitions in Review, 2012–13," *Library Resources & Technical Services* 60, no. 3 (2016): 169–81.

15. Elsa Anderson, "Electronic Resource Management Systems: A Workflow Approach," *Library Technology Reports* 50, no. 3 (2014): 1–2; Conger, *Collaborative Electronic Resource Management*; Lenore England and Stephen W. Miller, *Maximizing Electronic Resources Management in Libraries: Applying Business Process Management* (Oxford: Chandos, 2016).

16. Stachokas, "Electronic Resources and Mission Creep"; Kari Schmidt and Christine Korytnyk Dulaney, "From Print to Online: Revamping Technical Services with Centralized and Distributed Workflow Models," *Serials Librarian* 66, no 1–4 (2014): 65–75, doi:10.1080/0361526X.2014.879033.

17. Schmidt and Dulaney, "From Print to Online"; Vickery, "Reorganizing the British Library."

18. Maria D. D. Collins, "Staffing Trends and Issues in E-Resource Management," in *Managing the Transition from Print to Electronic Journals and Resources: A Guide for Library and Information Professionals,* ed. Maria Collins and Patrick Carr (New York: Routledge, 2008), 122.

19. Stephen C. Boss and Lawrence O. Schmidt, "Electronic Resources (ER) Management in the Academic Library: Process vs Function," *Collection Management* 32, no. 1–2 (2014):130, doi:10.1300/J105v32n01_09.

20. John Novak and Annette Day, "The Libraries They Are a-Changin': How Libraries Reorganize," *College and Undergraduate Libraries* 22, no. 3–4 (2015): 363, doi:10.1080/10691316.2015.1067663.

21. England and Miller, *Maximizing Electronic Resources Management.*

22. Jill Emery and Graham Stone, "TERMS: Techniques in Electronic Resources Management," WikiTerms, 2013, http://library.hud.ac.uk/wikiterms/Main_Page.

23. NASIG Core Competencies Task Force, "Core Competencies for Electronic Resources Librarians" (report), 2012, retrieved from North American Serials Interest Group website, www.nasig.org/site_page.cfm?pk_association_webpage_menu=310&pk_association_webpage=1225.

24. Eric Hartnett, "NASIG's Core Competencies for Electronic Resources Librarians Revisited: An Analysis of Job Advertisement Trends, 2000–2012," *The Journal of Academic Librarianship* 40, no. 3–4 (2014): 257, doi:10.1016/j.acalib.2014.03.013.

25. Lorelei Rutledge, Sarah LeMire, Melanie Hawks, and Alfred Mowdood, "Competency-Based Talent Management: Three Perspectives in an Academic Library," *Journal of Library Administration* 56, no. 3 (2016): 235–50, doi:10.1080/01930826.2015.1105051.

26. Paula Sullenger, "A Departmental Assessment Using the Core Competencies for Electronic Resources Librarians," *Serials Review* 40, no. 2 (2014): 88–96, doi:10.1080/00987913.2014.922377.

27. Clint Chamberlain and Derek Reece, "Library Reorganization, Chaos, and Using the Core Competencies as a Guide," *Serials Librarian* 66, no. 1–4 (2014): 248–52, doi:10.1080/0361526X.2014.881162; Novak and Day, "The Libraries They Are a-Changin'."

28. Rachel Erb, "Impact of Reorganization on Staff Using the Core Competencies as a Framework for Staff Training and Development," *Serials Librarian* 68, no. 1–4 (2015): 92–105, doi:10.1080/0361526X.2015.1017417.

29. Xiaohua Zhu, "Driven Adaptation: A Grounded Theory Study of Licensing Electronic Resources," *Library and Information Science Research* 38, no. 1 (2016): 76, doi:10.1016/j.lisr.2016.02.002.

30. Newton Miller, Sharp, and Jones, "70% and Climbing"; Novak and Day, "The Libraries They Are a-Changin'."

31. Boss and Schmidt, "ER Management in the Library," 132; Angela Rathmel, Liisa Mobley, Adam Chandler, and Buddy Pennington, "Tools, Techniques, and Training: Results of an E-Resources Troubleshooting Survey," *Journal of Electronic Resources Librarianship* 27, no. 2 (2015): 88–107, doi:10.1080/1941126X.2015.1029398.

32. Anne C. Elguindi and Kari Schmidt, *Electronic Resource Management: Practical Perspectives in a New Technical Services Model* (Oxford: Chandos, 2012); Schmidt and Dulaney, "From Print to Online."

33. England and Miller, *Maximizing Electronic Resources Management*, 24.

34. William Fisher, "Impact of Organizational Structure on Acquisitions in Review, 1996–2003," *Library Collections, Acquisitions, & Technical Services* 25 (2001): 409–19.

35. ARL statistics submitted for filled lending and borrowing requests were reviewed from the following four universities: Iowa, Missouri, North Carolina, and Oregon.

12

Managing Freely Available Electronic Resources

Chris Bulock

For traditional licensed electronic resources, one of the most difficult problems facing librarians is the delivery of licensed content to library patrons who discover resources on the Open Web rather than in the library's tools. If a researcher does not start from the library's website, then they're usually faced with the prospect of conducting their search again through the library's tools, unless they've installed a browser plug-in that can help to automate the process.[1] Even when researchers do use library search tools, they're faced with paywalls and proxy servers that can be an impediment to their work.

When appropriate resources are instead freely available on the Open Web, these particular problems are solved. No institutional credentials are necessary, and a user who discovers material through social media recommendations or search engines is typically able to access the content without any barriers. However, with freely available resources, the converse situation becomes problematic. In this case, researchers who do begin in the library's tools may have difficulty discovering and accessing appropriate free resources. Tools that are set up primarily to manage licensed resources with restrictions on access are not always well suited to the purpose of managing access to freely available materials.

A number of challenges arise in the management of freely available resources. Often, freely available resources are chosen for the library's collection through different processes than licensed resources. There is no acquisition process to speak of, and selections will not be made through an agent or book jobber's system. So the workflows for freely available resources may begin quite differently. Many libraries may decide to add huge swaths of free content at one time, and the availability of knowledge base collections, discovery index collections, and MARC record sets for free content encourages this approach. However, this method has the potential of introducing loads of inaccurate and unreliable metadata. On the other hand, more targeted approaches, with librarians selecting free titles one by one or rigorously providing their own metadata, are likely to consume large amounts of staff time.

This chapter will address some of the issues related to managing open access (OA) and other freely available electronic resources. While the focus is on OA journals and books, this chapter will generally use the phrase "freely available resources" to cover broader ground and avoid some of the definitional debates surrounding OA, including reuse rights and Creative Commons licenses. Within that broad view, this chapter will discuss quite a few types of content, including both fully open and hybrid journals, freely available books, and video resources. While managing these sources often seems to be an exercise in untangling an interrelated mess of format types and management tools, this chapter will attempt a clearer approach, first focusing on challenges arising from specific resource types, followed by a discussion of different management tools and strategies.

RESOURCE TYPES

Different types of resources will provide a range of varying challenges, so this part of the chapter sets out some useful categories to consider. While there are often some helpful distinctions to make between different formats, there are also parallels that arise when examining different resources within categories.

Journals and Articles

When discussing freely available electronic resources, OA journals are of central importance. Subscription journals have long occupied an outsized share of library budgets,[2] driven in part by the growing volume of journal articles published every year.[3] Many of the same forces that led to traditional electronic journals dominating library budgets and electronic resource management activity have also pushed OA journal articles to the head of the pack of freely available resources. That is, increasing costs coupled with rising scholarly output make OA journal article publication attractive for many researchers and libraries that wish to see a broad impact for scholarly work. Another key to the growth of OA journal articles has been the rise of OA publication mandates from many of the governmental agencies and foundations that fund research activities.[4] As a quick indicator of the volume of scholarly OA articles available, the Directory of Open Access Journals (DOAJ) currently includes over 2.3 million articles from over 9,000 journals,[5] while the Directory of Open Access Books (DOAB) includes only about 5,500 titles.[6]

There are a few different types of freely available journal content, with the main distinction being whether select articles are freely available or the entire journal is free. Fully OA journals are perhaps the easiest of these resources to manage, particularly when they come from publishers that have experience working with libraries and library software vendors. A library can include a journal or collection of journals of this sort in a knowledge base or catalog and know that its users will be able to access all of the associated articles. However, article-level linking can sometimes be hampered for journals that publish articles on an ongoing basis, rather than grouping articles into volumes or issues. This is fairly common among large OA-focused publishers such as Hindawi and the Public Library of Science[7] and makes sense given that they were never published as print serials. If libraries are making use of DOI (digital object identifier) linking in their link resolvers, and if all goes well with OpenURL requests sent from various databases and discovery points, then this problem can be overcome. However, it is a complication that can lead to diminished accessibility for some OA journals when managing them with traditional library tools.

The more problematic category of resources includes journals that mix subscription content with freely available content. This chapter won't discuss letters to the editor, errata, and other items that are sometimes freely available without a subscription, and will focus instead on full articles. In the easiest case of this type, journals provide free access at the issue level, such as the many free back issues available on HighWire Press.[8] Because access varies at the volume or issue level, this plays to the strengths of catalogs and discovery tools, and it's fairly easy to manage them. Often, the only complication is making sure to account for rolling back files that make an additional volume of content free each year.

Much more challenging are hybrid journals, which are subscription journals that offer selected articles for free, typically when the authors pay an article processing charge (APC).[9] An issue of a hybrid journal might contain an equal number of freely available and subscription articles, or it could consist entirely of subscription articles. The number of hybrid journals is quite high, and many publishers have chosen to make nearly all of their journals hybrid, possibly to meet the demand sparked by OA mandates discussed earlier.[10] Unfortunately, this poses a problem for tools that cannot track access at the article level, since librarians must choose whether to present their users with links to articles they may not access, or fail to present links to relevant OA materials. This problem will be discussed further in the section on knowledge bases.

Books

Scholarly books have been somewhat slower to enter the world of OA publications,[11] due in part to the high cost of publication compared to journal articles. As mentioned in regard to hybrid journals, OA publication is often funded in part by payments from authors to publishers. While it may be feasible for authors who have secured research grants to find money to pay an APC of $3,000 to publish an article, funding the publication of a book this way can be difficult. The University of California (UC) Press has launched its Luminos OA book program that requires most authors to secure $7,500, and this is likely to cover only half the costs of publication.[12] With this author-pays OA route likely less available for authors of monographs, growth has been a little slower for these resources.

That said, there are still thousands of freely available e-books from university presses, the National Academies Press,[13] and others. If OA titles are added to a library's collection on a title-by-title basis, then workflows will not vary much from purchased e-books. Similarly, if an entire book series or a whole publisher's output is freely available, then traditional library tools should work fairly well. However, there is another wrinkle with these resources. Many of these OA books come from publishers that do not have established workflows for getting e-book metadata to libraries. This can make it very difficult to manage OA e-books through link resolver knowledge bases or discovery tools due to limited or unreliable metadata. Thankfully, there are some efforts to assist academic publishers in this regard. The DOAB exists to aggregate and distribute book metadata in much the same way that DOAJ provides information on journals. Additionally, 2016 saw announcements from both Project Muse and JSTOR regarding services for publishing OA monographs.[14] The availability of OA books on platforms that already provide metadata to libraries and assist researchers with discovery should greatly ease the headaches of electronic resources librarians.

Other Media

There are numerous other types of freely available electronic resources, including streaming videos, streaming audio, archival collections, and gray literature. Unfortunately, both the purchased and OA categories of these resources can be difficult to manage with existing library tools. Part of this comes from the fact that many existing tools rely on identifiers such as the ISSN, ISBN, or DOI to identify and disambiguate between resources. ISSNs and ISBNs do not generally apply to this kind of media, and DOIs seem to be much less common. Catalog records are usually still able to capture relevant metadata and access details even when a set of videos or audio files may not be represented in a knowledge base,[15] and there is great potential for data sets and items from archival collections to be available through discovery tools. However, much work remains to be done in this regard.

MANAGEMENT TOOLS

Many academic libraries make use of a complex network of tools to enable the work of the researchers they serve. As already discussed, library collections include a diverse array of sources, and these are meant to serve an equally diverse set of information needs. One researcher might find a database from a subject guide and connect to the full text of a journal article through the library's link resolver. Another researcher might be searching for books in the catalog. Another might do all his research in the library's discovery tool, while still another prefers Google Scholar but makes extensive use of library resources through the link resolver.

When considering the roles each of these tools plays in discovery and access for freely available resources, it's important to think of them as complementary elements in a larger system. Often a discovery tool and catalog may both rely on the link resolver's knowledge base to determine whether a particular piece of content is available. It's also unlikely that any tool will become the sole discovery point for researchers. Try as we might to make the catalog or discovery tool a one-stop shop, there may be some resources and information needs that just don't fit well into these systems.

The goal of this section is to address many of the systems commonly used in library management of freely available resources, outline their strengths and weaknesses, and discuss what roles they play in this task. Not all libraries will make use of all these tools, and no one tool will be sufficient for fully incorporating freely available resources into the collection. However, it's possible to use one tool to fill in the weaknesses of another and make a good effort at incorporating open resources into the methods researchers are using to access library collections.

Knowledge Bases

Knowledge bases stand at the center of access and management for electronic resources in many systems. Whether they're part of a product primarily focused on link resolution and journal lists or part of a full-featured library service platform (LSP), their role is essentially the same. Knowledge bases allow librarians to track electronic inventory and provide access to entitled resources from multiple different discovery points. Knowledge bases do very well at tracking subscribed journal content, but there are some problems that arise when tracking freely available content. In some respects, the knowledge base is well suited to this task, since it includes package and journal-level metadata supplied by both vendors and a community of librarian users. Yet in practice, these systems have some problems tracking free content.

Any system is only as good as the metadata that it ingests. A 2014 survey of librarians found that there were many complaints about inaccurate and out-of-date metadata relating to free materials in link resolver knowledge bases.[16] This included inaccurate dates of availability, broken links, and the inclusion of subscription and hybrid materials in collections of supposedly freely available resources. These errors are most likely to pop up in large collections that include resources from many publishers, especially publishers that have smaller budgets and don't work closely with libraries. Many of those librarians surveyed were unwilling to dedicate substantial time to correcting errors in freely available collections, given no direct investment in that content from their library. With some knowledge base collections, librarians may need to choose between providing frequently erroneous access information or none at all. Each of these will present obstacles to researchers, and the choice may be difficult.

A similar problem occurs with hybrid OA journals. In a knowledge base, a librarian can typically indicate access at several different levels: the collection, the journal, the volume, the issue, or a range of dates. However, the case of hybrid journals can't be successfully handled at any of these levels, since access may vary within a single issue. Again, librarians must choose between indicating access when none exists or failing to indicate access even when the desired article is freely available. Mary Ann Jones has pointed out that this means users of library discovery tools and databases have an inferior experience when it comes to some freely available content and may be better served by tools such as Google Scholar in this case.[17] Without article-level metadata, link resolver knowledge bases seem unlikely to remain effective tools for access management if hybrid OA journals continue to thrive.

Discovery Tools

Discovery tools such as Summon, Primo, and EBSCO Discovery Service seem well positioned to correct many of the failings of knowledge bases, at least in theory. Discovery tools contain metadata at the article level, allowing them to get around the issue-level problems of a knowledge base. While discovery tools rely primarily on link resolvers for access to subscribed content, it might make more sense to include links to access freely available resources directly within a discovery record, since no institution-specific parameters or proxy links would be required. This could contribute to a loss of granular control, however, since discovery metadata is generally activated at a collection level, rather than the single-title level allowed in link resolvers. However, for institutions looking to quickly enable access to content from trusted providers, this could be a welcome solution.

Again, the main problems here tend to come from the quality of metadata provided to discovery vendors, as well as the ability of those vendors to ingest and make use of said metadata. In order for discovery tools to work as solutions for providing access to OA content within hybrid publications, content providers would need to indicate free access at the article level in the data streams they send to discovery providers. Facilitating this process is one of the goals of the Access License and Indicators (ALI) Recommended Practice from the National Information Standards Organization (NISO).[18] This Recommended Practice allows for a "free to read" metadata element that all parties could agree upon, thus simplifying the exchange of access metadata. Unfortunately, this metadata element does not seem to be in wide use. Christine Stohn, a member of the ALI Working Group and a product manager at Ex Libris, has mentioned that many content providers do not include the metadata element, while others do not communicate to discovery providers that they do make use of the element, preventing it from being properly ingested.[19] Until use of this element is widespread among discovery and content providers, it seems unlikely that discovery tools will live up to their promise of providing access to freely available resources.

One new development that could increase the availability of OA material in discovery tools is the integration of a product called oaFindr from 1science. This product is focused solely on finding appropriate OA copies of scholarly resources and relies on dynamic linking to route around broken links on the fly.[20] While oaFindr has its own search interface for finding OA material, that option requires users to know they are looking for OA material. Most researchers, however, would likely prefer to find OA and subscription material in a single interface, so it is encouraging to see that oaFindr is now being incorporated into discovery tools as well. The database has been included in EBSCO Discovery Service[21] and Summon[22] already. If implemented successfully and updated regularly across a wide range of library discovery tools, this could significantly benefit researchers.

Catalogs

Similar to using knowledge bases and link resolvers to manage freely available resources, library catalogs offer two different approaches. Libraries can select titles for inclusion one by one or take advantage of large sets of records for freely available content. Allyson Rodriquez of the University of North Texas has detailed one particular version of the former, more labor-intensive approach in a webinar sponsored by NISO.[23] In this approach, libraries proceed with OA collection development in much the same way they would with title-by-title monograph purchases. Individual titles are considered and vetted for quality and relevance to the institution and then added to the catalog one by one, with original cataloging if necessary. This effort is commendable and will likely appeal to institutions that seek greater control over the provision of freely available resources or have concerns regarding the quality of that material. However, the amount of time and labor required would make it difficult to cope with the growing volume of freely available resources.

It is also possible to load large sets of records, either from individual content providers or from entities that bring together records for many providers. One example of a record collection for a single provider is HathiTrust. HathiTrust provides bibliographic metadata through several different mechanisms, including OCLC's WorldCat, application programming interfaces (APIs), and tab delimited files.[24] Perhaps the biggest challenge associated with incorporating these records into a catalog is that the size of the collection may overwhelm the library's local collections. Of course, this problem is much less pronounced for smaller collections.

The Directory of Open Access Scholarly Resources (ROAD) from the ISSN International Centre provides an example of a record collection focusing on multiple different access providers. ROAD provides free access to bibliographic records for OA resources that have been assigned ISSNs.[25] ROAD might be an attractive option for libraries that wish to expand discoverability for OA journals, proceedings, and monographic series without sacrificing record quality. Of course, the utility of a set of catalog records like this is quite different from a link resolver (which can work with discovery tools, databases, and other sites) or a discovery tool (which can provide article-level data rather than journal-level data).

Database Lists and Guides

Finally, many librarians have added links to freely available content through database lists and subject guides. This approach avoids the numerous pitfalls previously mentioned. For example, linking to the HathiTrust search page avoids the situation where the local library catalog is overrun with millions of public domain records, primarily for items around a century old.[26] Linking to the search page for the DOAJ could assist libraries that are worried about keeping up with new serials records through a program like ROAD. Providing links to subject repositories could be useful for libraries that serve communities doing advanced or specialized research, for whom a general purpose discovery tool is less likely to be useful. Linking directly to oaFindr may be beneficial to researchers looking only for OA material, especially if sharing with colleagues who don't have any institutional affiliations.

Of course, as already mentioned, this approach will not be sufficient on its own to provide access to these materials. It's important to remember that links on a subject guide or database list will only be seen by a relatively small number of researchers, and that anyone using the library's catalog or discovery tool would likely benefit from more direct means of access.

CONCLUSION

Though freely available resources have long been a part of the landscape of electronic resources in libraries, recent developments in OA publishing have made this area vital to academic libraries. However, many library systems built to provide access to paid resources present problems when tasked with providing access to freely available resources. Online publication allows for many possibilities, including free access and hybrid publications, but these do not sit well with systems still built to fit print publication patterns.

As it stands, researchers seeking subscription material are best served by starting their search in library tools, while those seeking free material are often best served by starting in other tools on the Open Web. The problem with this is fairly obvious; researchers who are affiliated with a library are looking for materials that are germane to their research regardless of whether they're freely available or provided through library purchases. As it stands, a complex approach of providing access through multiple complementary systems is required just to reach a level of performance that still leaves much to be desired. Much remains to be done to make this a reality.

NOTES

1. The best example of this is LibX, available at http://libx.org/.
2. This is illustrated in the graph "Monograph & Serial Costs in ARL Libraries, 1986–2011," available at www.arl.org/storage/documents/monograph-serial-costs.pdf, and drawn from Martha Kyrillidou, Shaneka Morris, and Gary Roebuck, *ARL Statistics 2010–2011* (Washington, DC: Association of Research Libraries, 2012).
3. Mark Ware and Michael Mabe, *The STM Report: An Overview of Scientific and Scholarly Journal Publishing* (The Hague, Neth.: STM: International Association of Scientific, Technical and Medical Publishers, 2015), www.stm-assoc.org/2015_02_20_STM _Report_2015.pdf.
4. See lists and maps of these mandates at Registry of Open Access Repository Mandates and Policies (ROARMAP), http://roarmap.eprints.org/.
5. Updated count on the front page of Directory of Open Access Journals, https://doaj.org/.
6. Updated count on the front page of Directory of Open Access Books, www.doabooks.org/.
7. The Hindawi title *BioMed Research International* has several different topic sections and groups articles into one volume for each year (https://www.hindawi.com/journals/bmri/contents/), while *PLoS ONE* simply includes a publication date without any volume or issue information (http://journals.plos.org/plosone/).
8. See a list at HighWire Press Free Online Full-text Articles, http://highwire.stanford.edu/lists/freeart.dtl.
9. Bo-Christer Björk, "The Hybrid Model for Open Access Publication of Scholarly Articles: A Failed Experiment?" *The Journal of the Association for Information Science and Technology* 63 (2012): 1496, doi:10.1002/asi.22709.
10. For example, see Taylor and Francis's extensive list of Open Select titles at http://authorservices.taylorandfrancis.com/journal-list/, or Springer's assertion that their Springer Open Choice program allows authors "to publish open access in the majority of Springer's subscription-based journals" (https://www.springer.com/gp/open-access/springer-open-choice).
11. However, electronic texts have been made freely available through Project Gutenberg for several decades now, as recounted in Michael Hart, "The History and Philosophy of Project Gutenberg," August 1992, https://www.gutenberg.org/wiki/Gutenberg:The_History_and_Philosophy_of_Project_Gutenberg_by_Michael_Hart.
12. Part of the Author FAQs in "Frequently Asked Questions," Luminos, University of California Press' Open Access publishing program, www.luminosoa.org/site/faqs/#author-faqs-open-access.

13. For a description of the program and its reading interface, see Reid Dossinger, "Introducing a Great New Experience for Reading Books on NAP.edu," posted September 18, 2015, https://notes.nap.edu/2015/09/18/the-new-openbook-read-any -academies-report-online-for-free/.

14. JSTOR's program was announced in October at www.ithaka.org/news/open-access -ebooks-now-available-jstor, while the project at Project Muse was announced in July at http://musecommons.org/blog/2016/07/12/major-grant-to-develop-platform-to-host -oa-monographs-on-project-muse/.

15. See the slides of Hayden and Leffler's discussion of managing streaming video resources, in which they describe workflows that primarily rely on MARC records for metadata and access details. Jessica Hayden and Jennifer Leffler, "Juggling a New Format with Existing Tools: Incorporating Streaming Video into Technical Services Workflows," presented at the annual meeting for NASIG, Albuquerque, New Mexico, June 10, 2016. Slides accessed at https://nasig2016.sched.org/event/5mi8/concurrent-session -b5-juggling-a-new-format-with-existing-tools-incorporating-streaming-video-into -technical-services-workflows.

16. The survey results were presented at the NASIG annual conference. For a description, see the proceedings paper: Chris Bulock, Nathan Hosburgh, and Sanjeet Mann, "OA in the Library Collection: The Challenges of Identifying and Maintaining Open Access Resources," *Serials Librarian* 28 (2015): 79, doi:10.1080/0361526X.2015.1023690.

17. Mary Ann Jones, "Discovery of Open Access Articles in Hybrid Journals: What Role Does the Library Play?" presented at the annual meeting of the American Library Association, Las Vegas, Nevada, June 25–30. Summarized in Mavis B. Molto, "Discovering Open Access Articles: Maximum Access, Maximum Visibility! A Report of the ALCTS Continuing Resources Section Program, American Library Association Annual Conference, Las Vegas, June 2014," *Technical Services Quarterly* 32 (2015): 316, doi:10.1080/07317131.2015.1031605.

18. National Information Standards Organization, "Access License and Indicators: A Recommended Practice of the National Information Standards Organization" (Baltimore, MD: National Information Standards Organization, 2015), www.niso.org/ apps/group_public/download.php/14226/rp-22-2015_ALI.pdf.

19. Pascal Calarco, John G. Dove, and Christine Stohn, "Access All Around: A NISO Update on Open Access Discovery and Access-Related Projects," presented at the Charleston Library Conference, Charleston, South Carolina, November 1–5, 2016, https://2016charlestonconference.sched.org/event/89gB.

20. The author's institution subscribes to oaFindr, so much of this is taken from firsthand experience and communications from company representatives. More information on oaFindr is available at www.1science.com/oafindr.html.

21. A press release is available at 1science, Advanced Research Information Systems, https://1science.com/about-us/www.1science.com/press_3.html.

22. Included in the Summon release notes from December 15, 2016, at https://knowledge .exlibrisgroup.com/Summon/Release_Notes/Summon%3A_Release_Notes.

23. Allyson Rodriguez, "No Such Thing as a Free Lunch: Balancing Locally Curated Open Access Collections and Their Costs," presented at the NISO webinar on Open Access in Acquisitions, September 7, 2016. Slides available at www.slideshare.net/BaltimoreNISO/rodriguez-no-free-lunch-sept-7.

24. For details, see "Data Availability and APIs," HathiTrust, https://www.hathitrust.org/data.

25. For details, see this description of ROAD: http://road.issn.org/en/contenu/purposes-road-project.

26. HathiTrust, "HathiTrust Dates—Public Domain," https://www.hathitrust.org/visualizations_dates_pd.

13

Developing Staff Skills in E-Resource Troubleshooting

Training, Assessment, and Continuous Progress

Sunshine Carter and Stacie A. Traill

Electronic resources librarians are well acquainted with the multitude of challenges inherent in troubleshooting e-resource access issues. With the complicated mix of systems, data, and standards that must work together to provide and control access to resources, effective troubleshooting sometimes seems more art than science. The complexity involved in problem diagnosis and resolution can make developing troubleshooting skills in other staff seem like an insurmountable task. Faced with a growing number of problem reports and too few staff who could successfully resolve them, librarians at the University of Minnesota Libraries began exploring ways to develop staff troubleshooting skills. This chapter describes the planning, design, and implementation of a staff training program focused on assessment and ongoing skill development, and offers suggestions for how others might create their own training programs.

LITERATURE REVIEW

The number of electronic resources available to libraries has burgeoned over the past twenty years. Whether from native interfaces, OpenURLs, database

A-Z links, or ever-growing web-scale discovery services, the sheer quantity of links to e-resources has been constantly increasing since their inception. The growth in links corresponds to an increase in access issues. The propensity for e-resources to fail, and prohibit access to desired content, has been covered extensively in the literature.[1]

Troubleshooting in Libraries

Two surveys distributed in 2013 offered insight into the state of trouble-shooting in libraries: Samples and Healy surveyed Association of Research Libraries (ARL) members,[2] and Rathmel et al. surveyed a variety of libraries.[3] Both surveys suggested that troubleshooting practices could be improved by developing workflows, utilizing established tools to facilitate troubleshooting, and offering staff both basic and advanced levels of troubleshooting training. Respondents from the Rathmel et al. survey indicated that their top three training needs were basic troubleshooting (50 percent), a big-picture understanding of e-resources (33 percent), and advanced troubleshooting (27 percent).[4] Knowledge and staffing levels may not have kept pace with the growth in linking issues we see today in libraries. "The majority (138; 61%) [of reporting libraries] have between two to five employees with e-resources troubleshooting within their job responsibility. Strikingly, there are still over a third (75; 33%) who indicate having just one person handling e-resources troubleshooting, and that includes organizations with more than 50 employees."[5] Troubleshooting access issues is a difficult skill to master and one usually taught on the job.[6] Good communication skills, a knowledge of and access to e-resource technologies and systems, and a strong understanding of e-resource management are all required to troubleshoot problems effectively.[7]

Literature coverage on formalized troubleshooting training for staff is limited. Hart and Sugarman created an e-resources troubleshooting training program for public service staff.[8] At their institutions, public service staff triage access issues and act as first responders before forwarding the issues to technical services staff for resolution. Hart and Sugarman combed through older trouble tickets, identified areas of weakness, and created a map of potential points of failure, along with five important questions that public service staff should ask when investigating an access issue. Those five questions asked who the user was, where they were located, what content they were looking for, what happened when they tried to access the resource, and how the user got to the error. With this new knowledge, they designed and held a workshop for public services staff, consisting of four lecture/demonstration sessions. "The authors decided that while basic access issues would be addressed, greater emphasis would be placed on teaching the kind of information that attendees needed to provide in order to resolve problems, rather than teaching attendees how to technically resolve problems, given the complicated nature of access difficulties." So while Hart and Sugarman provided some training on resolving very basic access issues, their training focus was getting public services staff to collect and share with technical services staff information about the users and access issues scenario. The four sessions covered an overview of e-resources and the map, authentication, OpenURL and link resolvers, and lastly the map in context with the relevant e-resource systems (e.g., EZproxy, and the databases A-Z list). After the training, Hart and Sugarman reviewed the following year's trouble tickets to evaluate the effectiveness of their training program for public services. Based on the usually more descriptive information provided by public services staff, technical services staff resolved trouble tickets 59 percent more quickly (from 7.6 to 3.1 days).

Carter and Traill addressed the troubleshooting needs elucidated by the Samples and Healy and Rathmel et al. surveys within the specific confines of a complex web-scale discovery environment.[9] Carter and Traill discussed methods for tracking and reporting access issues, outlined approaches to documentation and training, and created a checklist of essential skills and knowledge for troubleshooting access problems. Carter and Traill argued that documenting and teaching others troubleshooting skills

> has a number of clear benefits. In addition to faster and more efficient problem resolution resulting in increased user satisfaction, a successful troubleshooting training program also demystifies the workings of the discovery system and empowers library staff with a much better understanding of the tools they and their users work with every day. Finally, a training program helps ensure continuity in the face of staff departures and retirements, allowing new staff to more quickly and effectively master the complexities of their library's discovery environment.[10]

Training Definitions and Methods

Training can be defined as "the planned and systematic activities designed to promote the acquisition of knowledge (i.e., need to know), skills (i.e., need to do), and attitudes (i.e., need to feel),"[11] but Ittner and Douds are careful to point out that the information provided in training is meant to be used, as opposed to providing information solely for the sake of learning.[12] *Training methods* are defined as "a set of systematic procedures, activities, or techniques that are designed to impart KASAs [knowledge, abilities, skills, or attitudes] to the participants that have direct utility in enhancing their job performance."[13]

Martin, Kolomitro, and Lam identified thirteen training methods via a comprehensive review of training literature. The training methods identified are case study, games-based training, internship, job rotation, job shadowing, lecture, mentoring and apprenticeship, programmed instruction, role-modeling, role play, simulation, stimulus-based training, and team-training.[14] Martin, Kolomitro, and Lam categorized these training methods based on criteria such as learning modality (doing, seeing, or hearing), training environment (natural, contrived, or simulated), presence of a trainer (yes or no), proximity to trainer (face-to-face or distance), interaction level (interactive, somewhat interactive, or not interactive), cost consideration (low, moderate, or high) and time demands of trainees (low, moderate, or high).[15] The paper highlighted the benefits and challenges of each training method, and concluded that providing a variety of training methods in a training program helps meet the needs of different learning styles, and reduces boredom.[16]

Effective Training

Salas et al. reviewed the literature on the effectiveness of organizational training and development. Their review of several meta-analyses on the effects of training "show that when training is designed systematically and based on the science of learning and training it yields positive results."[17] Pretraining, training design, and post-training activities are critical to teaching employees effectively. Pretraining tasks should include such things as performing needs analyses (on job-tasks, the organization and people) and establishing a positive learning climate. Clearly communicating the expectations, benefits, and needs of training and providing opportunities to practice or refresh skills all lend themselves to a positive environment.[18] During the design period, trainers should consider the individual characteristics of the trainees, appropriate pedagogical approaches, and the appropriateness of technology-based instruction.[19] Instructional strategies and principles should incorporate concepts such as information, demonstrations, practice, and feedback; should provide realistic and challenging practice opportunities; create tasks "designed so that trainees are more likely to commit errors"; model behavioral best practices; and encourage self-reflection and redirection.[20]

Post-training activities are just as important as the planning, design, and delivery stage of training; they should promote transfer of training ("the extent to which knowledge and skills acquired during training are applied to the job")[21] and provide evaluation opportunities. Salas et al. recommend the following post-training steps to increase effectiveness:

Ensure transfer of training
- Remove obstacles of transfer
- Provide tools and advice to supervisors
- Encourage use of real-world debriefs
- Provide other reinforcement and support mechanisms

Evaluate training
- Clearly specify the purpose of evaluation
- Consider evaluating training at multiple levels[22]

UNIVERSITY OF MINNESOTA LIBRARIES ENVIRONMENT

The University of Minnesota in the Twin Cities is a large public research university with over 30,000 undergraduate students, over 16,000 graduate and professional students, and almost 17,000 faculty and staff. The University of Minnesota Libraries (UL) provides access to hundreds of thousands of electronic resources, including electronic journals, electronic books, and subject-specific databases. The UL discovery environment relies in large part on tools from the vendor Ex Libris: the Alma library services platform (which includes a central knowledge base and link resolver alongside traditional ILS functions), the Primo discovery layer, and the Primo Central web-scale discovery index.

A library-wide reorganization in 2012 led to the creation of the E-Resource Management (ERM) Unit, with seven full-time staff. This unit, led by the electronic resources librarian, has primary responsibility for acquiring, licensing, activating, and troubleshooting e-resources. Staff in the UL Data Management and Access Department who manage systems and metadata also play a role in e-resource access and troubleshooting. ServiceNow is the University of Minnesota's issue-tracking system, used by UL staff to track and resolve discovery and access problems. Since March 2014, when the tracking of access issues began, the E-Resource Management Unit has resolved, on average, fifty-eight tickets per month.

As a result of the large influx of web-scale discovery records following system implementation in 2013, UL e-resources staff observed a sharp increase in the number of reported access issues. In November 2014, the authors began developing process flowchart job aids to provide visual descriptions of the institution's complex discovery ecosystem. These charts helped to encourage the sharing of different types of troubleshooting knowledge by revealing interconnections, boosting the confidence of troubleshooting staff, and fostering independent action. Shortly thereafter, the electronic resources librarian began meeting regularly with ERM unit staff to discuss troubleshooting. After the first workflow was completed, a second workflow was created, quickly followed by a third.

The confluence of these two activities—creating job aids and holding regular troubleshooting meetings—soon led to the identification of substantial local training needs. The authors then embarked upon the creation of a skills checklist consisting of all the essential skills and knowledge for troubleshooting access problems. They used this skills checklist, based on local needs and informed by best practices in the literature, as a curriculum outline for teaching troubleshooting skills to others, in response to the identified training needs.[23]

WORKSHOP PLANNING

The newly created curriculum outline provided the foundation for a ten-hour troubleshooting workshop that instructors presented to ERM staff in ten one-hour sessions, held from February to May 2016. Following the troubleshooting workshop, the authors conducted a troubleshooting skills development project between July and October 2016. ERM staff completed three surveys given over the course of the training program to measure their familiarity with e-resource system and troubleshooting topics. The authors wanted to learn whether a troubleshooting training program, including both a multi-session workshop and a skills development project, would increase staff familiarity with topics related to troubleshooting e-resources, as well as staff troubleshooting ability.

Curriculum development laid much of the groundwork for the workshop. The authors, who would also serve as workshop instructors, decided to break the workshop into ten one-hour sessions, with ample time between each workshop (a necessity of having to schedule workshop sessions around other commitments). The lengthy breaks between workshop sessions were not ideal in some ways, but they did have two major positive outcomes. First, staff had plenty of time to review and put into practice what they had learned during each session before the next. Second, instructors had time to adjust the content of upcoming workshops based on their experiences during each workshop session and feedback from staff.

Instructors originally planned one hour for each of the ten major curriculum topics, but quickly realized that some topics required much more than one hour to cover adequately, while others needed less time. While ten hours turned out to be enough time to cover the planned workshop content in full, instructors had to be flexible in shifting content between sessions. Potential future workshops would follow a more realistic schedule based on instructor experiences during the initial workshop offering.

To create content for each workshop session, instructors met to outline the specific concepts, tools, practical information, demonstrations, and scenarios to plan for each session, then divided the content so each could prepare their assigned portions individually. In an effort to make the content accessible and relatable to staff participating in the training, the instructors placed heavy emphasis on concrete examples, details of local system implementations, policies and procedures, and real-world troubleshooting examples. Troubleshooting tools, including both established third-party tools and locally developed tools, played a significant role in workshop sessions. The introduction of each tool in the context of the workshop provided a natural opportunity to demonstrate it in use to diagnose or resolve an access problem.

The troubleshooting training program at UL included case studies, lectures, and mentoring/apprenticeship, along with role-modeling and team-training methods. In practice, the largest portion of group training time consisted of lectures. Most workshop sessions followed a common structure: they began with a brief review of the previous session, followed by the introduction of a key concept. After introducing a concept, instructors presented applications, examples, and demonstrations of that concept in the local discovery environment, and discussed useful tools for diagnosing and solving problems related to the basic concept. Finally, instructors presented issue scenarios that the group worked through together. Instructors combined the various content elements in the way that seemed most logical for each workshop session.

WORKSHOP CONTENT

Pre-Readings

Selected readings on general workshop concepts or topics are a worthwhile learning tool for some staff. At UL, staff received one or two short reading selections before most of the hour-long workshop sessions that introduced concepts or topics covered in that session. The selected readings ranged from brief articles in peer-reviewed journals to web pages offering informal overviews of a particular topic. For some workshops, instructors were unable to find any readings that addressed relevant topics at an appropriate level, but instructors selected at least one pre-workshop reading whenever possible. The goal was not to overwhelm staff with preparatory work, but to help those who prefer to learn by reading, and to provide context extending beyond the scope of an hour-long workshop session.

Concepts

Staff must learn and understand a number of concepts before they are able to solve electronic resource access problems successfully on their own. Workshops should devote substantial time to the teaching of conceptual information in a number of areas. The checklist, serving as the blueprint for workshop content, outlines most of the major concepts that workshops should cover. At UL, instructors emphasized several e-resource management and access concepts in workshop sessions, most extrapolated from the curriculum outline:

- Link resolvers, knowledge bases, and OpenURL construction and linking
- Linking methods and parsers
- Web-scale discovery systems
- Authentication and access control, including proxying and other methods of IP-based authentication
- Content access models (open access/free and licensed)
- How metadata works and what it controls in discovery systems and link resolvers
- Structure and relationship of e-resource administrative, discovery, and access metadata in local systems

Instructors used preassigned readings to introduce many of these concepts, and then reinforced and expanded on them in workshop sessions. Instructors typically followed the discussion of new concepts with real-world examples and practical demonstrations of the concept at work in local systems.

Practical and Factual Information

Most of the workshop time should be devoted to delivering practical and factual information that staff will need in order to become effective problem solvers. The training should cover the specifics of local system implementations and the local discovery environment, as well as local policies and procedures for relevant functions in electronic resources management, problem tracking, and communication. At the University of Minnesota, instructors covered a long list of specific topics in several broad subject areas, including but not limited to the following:

- Component systems of the local discovery environment and communication among those systems
- Update schedules for each system, and staff/units responsible for the maintenance of each system
- Information display and presentation in the public user interface
- Common access problems and their likely causes
- How access to resources is controlled, and which groups of affiliate and nonaffiliate users have access to which resources
- Local policies for activation of resources in the link resolver knowledge base and web-scale discovery system
- Data sources that provide content in the discovery layer, and the degree of local control over those data sources
- Tools to diagnose specific problems (OpenURL deconstructor, link resolver context object viewer, HTTP headers viewing tools)
- Local policies and procedures for problem tracking and escalation
- Best practices for reporting problems to system and content vendors
- Best practices for communicating with end users when problems are resolved

Practical topics follow on from the concepts they demonstrate. For example, authentication concepts lead naturally to a detailed discussion of access control for various user groups at a specific institution, and web-scale discovery concepts naturally lead to a discussion of discovery system data sources and metadata.

Demonstrations

Demonstrations of basic troubleshooting techniques and tools should be included in workshop sessions when appropriate. Practical demonstrations are extremely effective at showing how conceptual and practical information enables real-world problem-solving. Instructors can demonstrate tools and techniques not easily shown in a classroom setting at other times, such as during one-on-one training sessions with staff. Some advance preparation may be necessary for demonstrations, especially when demonstrating tools that require local installation. Screencasts of a technique or tool in action to be played during a classroom session (or afterwards for review) are one way to overcome technology issues, complicated scenario setups, differences in computer installations, and failures that might occur during a live demonstration.

Whether shown live or recorded for later, demonstrations require an example of a known issue from which to work. It can be difficult to find an example of a known issue "on the fly," especially for rare, intermittent, or location-dependent issues. Building a collection of known issues before any instruction takes place will benefit testing, training, and demonstrating, and will make all of these activities more efficient.

For example, evaluating HTTP headers of websites proved to be a useful troubleshooting skill. During the fourth workshop session, on OpenURL and link resolvers, workshop instructors demonstrated the Firefox Chrome extension "HTTP Live Headers" to track the HTTP header history when navigating from a licensed database to full-text content via the OpenURL resolver. Instructors tracked the headers by activating the extension, navigating through to the full text, reviewed the HTTP header logs with attendees, and highlighted any useful or erroneous pieces of information. All staff attendees were encouraged to install the extension on their computers in order to practice reviewing HTTP headers on their own.

Diagrams and Workflows

Diagrams and flowcharts are effective training tools for visual learners and others because they can convey multiple complex relationships or decision-making processes in a constrained amount of space. At UL, workshop instructors used charts created during the training project's exploratory phase as a starting point for diagrams to show communication paths and relationships among various systems in the discovery ecosystem, as well as flowcharts to show troubleshooting steps for several common types of access problems. Charts and diagrams can serve as a bridge between conceptual and practical information and demonstrations, offering a high-level overview of a concept's local relevance before delving into the details. Instructors can also reuse charts and diagrams many times over the course of a multi-hour workshop. Charts and diagrams can serve as reminders or memory aids for staff of topics previously covered, and they can help orient staff to which local system(s) play a role in the specific topic, demonstration, or scenario under discussion at any given moment.

Scenarios

Crafted scenarios or case studies are useful for illustration and teaching. They can introduce or wrap up a training topic, initiate small-group discussions, or test knowledge. Depending on the goals for troubleshooting training, scenarios should include various pieces of information, such as

- The issue experienced by the user
- Information about the user (institutional affiliation, location, etc.)
- Additional information pertinent to the particular issue
- Initial results of troubleshooting

For example, in a troubleshooting workshop session on authentication, UL instructors presented staff with this scenario:

> Reported Issue: An off-campus user is having problems accessing articles on the [publisher platform]. They are not having problems getting into [the publisher platform] when coming from a Primo/Alma services page, but if they try to browse to another article inside [the publisher platform] they are asked to pay for the other article. What is going on?

This scenario could have been used by itself as a solo or group exercise, but instructors instead offered more information to further the discussion, elaborating on the above scenario as follows:

> Investigation: You check the EZProxy configuration file, and the [publisher platform] stanza looks correct, and is the recommended entry provided by the vendor. The troubleshooter tests using an off-campus IP and sees the issue. Is this a proxy issue?

Scenarios should be created with an end result in mind. Trainers should be aware that trying to elicit a specific answer or discussion requires a specific scenario with many details. In cases where a broad answer with multiple outcomes is adequate, scenarios can be less specific.

ASSESSMENT

Pre- and Post-Surveys

Pre- and post-surveys for workshop attendees are an easy and effective way to determine whether the goals of the workshop have been met. To achieve this, identical surveys should be given just prior to and immediately after the workshops take place. Pre-workshop survey results should be used to identify topics that may require more time to cover; post-workshop results help to identify topics where staff need further reinforcement. Of course, survey results also provide one method that instructors can use to assess staff progress and knowledge gains once the workshop has been completed.

Various types of surveys could serve these purposes. At UL, workshop instructors opted to use a Likert-type scale,[24] since it is simple to use and allows for easy analysis. Instructors surveyed staff on their familiarity with broad topics related to e-resources, troubleshooting, and the local web-scale discovery environment (see table 13.1). The Likert scale spanned five choices ranging from "Not at All Familiar" to "Extremely Familiar" (or on a scale of 1 to 5, respectively). Staff rated their familiarity with the following areas:

- A high-level overview of our discovery and access environment
- Common points of failure
- Authentication and authorization
- OpenURL and link resolvers
- Differences and similarities between access for OA/free resources and licensed/paid resources
- Discovery index content, activations, and linking mechanisms
- Metadata sources, quality, and impact on access
- Detailed interaction between the link resolver, discovery index, discovery layer, and LMS
- Distinguishing isolated issues from widespread problems
- Effective communication with system vendors and content providers

Workshop instructors intentionally provided no elaboration on or definitions of the topics, leaving it up to each staff member to construct the meaning themselves. Attendees received the pre-survey twenty-eight workdays before the workshop sessions began. The post-survey was distributed seven workdays after the workshop sessions completed. All attendees (n = 6) completed both surveys. The non-supervisor workshop instructor matched each attendee's pre- and post-survey results for comparison. The instructor then anonymized the resulting comparison data and destroyed the original survey results. The average pre-survey score was 2.68, while the average post-survey score was 4.17, an increase of 1.49. There was a significant increase in average familiarity scores (P-value < 0.000001 by two-tailed t-test). Additionally, all but two of the individual questions had significant increases in familiarity (P-value < 0.05 by two-tailed t-test). The two questions without significant increases were about authentication and authorization (P-value = 0.062) and distinguishing between isolated and widespread problems (P-value = 0.084). While these changes were nearly significant, one likely reason to explain a more minor effect could be that staff were most familiar with these two topics and had less to gain from a session on this topic.

Table 13.1 | **Average staff familiarity with troubleshooting topics**

QUESTION	PRE-WORKSHOP FAMILIARITY	POST-WORKSHOP FAMILIARITY	+/-	P-VALUE
1. Overview of discovery and access environment	3.00	4.33	1.33	**0.025**
2. Common points of failure	2.67	4.00	1.33	**0.043**
3. Authentication and authorization	2.83	4.17	1.34	0.062
4. OpenURL and link resolvers	2.67	4.00	1.33	**0.010**
5. Differences and similarities between access for OA/free resources and licensed/paid resources	3.00	4.50	1.50	**0.007**
6. Discovery index content, activations, and linking mechanisms	2.33	4.00	1.67	**0.001**
7. Metadata sources, quality, and impact on access	2.33	4.00	1.67	**0.011**
8. Detailed interaction between link resolver, discovery index, discovery layer, and LMS	1.67	3.83	2.16	**0.001**
9. Distinguishing isolated issues from widespread problems	3.00	4.17	1.17	0.084
10. Effective communication with system vendors and content providers	3.33	4.67	1.34	**0.025**
Average	2.68	4.17	1.49	**0.000**

*(1 = Not at all; 5 = Extremely). N = 10 questions by 6 respondents. Bolded P-values = statistically significant values.

Minute Surveys

Short surveys administered immediately after each individual workshop session can help identify areas of confusion, provide an opportunity for immediate feedback, and offer a quick snapshot of attendees' thoughts on the session. Additionally, instructors can use the feedback from these surveys to improve the curriculum and pedagogy for future workshops. At UL, instructors administered "minute" surveys[25] during the last few minutes of each of the ten workshop sessions. These surveys were anonymous and asked the same four questions:

1. What session are you reviewing?
2. Without looking at your notes, what was most memorable or stands out in your mind about today's session?
3. During today's session, what idea(s) struck you as things you could or should put into practice?
4. For you, what interesting questions remain unanswered about today's topic?

Minute survey questions should help answer any questions that workshop instructors might have about the content and delivery of workshop sessions. For multiple-session workshops offered over a period of days or weeks, minute survey responses can give instructors the opportunity to fine-tune training as it progresses, making it possible to revisit or reinforce topics that attendees did not fully understand when initially presented.

ONGOING DEVELOPMENT

Group Troubleshooting Sessions

Group troubleshooting sessions are useful to gather and tackle issues collaboratively. They also provide an opportunity to discuss any new issues that require deeper explanation, to delve deeper into a new problem-solving or diagnosis technique, or to work on a thorny issue together. The UL E-Resource Management unit has a standing monthly meeting to discuss troubleshooting issues. Typically, these meetings offer a chance to review specific reported but unresolved issues submitted via the ticketing system, or to discuss troubleshooting strategies and "hot topics." The meetings also provide a forum for the unit manager to address pending changes to the system (e.g., changes to authentication methods, system release functionality or bugs, etc.), so staff can better prepare for potential issues that may result from the changes. Group troubleshooting sessions should ideally be held in a room where there is access to a presenter's workstation with all of the necessary troubleshooting tools installed.

Skill Development

Staff must put troubleshooting skills and knowledge into everyday practice to help with retention and to establish concrete understanding. Access issues can be hard to come by; they can be nonexistent one week and plentiful the next. It is not always easy to predict or plan for practice opportunities while reactively addressing access issues as they are reported or discovered. At UL, instructors opted instead to proactively seek out potential access issues in order to give staff problems to diagnose and solve as they continued to develop their troubleshooting skills. As part of another project, technical staff provided a list of 400 random OpenURLs generated by library patrons attempting to link to resources via third-party databases in May 2016. Each staff member tested a subset of these OpenURLs for successful linking to full text. A total of 314 of the OpenURLs offered full text, and 56 (17.8 percent) of these had at least one malfunctioning link to full text. This gave E-Resource Management unit staff an opportunity to exercise their troubleshooting skills in a compressed and intensified time line. Not only did staff identify the 56 OpenURLs with broken links, but they also reviewed these links to determine the cause of the issue, reported or fixed the issue as appropriate, and saw the issue through to resolution. Staff completed proactive troubleshooting (testing, diagnosis, and resolution) by December 1.

During this skill development phase of the training, each staff member had two one-hour one-on-one troubleshooting sessions with the electronic resources librarian. This was an opportunity to discuss, diagnose, test, and begin resolution of the access issues.

After the skill development phase of the training was complete, the non-supervisor instructor distributed a third survey (a post-post-survey) to staff in order to evaluate the staff's familiarity with the same ten e-resource topics (see table 13.2 and figure 13.1). The post-troubleshooting survey was distributed

Table 13.2 | **Average post-workshop and post-troubleshooting staff familiarity with troubleshooting topics**

QUESTION	POST-WORKSHOP FAMILIARITY	POST-TROUBLESHOOTING FAMILIARITY	+/-	P-VALUE
1. Overview of discovery and access environment	4.33	4.50	0.17	0.363
2. Common points of failure	4.00	4.50	0.50	0.203
3. Authentication and authorization	4.17	4.33	0.16	0.363
4. OpenURL and link resolvers	4.00	4.17	0.17	0.363
5. Differences and similarities between access for OA/free resources and licensed/paid resources	4.50	4.83	0.33	0.175
6. Discovery index content, activations, and linking mechanisms	4.00	4.00	0.00	1.000
7. Metadata sources, quality, and impact on access	4.00	4.17	0.17	0.611
8. Detailed interaction between link resolver, discovery index, discovery layer, and LMS	3.83	3.83	0.00	1.000
9. Distinguishing isolated issues from widespread problems	4.17	4.50	0.33	0.175
10. Effective communication with system vendors and content providers	4.67	4.33	-0.34	0.175
Average	4.17	4.32	0.15	0.068

*(1 = Not at all; 5 = Extremely). N = 10 questions by 6 respondents. Bolded P-values = statistically significant values.

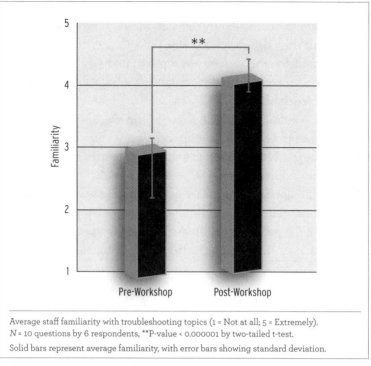

Average staff familiarity with troubleshooting topics (1 = Not at all; 5 = Extremely).
N = 10 questions by 6 respondents, **P-value < 0.000001 by two-tailed t-test.
Solid bars represent average familiarity, with error bars showing standard deviation.

Figure 13.1 | **Post-post survey**

143 workdays after the workshop ended and 7 workdays after proactive trouble shooting ended. All attendees (n = 6) completed the post-troubleshooting survey. The non-supervisor workshop instructor matched each attendee's post-workshop and post-troubleshooting results for comparison. The instructor then anonymized the resulting comparison data and destroyed the original survey results. The average post-workshop score was 4.17, while the average post-troubleshooting score was 4.32, an increase of 0.15. The average score for seven of the ten questions increased; two questions had no change, and one question had a decrease. None of the individual questions had significant differences in familiarity, and there was no significant difference in average familiarity scores for the post-troubleshooting survey. Even though the survey did not show significant differences in self-assessed familiarity after proactive troubleshooting, informal feedback indicated that the experience was overall a positive one for staff. Due to the varied nature of the randomly selected OpenURLs for proactive troubleshooting and the long lag time between workshop and troubleshooting completion, staff may not have felt that their familiarity with some topics increased as a result of the project. Additionally,

staff may have encountered specific issues not covered in the workshop, in which instructors demonstrated broad topics with "hand-picked" examples.

CONCLUSION

Creating an effective staff-training program for electronic resources trouble-shooting requires a substantial investment of time and effort on the part of both instructors and staff learners. However, for institutions willing to invest the necessary resources in such a project, the payoff can be great. Having a larger number of staff who are sophisticated e-resource troubleshooters means better service for library patrons, who will see their access problems resolved more quickly and efficiently. Reducing bottlenecks in problem-solving queues also makes it possible for e-resource support units to manage their workloads more effectively. Libraries become less dependent on a small number of individuals who hold the specialized skills and knowledge needed for troubleshooting, making succession planning and staff departures easier to manage. Finally, a training program is rewarding for both staff and instructors. Instructors improve and enhance their own skills through the process of teaching others, while staff members build confidence as they acquire new skills, which can position them to progress in their own careers and take on new opportunities as they arise. At the University of Minnesota Libraries, the authors and e-resources staff continue to learn together as systems evolve and new problems arise, but all are better off for participating in the process.

NOTES

1. Beth Ashmore, Emily Allee, and Rebekah Wood, "Identifying and Troubleshooting Link-Resolution Issues with ILL Data," *Serials Review* 41, no. 1 (2015): 23–29, doi: 10.1080/00987913.2014.1001506; Sarah Glasser, "Broken Links and Failed Access," *Library Resources & Technical Services* 56, no. 1 (2012): 14–23, doi:10.5860/lrts.56n1.14; Tess Graham and Nate Hosburgh, "A User-Centered Approach to Addressing Issues of Discoverability and Access," *The Serials Librarian* 67, no. 1 (2014): 48–51, doi:10.1 080/0361526X.2014.899290; Patricia A. Headlee and Sandra C. Lahtinen, "Callisto Basic and Callisto Pro," *Journal of the Medical Library Association: JMLA* 102, no. 4 (2014): 305–6, doi:10.3163/1536–5050.102.4.018; Sanjeet Mann, "Electronic Resource Availability Studies: An Effective Way to Discover Access Errors," *Evidence Based Library and Information Practice* 10, no. 3 (2015): 30–49. doi:10.18438/B88C82; Denise Pan, Gayle Bradbeer, and Elaine Jurries, "From Communication to Collaboration: Blogging to Troubleshoot E-Resources," *The Electronic Library* 29, no. 3 (2011): 344–53, doi:10.1108/02640471111141089; Kenyon Stuart, Ken Varnum, and Judith Ahronheim, "Measuring Journal Linking Success from a Discovery Service." *Information Technology*

and Libraries 34, no. 1 (2015): 52–76, doi:10.6017/ital.v34i1.5607; Susan Davis et al., "Who Ya Gonna Call? Troubleshooting Strategies for E-Resources Access Problems," *The Serials Librarian* 62, no. 1–4 (2012): 24–32, doi:10.1080/0361526X.2012.652459; Rebecca Donlan, "Boulevard of Broken Links: Keeping Users Connected to E-Journal Content," *Reference Librarian* 48, no. 1 (2007): 99–104, doi:10.1300/J120v48n99_08; Sanjeet Mann and Sarah Sutton, "Why Can't Students Get the Sources They Need? Results from a Real Electronic Resources Availability Study," *The Serials Librarian* 68, no. 1–4 (2015): 180–90, doi:10.1080/0361526X.2015.1017419; Cindi Trainor and Jason Price, "Digging into the Data: Exposing the Causes of Resolver Failure," *Library Technology Reports* 46, no. 7 (2010): 15–26; Maria Collins and William T. Murray, "SEESAU: University of Georgia's Electronic Journal Verification System," *Serials Review* 35, no. 2 (2009): 80–87, doi:10.1080/00987913.2009.10765216; Jina Choi Wakimoto, David S. Walker, and Katherine S. Dabbour, "The Myths and Realities of SFX in Academic Libraries," *The Journal of Academic Librarianship* 32, no. 2 (2006): 127–36, doi:10.1016/j.acalib.2005.12.008.

2. Jacquie Samples and Ciara Healy, "Making It Look Easy: Maintaining the Magic of Access," *Serials Review* 40, no. 2 (2014): 105–17, doi: 10.1080/00987913.2014.929483.

3. Angela Rathmel et al., "Tools, Techniques, and Training: Results of an E-Resources Troubleshooting Survey," *Journal of Electronic Resources Librarianship* 27, no. 2 (2015): 88–107, doi:10.1080/1941126X.2015.1029398.

4. Ibid., 103.

5. Ibid., 99–100.

6. Taryn Resnick, "Core Competencies for Electronic Resource Access Services," *Journal of Electronic Resources in Medical Libraries* 6, no. 2 (2009): 101–22, doi:10.1080/15424060902932185; Sarah Sutton, "Identifying Core Competencies for Electronic Resources Librarians in the Twenty-First Century Library" (PhD diss., Texas Woman's University, 2011); Emma Lawson, Roën Janyk, and Rachel A. Erb, "Getting to the Core of the Matter: Competencies for New E-Resources Librarians," *The Serials Librarian* 66, no. 1–4 (2014): 153–60, doi: 10.1080/0361526X.2014.879639.

7. Jeffrey Perkins, "Solving Electronic Journal Problems Effectively: A Short Guide," *Journal of Electronic Resources in Medical Libraries* 5, no. 3 (2008): 267–73, doi:10.1080/15424060802222471; Davis et al., "Who Ya Gonna Call?"; Resnick, "Core Competencies for Electronic Resource Access Services."

8. Katherine A. Hart and Tammy S. Sugarman, "Developing an Interdepartmental Training Program for E-Resources Troubleshooting," *The Serials Librarian* 71, no. 1 (2016): 25–38, doi:10.1080/0361526X.2016.1169569.

9. Sunshine Carter and Stacie Traill, "Essential Skills and Knowledge for Troubleshooting E-Resources Access Issues in a Web-Scale Discovery Environment," *Journal of Electronic Resources Librarianship* 29, no. 1 (2017): doi:10.1080/1941126X.2017.1270096.

10. Ibid., 13.

11. Eduardo Salas et al., "The Science of Training and Development in Organizations: What Matters in Practice," *Psychological Science in the Public Interest* 13, no. 2 (2012): 77, doi:10.1177/1529100612436661.

12. Penny L. Ittner and Alex F. Douds, *Train the Trainer: Practical Skills That Work (Coursebook)* (Amherst, MA: Human Resource Development, 1988), 1.4.

13. Barbara Ostrowski Martin, Klodiana Kolomitro, and Tony C. M. Lam, "Training Methods: A Review and Analysis," *Human Resource Development Review* 13, no. 1 (2014): 12, doi:10.1177/1534484313497947.

14. Ibid., 16–17.

15. Ibid., 15–20.

16. Ibid., 21–31.

17. Salas et al., "The Science of Training and Development in Organizations," 74.

18. Ibid., 80–83.

19. Ibid., 84–88.

20. Ibid., 85–87.

21. Ibid., 88.

22. Ibid., 92.

23. Carter and Traill, "Essential Skills and Knowledge for Troubleshooting E-Resources Access Issues," 6–11.

24. Wade M. Vagias, "Likert-Type Scale Response Anchors," Clemson International Institute for Tourism & Research Development, Department of Parks, Recreation and Tourism Management, Clemson University, www.marquette.edu/dsa/assessment/documents/Sample-Likert-Scales.pdf.

25. Thomas A. Angelo and K. Patricia Cross, *Classroom Assessment Techniques: A Handbook for College Teachers* (San Francisco: Jossey-Bass, 1993).

SUSHI
Automating the Retrieval of COUNTER Usage Data

Oliver Pesch

The Standardized Usage Statistics Harvesting Initiative (SUSHI) is an ANSI-accredited standard (Z39.83–2014) developed by the National Information Standards Organization (NISO) to define an "automated request and response model for harvesting e-resource usage data . . . designed to work with COUNTER, the most frequently retrieved usage reports."[1]

OVERVIEW AND HISTORY

COUNTER usage reports, discussed in detail in earlier chapters, are the product of collaboration between publishers, librarians, and aggregators that is focused on providing consistent, credible, and comparable usage statistics for scholarly information. The time line in figure 14.1 shows the evolution of both COUNTER and SUSHI. The initiative that resulted in SUSHI began in 2004, and SUSHI was released as an approved ANSI standard in 2007 after the release 1 of the COUNTER Code of Practice was published.

The timing of the SUSHI initiative was not purely coincidental. In the early 2000s the Electronic Resource Management Initiative[2] (ERMI) was a project with an objective of "developing common specifications and tools for

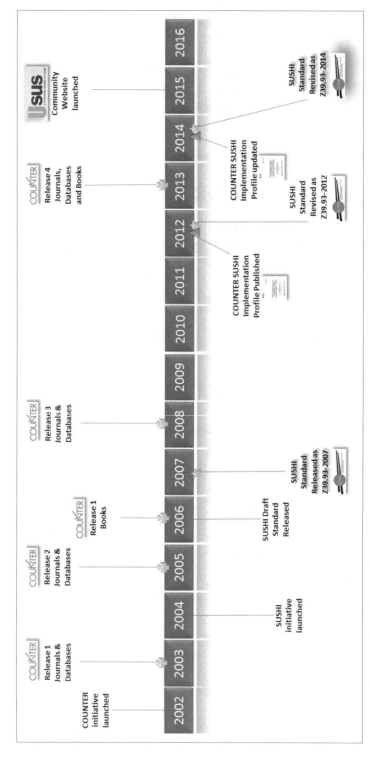

Figure 14.1 | A time line for the development of COUNTER and SUSHI

managing the license agreements, related administrative information, and internal processes associated with collections of licensed electronic resources." The resulting report imagined that e-resource management systems built to the ERMI specifications would support the "management of and access to usage statistics."[3] The ERMI report, published in 2004, became the foundation for many electronic resource management (ERM) systems. When it came time to implement the usage statistics' functionality, COUNTER reports were the natural solution, since they offered the potential of a standardization of usage reports across all content providers. However, as work began to add COUNTER usage statistics to ERMs, it became clear that not only was the effort of downloading individual COUNTER reports from dozens of reporting sites not scalable, but the resulting reports were not really as compatible with each other as was hoped.

COUNTER reports were originally designed to be read by humans and not computers. Minor differences in formatting, which the human reader would not even notice, would trip up computer logic trying to ingest those reports into an ERM. Scalability could only come if the ERM was able to automatically harvest and ingest the COUNTER reports and load the usage statistics without library staff intervention. The problem was brought to NISO[4] in the summer of 2004 and a working group was formed. Within six months a working prototype implementing what would later become known as SUSHI was in production delivering COUNTER reports. The NISO working group had two primary goals: to develop a mechanism that would allow automated harvesting of COUNTER reports, and to create a formal data schema that would ensure compatibility between content providers.

The working group chose to design SUSHI as a web service implemented using the Simple Object Access Protocol[5] (SOAP) exchange COUNTER Usage data as XML.[6] The web service approach would allow report harvesting to be performed on a scheduled basis without human intervention, and the choice of XML as a delivery format meant that the COUNTER data could be machine-validated to ensure accuracy.

TECHNICAL DETAILS

As a web service, SUSHI uses a client-server approach to harvesting COUNTER reports. To be COUNTER-compliant, content providers must provide a SUSHI server so that their customers can automatically harvest COUNTER reports using a SUSHI client of their choice. Figure 14.2 shows SUSHI's basic architecture and flow.

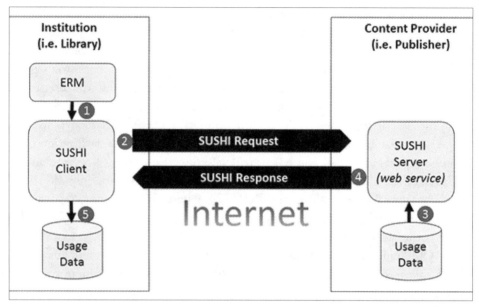

Figure 14.2 | **SUSHI architecture and flow**

In this diagram, the SUSHI client is a component of an ERM system. When it is time to harvest the usage statistics, the ERM passes information to the client (1) identifying the URL of the server, which report to ask for, and other configuration details; the client sends the request to the content provider's SUSHI server (2); which fetches the COUNTER data from its usage report data (3); formats the COUNTER report as XML and sends it back to the client as part of the SUSHI response (4); and finally, the SUSHI client extracts the COUNTER usage data from the response and loads it into its own usage data repository (5) to be ready for performing analysis and consolidated reporting.

To better understand how to successfully use SUSHI, it is good to have an understanding of the details of the SUSHI Request and Response. Table 14.1 shows the four key elements of the SUSHI Request: the Requestor (identifies who is asking for the report); the Customer (identifies which institution's usage is desired); the Report Information (the COUNTER report to return); and Filters (the date range for the usage desired). This, along with the URL for the content provider's SUSHI service, is generally all that is needed for a SUSHI client to retrieve a COUNTER report.

Table 14.1 | **Elements in a SUSHI Request**

REQUEST ELEMENT	DEFINITION	HOW IT APPEARS IN THE REQUEST

REQUESTOR	A unique identifier of the SUSHI client instance, as assigned by the content provider, along with a name and e-mail contact. The Requestor ID functions in many ways like an API-key in that it grants the client software the rights to use the server.	`<Requestor>`
		  `<ID>`*requestor_id*`</ID`
		  `<Name>`*requestor_name*`</Name>`
		  `<Email>`*contact_email*`</Email>`
		`</Requestor>`

CUSTOMER	A unique identifier and customer name for the institution for which usage statistics are being requested. The Customer ID will be the unique identifier assigned by the content provider. For example, when retrieving usage for EBSCOhost, the Customer ID is that institution's EBSCOhost customer ID.	`<CustomerReference>`
		  `<ID>`*customer_id*`</ID`
		  `<Name>`*customer_name*`</Name>`
		`</CustomerReference>`

REPORT INFORMATION	The name of the report being requested and its release information.	`<ReportDefinition  Name=`*report_id*
		`Release=`*release_number*`>`
		  ...
		`</ReportDefinition>`

FILTERS	The date range of the usage to be retrieved expressed as full dates in international date format (yyyy-mm-dd). Note that COUNTER reports are for full months, so the expectation is that the day value for the Begin date is "01" and the day value for the End date is the last day of the month.	`<ReportDefinition ...>`
		  `<Filters>`
		    `<UsageDateRange>`
		      `<Begin>`*yyyy-mm-dd*`</Begin>`
		      `<End>`*yyyy-mm-dd*`</End>`
		    `</UsageDateRange>`
		  `</Filters>`
		`</ReportDefinition>`

Putting this all together, the XML of a request to EBSCOhost for Journal Report 1 for 2016 for Mt. Laurel University would look something like this:

```
<ReportRequest>
  <Requestor>
  <ID>12a2–2fd42a-0dc42s</ID>
  <Name>Example ERM System</Name>
  <Email>support@example.com</Email>
  </Requestor>
  <CustomerReference>
  <ID>z12345</ID
  <Name>Mt. Laurel University</Name>
  </CustomerReference>
  <ReportDefinition Name="JR1" Release="4">
  <Filters>
  <UsageDateRange>
  <Begin>2016–01–01</Begin>
  <End>2016–12–31</End>
  </UsageDateRange>
  </Filters>
  </ReportDefinition>
</ReportRequest>
```

Without going into too much detail, the SUSHI Response is very similar to the Request. The Response mirrors the Request elements and also includes the Report. Figure 14.3 shows graphical representation of the response.

UNDERSTANDING AND MANAGING SUSHI CREDENTIALS

The successful use of SUSHI requires a certain level of understanding of SUSHI Credentials—the information needed to successfully harvest a COUNTER report via SUSHI. Since most of the individual elements were discussed in the previous section, the following are some important notes:

> Customer IDs and Requestor IDs are assigned by the content provider; therefore, it will be necessary to gather and track these elements for each platform.

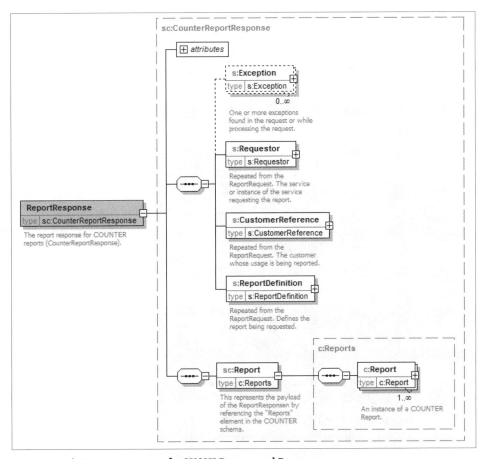

Figure 14.3 | **Representation of a SUSHI Report and Response**

Each content provider (platform) will have its own URL; therefore, it will be necessary to gather and record the unique URL for each platform in order to harvest that platform's usage statistics.

Some content providers also impose additional authentication, such as IP Address validation; therefore, the IP Address of the SUSHI client may need to be registered with the content provider.

Usage data is considered private, so to ensure the security of the usage data, a customer is often required to "activate" SUSHI harvesting from within the content provider's administrative module. During this activation, the customer may have to indicate which SUSHI client is being used, and the IP Address of that client may also need to be registered, since some content providers also impose additional IP Address authentication.

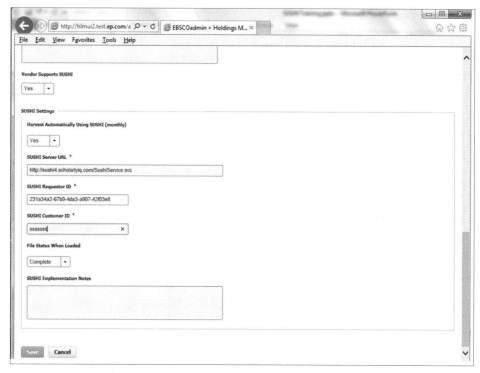

Figure 14.4 | **Example of a SUSHI configuration screen**

If reports are being harvested automatically, it is important to know what day of the month usage for the prior month will be ready. COUNTER allows content providers up to 28 days to prepare the prior month's usage. If you are not sure what day of the month a content provider's usage is ready, harvest the COUNTER reports on the 28th day of the following month.

Library staff using an ERM or usage consolidation module will have an interface, similar to the one shown in figure 14.4, where the SUSHI credentials are entered.

SUSHI credentials must be added for each platform. The best source of these credentials is the content provider themselves; this is often discoverable through their administration/reporting module. Figure 14.5 provides an example of a content provider's administrative module showing the SUSHI credentials. While the effort of collecting and recording the necessary credentials from dozens of content-provider platforms is not trivial, it generally only needs to be done once, and it will greatly simplify loading COUNTER statistics going forward, so it is well worth the effort. Note that some providers

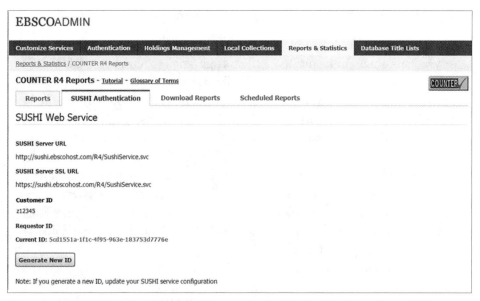

Figure 14.5 | **SUSHI credentials shown in content provider's administration module**

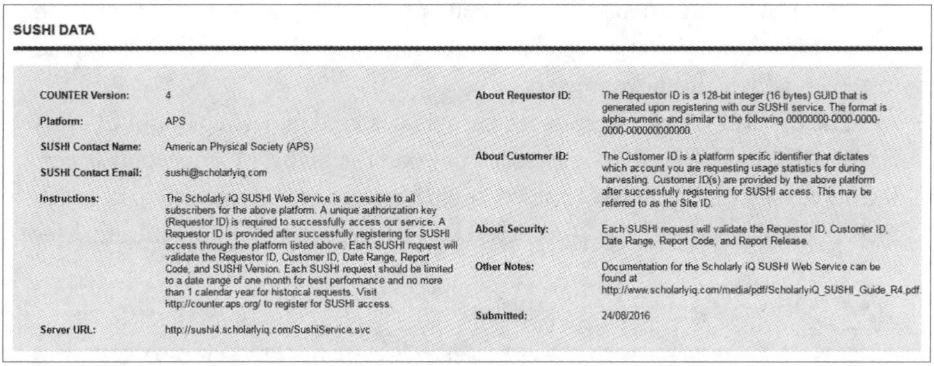

Figure 14.6 | **COUNTER registries of compliance SUSHI data**

of usage consolidation products may locate and load credentials on your behalf as part of the subscription fee.

COUNTER's Registries of Compliance[7] page is an excellent resource for library staff who are charged with locating SUSHI credentials. The COUNTER registry data, as shown in figure 14.6, provides critical details such as the SUSHI server URL; instructions for activating SUSHI; information about the requirements/expectations for Customer ID and Requestor ID; and the list of reports supported.

SUSHI CLIENTS AND HOW THEY WORK

The SUSHI standard describes how two computer programs (a client and a server) can communicate to allow a client application to retrieve a COUNTER report from a server application. The SUSHI standard is an enabler and doesn't actually do the work. To retrieve COUNTER reports via SUSHI requires a SUSHI client. Several options exist for SUSHI clients, ranging from commercial offerings from various library automation vendors (i.e., Intota from ProQuest and Usage Consolidation from EBSCO), to open source solutions (i.e., CORAL ERM and MISO open source client), to in-house development.

To demonstrate the operation of a SUSHI client, the following few figures are screenshots that use the CORAL[8] demo to show the process from beginning to end. CORAL is an open source ERM that includes a usage statistics module that supports SUSHI.

Starting with the SUSHI Connection screen shown in figure 14.7, the SUSHI configuration information is added for a new platform (this screen is accessed using the "Add New Platform for SUSHI" link on the SUSHI tab in CORAL's Usage Statistics module).

Once SUSHI credentials have been entered, the platform will appear on the SUSHI Administration screen as shown in figure 14.8—EBSCOhost had just been added and now appears.

The SUSHI Administration screen acts as a kind of dashboard for SUSHI activity. When EBSCOhost was added to using the SUSHI Connection screen, the Service Day indicates that reports are to be requested on the fifth day of each month; therefore, the EBSCOhost COUNTER reports will automatically show

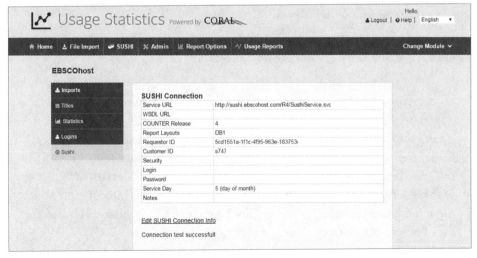

Figure 14.7 | **SUSHI Connection screen from CORAL**

in the "Outstanding Import Queue" on that date. Alternatively, COUNTER reports can be manually retrieved immediately by clicking the "Run Now" link in the "All SUSHI Services" section of the screen. The user is prompted to enter a date range for the usage to be harvested.

Clicking the "View to Process" link in the "Outstanding Import Queue" section displays the report details. Figure 14.9 shows the results of the EBSCO-host Database Report 1 (DB1) harvest using SUSHI.

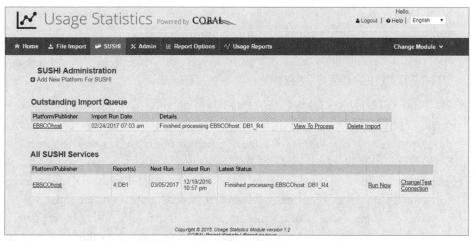

Figure 14.8 | **SUSHI Administration screen from CORAL**

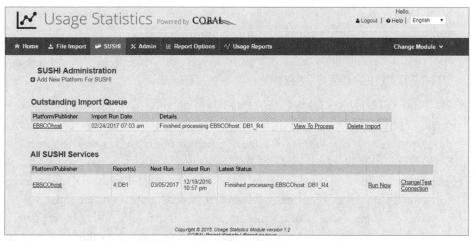

Figure 14.9 | **SUSHI Import Confirmation screen from CORAL**

The user would scroll to the bottom of this screen and, if all is okay with the report and its data, they would click "Confirm" on this screen and the usage data would be loaded into CORAL's reporting system.

The above examples demonstrate how one open-source SUSHI client works. Other open-source options are listed on the NISO SUSHI "Tools" page, along with some samples and guidance for developers wishing to create their own SUSHI client.

Developers and other interested parties are encouraged to join the NISO SUSHI developer list,[9] where they can submit questions to other developers and follow discussions related to implementing SUSHI.

THE FUTURE OF SUSHI

The NISO SUSHI Standing Committee[10] is in the process of developing a new version of SUSHI that can be easily integrated into applications that have been developed using today's most in-demand programming languages. The current SUSHI standard is based on the SOAP web service model exchanging XML. The new version of SUSHI, currently known as SUSHI-Lite, takes the more common approach of employing REpresentational State Transfer (REST)[11] or RESTful web services that exchange data using the JSON[12] (JavaScript Object Notation) format. The advantage of REST is that it uses the http/https protocol to request and retrieve data—essentially an Internet browser can be used to retrieve a COUNTER report—and the benefit of JSON is that it is a format native to most modern web programming languages, making it easy to work with, along with the fact that most developers are very familiar with it.

In addition to being easier to implement, SUSHI-Lite is also designed to allow snippets of usage to be retrieved. For example, with SUSHI-Lite, it would be possible to retrieve usage for just one journal, allowing an application like a serials module or subscription management system to directly integrate usage data into the librarian workflow and help support decisions.

In 2016, an early version of SUSHI-Lite was submitted to the community as a draft recommended practice. At the time of writing, SUSHI-Lite was being refined based on the feedback received during the comment period, and to accommodate changes required to support COUNTER Release 5. The goal was to have an updated SUSHI-Lite recommended practice available shortly after COUNTER Release 5 was published in 2017.

SUSHI is a requirement for COUNTER compliance, and with well over 100 platforms supporting SUSHI, usage from tens of thousands of journals and hundreds of thousands of books can be harvested automatically. Release 5 of the COUNTER Code of Practice will lead to even wider adoption, and the updated SUSHI protocol will improve both the quality and ease of implementation. SUSHI will continue to play an increasingly valuable role in collection assessment by enabling the automation of the retrieval of COUNTER usage data that is so important to the process.

More information on SUSHI is available from the NISO SUSHI website (www.niso.org/workrooms/sushi).

NOTES

1. "SUSHI," NISO, www.niso.org/workrooms/sushi/.
2. DLF Electronic Resource Management Initiative, https://old.diglib.org/standards/dlf-erm02.htm.
3. "Electronic Resource Management: Report of the DLF ERM Initiative," p. 58, https://old.diglib.org/pubs/dlf102/ERMFINAL.pdf.
4. NISO, www.niso.org.
5. "Simple Object Access Protocol," Wikipedia definition, https://en.wikipedia.org/wiki/SOAP.
6. "XML," Wikipedia definition, https://en.wikipedia.org/wiki/XML.
7. "COUNTER Registries of Compliance," COUNTER, https://www.projectcounter.org/about/register/.
8. "CORAL Usage Statistics," CORAL, http://coral-erm.org/usage/.
9. "Join the Developer List," NISO SUSHI, www.niso.org/workrooms/sushi/developers _list/.
10. "NISO SUSHI Standing Committee," NISO, www.niso.org/workrooms/sushi/.
11. "Representative state transfer," Wikipedia definition, https://en.wikipedia.org/wiki/Representational_state_transfer.
12. "JSON," Wikipedia definition, https://en.wikipedia.org/wiki/JSON.

Analytics and Assessment of Electronic Resources

Geoffrey Timms

nalytics is a process of gathering and analyzing data for meaningful use. In the context of electronic resources (e-resources) management, analytics involves obtaining a variety of data points from various data sources; organizing and preserving them; processing and analyzing statistics; and communicating information in a meaningful way for decision-makers who may not be familiar with the intricacies of interpreting the data. The terms *data* and *statistics* are often used interchangeably when describing the assessment of electronic resources. For the purpose of this chapter, however, the following distinction is made: *data* is raw and unprocessed, sometimes numerical output from reporting tools of electronic resources, while at other times data might be evaluative and subjective human responses to surveys that are evaluated or rated into numerical representation. *Statistics* are generated by combining multiple data items in order to generate numerical representations of more complex concepts. For example, the venerated cost-per-use statistic is generated from price and use data to represent the concept of return on investment or value.

WHY ASSESS E-RESOURCES?

Assessment is steadily permeating workflows in libraries. Librarians compete for finite funds with other departments in academic institutions, local governments, and corporations, and these funding entities increasingly require evidence of a return on their investment. Assessment is not simply driven by a need for justification, however. Across all types of libraries, librarians strive to meet the needs of their constituents and rely on quantitative and qualitative feedback to help guide the strategies and decisions they make in satisfying information needs effectively.

The assessment of e-resources does not only involve evaluating what the library already offers; it also involves evaluating e-resources in which the library may choose to invest. Such assessment is necessary to ensure (and prove) that funds are being, or will be, expended wisely and that constituents are being provided with what they need. The very nature of e-resources offers many opportunities to engage in assessment through the use of analytics, which is possible due to the perpetual gathering of data as online indexes, articles, e-books, images, and streaming media (to name but a few e-resources) are used. The assessment of e-resources is certainly driven, in part, out of a need to justify expenditure. Libraries have endured significant budget challenges since the Great Recession of 2008, and budgets continue to struggle for a variety of reasons as institutions adapt to new economic realities.

An annual survey conducted in 2015 predicted that North American library budgets, across all types of libraries, would increase on average by 1 percent in 2016, while Europe would experience a 0.1 percent decrease. Serials and books budgets were anticipated to increase by 0.2 percent and 1.9 percent respectively in North America but increase 0.3 percent and decrease 0.4 percent respectively in Europe. Respondents reported that the percentage of serials expenditure made upon electronic serials increased between 2006 and 2015 from 26 percent to 77 percent in North America and from 36 percent to 58 percent in Europe. The percentage of book budgets spent on electronic books in surveyed libraries worldwide increased from 3.1 percent in 2006 to 29.7 percent in 2015.[1] Within their purchasing and subscribing capacities, libraries are showing evidence of transitioning to electronic content at an increasing rate.

While the transition to electronic content expands access potential and is supportive of hybrid and blended learning, the inflation in the prices of electronic resources continues to be a cause for concern to decision-makers. Serials prices increased, on average, 4–6 percent from 2015 to 2016 with a comparable projection for 2017.[2] US-published periodicals were, on average, 32.1 percent more expensive in 2015 compared to 2010. US-published e-book prices have changed variably, based upon subject, during this time, while academic e-books have generally increased in price at substantially varying annual rates between 2010 and 2013.[3] Contrasting these price changes with recent budget histories and predictions demonstrates that increasing proportions of budgets are, and must be, spent on electronic resources to maintain existing purchasing and licensing patterns. Assessment is particularly necessary, therefore, to justify the increase in budgeted expenditure on electronic resources at the expense of other aspects of library operations. Proof must be offered that the continued investment in these virtual materials is worth the cost of the alternative foregone.

Electronic resources also present users with a variety of challenges, so user behavior and usability are important components of assessment. Familiarity with multiple interfaces, search tools, linking tools, and access or delivery points is now necessary to access content that formerly resided in print upon a shelf. Thus, the process of achieving access is a facet of assessment that must be integrated with the assessment of content and its use. Librarians, when assessing whether the needs of constituents are being met, need to know not only if the right information is being offered, but also if it is being offered in the best way. Indiana University librarians deployed usage statistics and Google Analytics data from their discovery service to assess user behavior and inform information literacy instruction needs, as well as to identify a need to improve three aspects of the discovery service platform.[4] University of Huddersfield librarians utilized e-resource usage data, in addition to other usage and qualitative data about library services and use, to confirm a statistically significant relationship between library use and student achievement.[5] The use of Florida Electronic Library databases and user demographics were assessed in an extensive project undertaken for the purpose of guiding county and library system-specific marketing strategies in order to promote future database use.[6] Analytics, therefore, can be of strategic value beyond collection development departments.

DATA FOR THE ASSESSMENT OF E-RESOURCES

Data is generally divided into two broad categories: quantitative data represent measurable and numerically quantifiable observations, while qualitative data represent more abstract, and often evaluative, observations. A broad array of quantitative and qualitative observations can be made for the purpose of assessing electronic resources.

Quantitative Data

The quantitative data available for the assessment of e-resources relate both to a given e-resource relative to an institution and its users, and to the e-resource relative to other information resources. In other words, data represent both the use of e-resources by an institution's constituents and the relative quality or esteem and uniqueness of a given e-resource compared to other available e-resources.

Quantitative Measures of Institutional Use

Perhaps the most widely collected quantitative data regarding existing e-resources are usage data. The greatest assurance sought after investing in electronic resources is that they are being used, which might be considered a basic indicator of value to users, or return on investment. Quantitative data is generally available from publishers and vendors related to the e-resources which they provide, as well as from third-party and subscribing institutions' local systems used for discovery, user authentication, and delivery.

Vendor-Provided Usage Data

As discussed in a previous chapter, the issue of standardization of usage data through the Project COUNTER (https://www.projectcounter.org/) initiative continues to make great strides in improving data integrity and comparability, as well as in accounting for non-textual media. Currently in release 4, with a deadline of January 1 2019 to transition to release 5 published in 2017, the number of COUNTER reports defined has grown over the various releases of the standards. A COUNTER-compliant vendor, however, is not required to provide all of the reports appropriate to the e-resource type and format. While many reports are potentially available across e-resource types and with parallel reports now offered for mobile device use, the data remains focused on four areas of interest at the platform, database, and title levels as applicable:

- Searches
- Access denials
- Successful artifact accesses (full text article/book/chapter, image/video/audio, and article record in an index)
- Result clicks (in the case of search interfaces, particularly of index/abstract-only databases)

Another benefit of COUNTER data is the consistency of downloadable report formats due to the extensive specifications provided by the standard.[7] This facilitates the manual and automated aggregation of data for preservation and processing. In addition, the SUSHI (www.niso.org/workrooms/sushi/) protocol enables the automated harvesting of COUNTER-compliant usage data by third-party services from vendors that make usage data available in the COUNTER XML standard.[8]

Not all vendors provide COUNTER-compliant usage data, while a handful have started to but have not yet completed the audit process. Noncompliant usage reports and data may seem comparable to COUNTER data in terms of nomenclature with sessions, searches, downloads, and so on being provided. However, there are numerous underlying aspects of this data that should be considered. The current COUNTER standard identifies issues that have been addressed in the latest release, including double-clicking and federated search or robot inflation of usage counts, to ensure that usage data "should meet the basic requirement that only intended usage is recorded and that all requests that are not intended by the user are removed."[9] Some scholarship has been devoted in recent years to issues of usage data integrity and the behavior of search interfaces which can impact the validity, comparison, and interpretation of usage data, including the ratio of searches to sessions in the case of federated searching.[10] The default display of HTML versions of articles on some search platforms can also inflate the count of full-text views.[11] While COUNTER-compliancy has alleviated many of these issues, they continue to be of concern to nonparticipating vendors.

Authentication Data

Remote access authentication systems, such as OCLC EZProxy, Shibboleth, and Virtual Private Networks, can generate activity logs which can be analyzed for information about e-resource use by authenticated patrons. Depending upon the configuration of the authentication system, however, it is important to note that only authenticated (that is, remote) users' activity may be recorded. Log files provide predictably formatted entries reflecting user activity and can often be customized in the software configuration. EZProxy, in its default configuration, generates logs in the format

132.174.1.1—[14 /Mar/2014:09:39:18 -0700] "GET www.somedb
.com:80/index.html HTTP/1.0" 200 1234

where the IP address, date and time, URL, status, and byte size of the request are documented.[12] The number of entries for a single user's activity may be extensive, particularly when individual web pages load images and other content from various distinct URLs.

Reading log files may be accomplished either by using existing log file analysis software, or by developing a custom script to read log files and report the findings. The challenge in both cases is to account for all possible URL structures across a range of e-resource providers, ensuring that key data is collected and that tangential or unimportant data is not reported. The data obtained from an authentication system may be useful as a supplement to vendor-provided usage data and as a means to study user behavior.

Link Resolver Data

A link resolver is software used to bridge the gap between the discovery of scholarship in an online index where the full text to a particular item cannot be found and potential sources of full text, including online and print holdings, as well as sources beyond the institution through interlibrary loan (ILL). Examples of proprietary link resolvers include Serials Solutions 360 Link, EBSCO LinkSource, and Ovid LinkSolver, while a small number of open-source link resolvers, such as Simon Fraser University's GODOT link resolver using the CUFTS knowledge base (www.lib.sfu.ca/about/initiatives/researcher), both of which were scheduled to be decommissioned in late 2017, have also been developed. Data obtained from a link resolver represents attempts to locate full-text access to scholarship of interest. Link resolver data consists of two key parts: the origin or source of the citation, and the chosen target of the full-text content for the citation. The link resolver cannot provide information about the final outcome of the attempt to locate full-text content. However, it does offer insight into where people are searching for content and, in cases where more than one target option exists, where people are choosing to access full text. Additionally, a link resolver may not provide sufficiently granular data for analysis at the individual title level. Rather, it may be most useful for studying the origin and target by database or platform.

Interlibrary Loan Borrowing Data

Interlibrary loan borrowing data is usually obtainable through the library's ILL software, such as Atlas Systems ILLiad (distributed by OCLC), Clio Software Clio System, and OCLC WorldShare Interlibrary Loan, which are used to submit, process, and manage requests. Borrowing data, unlike most other data considered above, represents the use by an institution's affiliates of items not accessible through the institution. It is, therefore, data that reflects either the inadequacy or the strategic selectiveness of a collection and thus offers valuable insight for future collection management strategies.

ILL borrowing data is particularly useful when contrasted with data about acquisition costs and information about institutional needs, particularly with regard to timeliness of access. It follows that a collection management strategy may rely on ILL to mitigate subscription costs, particularly for low-use titles with no urgency for immediate access. With changes in an institution's clientele, faculty, research emphases, or financial stability over time, it is prudent to revisit collection evaluation in conjunction with ILL data in order to ensure that previous decisions and resource profiles remain appropriate for the existing research and fiscal climate.

Institutional Sources-Cited Data

Evidence of the citation of information resources in the scholarship generated within an institution is a reliable indicator of the use of scholarship, where the evidence of intent, as indicated by searches and downloads, is confirmed by the proof of its use. Citation analysis within an institution may be undertaken by direct analysis of the scholarly works of its affiliates. This may be achieved using citation databases that include works-cited data for books and articles, or by the systematic extraction of bibliographies from online or print documents.

For example, the author is currently assessing the use of serials by marine biology graduate students in their theses over the past ten years at his institution. Bibliographies were downloaded from online theses and scans were made of bibliographies that were only available in print form. Each bibliography was converted to a Comma Separated Value spreadsheet and non-serial citations were removed. Information such as publication year, serial title, and the remainder of the citation were manually extracted and standardized in format. These sheets were then read by a Python script written to ingest the data into an SQL database for future analysis.

Such data processing can be a time-consuming process. A script had to be prepared to read, process, and store the data in a database. Particular challenges included the standardization of serial titles where titles had changed or been separated into two or more different publications. Additionally, errors existed in many citations, especially with the inaccurate abbreviation or expansion of journal titles. This necessitated the creation of a translation table to be used during automated processing, in order to ensure the correct standardization and matching of erroneous titles to accurate ones. However, once the data is processed and stored, SQL queries can be run to gain insight into the sources, online availability, and currency of information used by students, and patterns between date, source, subdiscipline, and so on can be analyzed.

The analysis of citations in a selection of articles is more efficient when the article citations are available within a citation database such as Web of Science. The process of downloading and aggregating data over many articles is still onerous, but the advantage over raw data analysis is that citations in such databases are usually more consistent in form.

Institutional Publication Outlet Data

If an understanding of the sources cited by an institution's authors is useful for collection management decisions, then it is also wise to maintain awareness of the publications in which those authors publish. Scholarship is created to be shared with others in the profession, and it follows that authors would seek to convey their scholarship through the most appropriate professional outlets available. This being so, the case for subscribing to online access for these titles is enhanced. It must be acknowledged, however, that there are factors, both within and beyond the immediate control of the author(s), which may influence the final choice of publication in which to present their scholarship. Numerous databases across many disciplines facilitate the searching of authors by their institutional affiliation in order to locate their scholarship. From a resulting set of articles, it is often reasonably simple to produce a ranked list of publication source titles.

Quantitative Measures of Quality or Esteem

Researchers have long been concerned with the quality or esteem of published scholarly and creative works. Naturally, those engaged in the creation of scholarship want to ensure that access to the best existing scholarship is available in order to continue producing high-quality research. In the academic world, in particular, scholars strive to ensure that their own publications have the greatest impact both as a contribution to scholarship in their fields, and also to ensure success in career advancement—namely tenure and post-tenure review.

Quantitative measures of the quality of scholarship primarily focus on articles published in journals, which have been the traditional forum for publishing primary research. Many other forms of scholarship, such as books, creative works, and media, are evaluated in the qualitative form of reviews that are made available in the serial publications of the discipline. Quantitative indicators of journal quality are developed using a variety of techniques and are evolving. Here, some of the most readily accessible and well-established indicators are considered.

Price

Perhaps the most basic and traditional indicator of quality is price. Assuming freedom of choice and a free market, one might surmise that the basic principles of supply and demand cause journal prices to find a natural level based upon their value to their audiences. High perceived value can command a high price and result in high demand. However, there are numerous factors that can bring this assumption into question. A journal that enjoys limited competition from other publications in terms of scope and content matter may benefit from the market attributes of a monopoly where prices may be held artificially high. Additionally, the discipline of a journal has a strong impact on price. The average prices of scientific journals, according to the Library Journal Periodicals Price Survey 2016, are substantially higher than those in the arts and humanities.[13] This causes price to be of little merit for interdisciplinary comparison of value. Lastly, the gradual move towards open-access articles and journals renders subscription price irrelevant for evaluation. For similar reasons, it is unlikely that the price paid by an author to publish within an open-access journal will become indicative of its quality.

Impact Factor

Perhaps one of the most ubiquitous indicators of quality, the then Institute for Scientific Information's (ISI, until recently Thomson Reuters, and now Clarivate Analytics) impact factor statistic was developed in the early 1960s by Garfield and Sher with the purpose of identifying the most significant scientific publications to include in the Science Citation Index. The impact factor is calculated "based on two elements: the numerator, which is the number of cites in the current year to any items published in the journal in the previous 2 years; and the denominator, the number of substantive articles (source items) published in the same 2 years."[14] Five-year impact factors have more recently been developed. Impact factors themselves are marketable, and Clarivate Analytics licenses a product entitled Journal Citation Reports (JCR, http://ipscience.thomsonreuters.com/product/journal-citation-reports/). High impact factors are still promoted by publishers whose journals are so evaluated by the metric. Criticism about potential bias in the calculation of impact factors as well as their potential influence on research decisions and strategies continue to cause angst about the prevalent use of this statistic.[15] Concern about the use of impact factors by administrators and decision-makers has been increasingly vocal among researchers whose work is often judged by the impact factor of the publication to which they contribute their work.[16] To their credit, Garfield and ISI/Thomson Reuters have long promoted the appropriate and contextual use of impact factors and encouraged the recognition of differences in citation activities and patterns among disciplines.

Eigenfactor Score, Article Influence Score, and Cost Effectiveness

Launched in 2007, the Eigenfactor Project sought to improve the process of evaluating the quality, or influence, of scholarly journals.[17] Using a ranking system similar to Google's page ranking, "Eigenfactor measures the total influence of a journal on the scholarly literature or, comparably, the total value provided by all of the articles published in that journal in a year. This seems the appropriate metric for making subscription decisions."[18] The Eigenfactor (EF) is calculated using five years of JCR citation data to ensure greater reliability than the original two-year span used for the impact factor. The original EF statistic represents a title's influence among all publications represented, where the sum of all EFs is equal to 100.[19] For example, in 2014 the second highest-ranked journal, *Nature,* had an EF of 1.499.

Criticism of the Eigenfactor includes the fact that it is not adjusted for journal size, so that larger journals tend towards higher EF scores.[20] Some would judge that a larger journal is larger because of its influence in the field. The EF scaling also makes the actual score a little challenging to interpret or compare. However, with the 2013 data set release, a Normalized Eigenfactor (EFn) was introduced to assist with interpretation. Normalization involves adjusting the EF score so that the mean score of all the journals assessed is 1. Therefore, *Nature*'s 2014 EFn of 167.9 demonstrates that its influence is 167.9 times more than the mean.

The article influence (AI) score is a metric developed to rank journals by the average article influence rather than the total influence of all articles. The AI metric is, like EFn, normalized so that the mean score of all articles assessed is 1. *Nature*'s 2014 AI score is 22.0, demonstrating that the average article in *Nature* has 22 times the influence of the mean article in JCR.

EF, EFn, and AI scores are freely available on the Eigenfactor Project website (http://eigenfactor.org) and are also incorporated into the JCR product. The partnership between the Eigenfactor Project and Thomson Reuters as well as the use of JCR proprietary data, however, means that EF, EFn, and AI metrics are not made freely available until six months after they appear in JCR.[21]

The Eigenfactor Project has also launched two useful cost-based tools that address subscription and open access journals. The cost effectiveness (CE) metric (conceptually the cost per Eigenfactor) is another normalized statistic where the mean cost effectiveness of all journals assessed is 1. Unlike EFn and AI, however, the lower the CE metric, the better the value for one's money. CE data is less current than the other metrics discussed so far. In 2011, *Nature*'s CE was 0.0887—significantly less than the mean. This could be interpreted as strong value for the investment in the subscription.

The metric for the cost effectiveness of publishing in an open access journal is calculated in a similar way, but is not normalized as is CE:

$$\text{Open Access CE} = 1000 * \text{Article Influence/article processing charges}$$

The Open Access CE metric is only available for fully open-access (non-hybrid) titles which are also included in JCR.[22] The interpretation of this metric is somewhat opposite to CE, in that the higher the CE is for open access journals, the better the value for one's money.

The relationship between cost and use has been a mainstay of statistics generated by librarians. Increasingly, the relationship between cost and metrics representing quality is being investigated. One regression study investigating the relationship between five metrics representing use or prestige and cost across three scientific fields found that Eigenfactor was the best predictor of price among sociology journals, while total cites was the best predictor in the fields of aquatic science and immunology. This study affirms the notion that varying citation patterns across disciplines render single or universal assessment tools inappropriate.[23]

CiteScore

The newest journal rating metric, CiteScore, was launched in 2016 by Elsevier and is freely available online along with data from the current SCImago Journal & Country Rank and Source Normalized Impact per Paper (https://journal metrics.scopus.com). CiteScore is conceptually similar to the impact factor in that it "calculates the average number of citations received in a calendar year by all items published in that journal in the preceding three years."[24] Impact factor, as already discussed, is based upon the number of items published in the preceding two years, or five years in the case of the five-year impact factor. Like impact factor, CiteScore is only available for a given year after that year has passed and calculations have been processed. Currently, CiteScore is available back to 2011. An additional current and dynamic metric, CiteScoreTracker, however, provides monthly updates for titles during the course of the current year. Additionally, percentile rankings within Scopus subject categories are listed. There remain, however, a number of fundamental differences between CiteScore and impact factor which are embodied by the data used in the calculations.

As competitors in the scholarly information market, Elsevier and Clarivate Analytics both produce leading indexing and abstracting products (Scopus and Web of Science respectively). CiteScore is calculated using Scopus data, while impact factor uses Journal Citation Reports (JCR) data. Elsevier claims that "Scopus has a broader coverage than the Journal Citation Reports, so that the amount of citations captured per serial title is on average around 10% higher."[25] Similarly, the scope of documents included in the data for the number of items published is broader in CiteScore than in impact factor, with CiteScore intentionally including everything from primary research articles to letters and errata, compared to impact factor's greater selectivity.[26]

As is appropriate, Elsevier, in introducing this new metric, explains at length the importance of not relying on a single metric for the assessment of a journal and not trying to compare CiteScores across disciplines that have differing publication and citation patterns. In acknowledging the similarities and distinctions between CiteScore and impact factor, the comparability of their respective journal rankings is also recognized to be challenging due to the differing subject categories and journal title counts therein.[27]

Hirsch H-Index

Developed in 2005, Hirsch's h-index was designed to quantitatively represent the impact of individual researchers, providing "an estimate of the importance, significance, and broad impact of a scientist's cumulative research contributions."[28] Shortly thereafter, the application of the h-index to journals as a complement to (not a substitute for) the impact factor was proposed, where a journal has an h-index of h when h of its papers have at least h citations. This is calculated by obtaining a list of all items published in a journal for a given time frame, sorting them according to times cited, and identifying "the highest rank number which is still lower than the corresponding 'Times Cited' value."[29]

Initial h-index studies typically used Web of Science/JCR data. As with other metrics, the publishing and citing characteristics of individual disciplines must be taken into account when making interdisciplinary comparisons, and the h-index has its strengths and weaknesses. By virtue of its calculation, a high h-index cannot be achieved for journals that publish few articles, regardless of their quality and impact, while their impact factor may be high. Conversely, the h-index is less influenced by outliers in the data compared to impact factor.[30]

The use of metrics based on Clarivate Analytics JCR is limited by the highly selective coverage of Clarivate Analytics indexes, a characteristic of its distinction. However, this does present a problem for fields not extensively represented in these indexes. With Google Scholar's (GS) rise in popularity, a study comparing h-index using GS data with impact factor for business and economics titles found strong correlation between the two measures for titles represented in both data sources, but also identified discipline-specific characteristics which caused divergence between them. The authors also note the inherent differences between source coverage in JCR and Google Scholar which, in the case of JCR, introduces bias towards sources published in the English language, published in the United States, and of the journal source type.[31] Perhaps this difference will diminish in the future as Clarivate Analytics continues to launch new indexes, including those representing publication in other countries, as with its Chinese and Russian Science Citation Indexes, KCI-Korean Journal Database, and SciELO Citation Index.

SCImago Journal Rank

Another journal rating system based upon Google Page Ranking, the SCImago Journal Rank Indicator (SJR), is freely available on the SCImago Journal & Country Rank platform at www.scimagojr.com/. Calculated from data in the Scopus database, SJR indicators are available from 1999 onwards and may be analyzed broadly by theme, selectively by subject, or by country.[32] The platform also provides an h-index metric for the journals assessed.

SJR is an indicator of prestige that is "designed to weight the citations according to the prestige of the citing journal, also taking into account the thematic closeness of the citing and the cited journals."[33] This method lends new value to citation analysis by deepening the analysis beyond basic citation counts and emphasizing interrelatedness according to discipline. Bias in assigned prestige due to journal size is mathematically eliminated by normalizing the overall calculated prestige of a journal using its ratio of citable documents compared to all citable documents in the data set.[34]

Source Normalized Impact per Paper

Continuing the pursuit of a journal impact metric that accounts for differences in citation practices among disciplines, the Source Normalized Impact per Paper (SNIP) was created to "measure[s] a journal's contextual citation impact, taking into account characteristics of its subject field, especially the frequency at which authors cite other papers in their reference lists, the rapidity of maturing of citation impact, and the extent to which the database used for the assessment covers the field's literature."[35] Elsevier freely provides current SNIP data along with CiteScore and SJR data at https://journalmetrics.scopus.com/.

Accounting for interdisciplinary differences in citation rates, SNIP gains credibility for its objective statistical comparison of journal impact across disciplines. SNIP is calculated as the ratio of raw impact per paper (RIP) to its database citation potential (DCP) over the preceding three years for a given year of analysis. DCP is calculated in the context of the data set, that is, Scopus, being used.[36] It follows that two journals with the same RIP but coming from fields with distinctly different citation patterns (represented by DCP) will have different SNIP values. In other words, the journal with the lower likelihood of being cited will have a lower DCP and, by definition, a higher SNIP. It is, in a sense, a system in which reward is issued for overcoming the odds against accomplishment.

Hybrid Metrics

Hybrid metrics have also been developed that involve the combination of two or more existing metrics. The rationale behind combining multiple metrics is to mitigate the different rankings resulting from the varying principles and calculations underlying each of them. Hsu et al. developed a Standardized Average (SA) Index based upon Borda counting principles by simply averaging the relative journal impact (JIF) factor and h-index values for journals. The authors found that in the field of health care science, the SA index has a high correlation with impact factor and h-index and is more accurate than the h-index. They also assert that the metric can be used for interdisciplinary comparison.[37]

Unlike Hsu et al., Bradshaw and Brook used journal ranks, rather than relative metric values, from five different metrics (impact factor, Immediacy Index, SNIP, SJR, and GS h-index) to develop a κ-resampled composite journal rank of scientific journals in six small sample groups. When the composite ranked titles for a small ecology and multidisciplinary journal set were compared to the same set qualitatively ranked by publishing ecologists, the new metric was validated for the field of ecology.[38]

Journal Usage Factor

Implemented by the United Kingdom Serials Group (UKSG) and Project COUNTER in 2007 and currently in beta with Project COUNTER at the time of writing, the Journal Usage Factor (UFJ) statistic differs fundamentally from citation-based metrics in that it is based on the principle that the impact of a journal can be judged by how much it is read, not merely by how often it is cited.[39] The concept of the usage factor can be applicable to numerous formats of online publication, and the first release of the COUNTER Code of Practice for Usage Factors in 2014 is structured to reflect this.[40] Usage Factors represent the overall use of a publication, rather than institution-specific use, as is the case with other COUNTER metrics.

The Code of Practice specifies UFJ to be calculated as "the Median Value in a set of ordered full text article usage data (i.e., the number of successful full text article requests) for a specified Usage Period of articles published in a journal during a specified Publication Period."[41] The use of a median value eliminates the skewing of data by a few highly used articles, including mitigating the effect of "gaming" of articles to boost usage counts.[42] The Code of Practice also specifies which content types and article versions may be included in the data for two UFJs (UFJ1a: All Content, and UFJ1b: Articles Only), which is collected over a period of two calendar years. Thus, the UFJ is specified, for example, as 2015/2016. A central registry of Usage Factors is intended to provide open access to these metrics.[43]

Web of Science Usage Count

Thomson Reuters, in release 5.19 of its Web of Science platform in 2015, began providing two indicators of usage: Usage Count—Last 180 Days (a rolling, current indicator) and Usage Count—Since 2013 (cumulative data since February 1, 2013, when data began to be gathered).[44] A subscription product, Web of Science provides indexes with no full-text content, but is certainly a premier discovery tool for scholarly research. The Web of Science Usage Count, therefore, represents an analysis further upstream in documenting use than the UFJ and further yet than citation metrics. A subscription to content on Web of Science is required to be able to access Usage Count data.

The Usage Count definition of use is based upon a perceived level of interest based upon user behavior. This is a useful data point, particularly in the context of a citation index. It should be noted that there is no one definition of use for scholarly resources. Whether a document is cited or not, its value to the researcher should not be taken for granted. Also, until a publication is actually cited there can be no certainty that it has been read, and even then, a citation still does not provide any guarantee that an article was, in fact, read.[45] In Web of Science, a use is documented when a user attempts to link out to full text from the item record or result list or when the user saves or exports the article metadata. The Usage Count is an integer representing the number of times the article record was used. Safeguards are implemented to eliminate automated or unintentional activity.[46]

Developing Indicators—Social Media

While academic journals were the traditional outlets for researchers to present and discuss research, current communication technology offers the potential for exceedingly fast engagement with research. Social media have revolutionized the speed and scope of communication in society today. When an article is published online, the scholarly conversation may be started immediately with sharing, critiquing, and building upon the latest research among socially networked readers months before the first citing article is ever published. This interest in specific articles is beginning to be documented in online platforms in the form of article-level social media metrics. For example, Elsevier's Scopus platform includes information provided by Altmetric.com (http://altmetric.com) about research mentioned in social media and other informal online publications, like blogs.[47] This data is indicative of early interest in published articles and may provide early insight into the rate at which articles in specific publications are engaged by readers soon after publication.

Measures of Uniqueness

The combination of individual and big deal subscriptions along with aggregated full-text databases typically results in duplicated access to some online resources. Duplicate access is not necessarily complete in terms of the extent of coverage of a title. The variety of available e-resource acquisition models such as complete coverage, cumulative current coverage, rolling current coverage, and archival coverage may result in some duplication while potentially necessitating more than one access point or platform to achieve the desired breadth of access to a particular title. Management of e-resources, particularly during times of static or cut budgets, includes the cessation of subscriptions to save money. In order to minimize the negative impact of deselection upon the researchers served, overlap analysis is undertaken to identify existing alternate access points.

E-resource management and delivery tools, such as Serials Solutions 360 Core or EBSCO A-to-Z (transitioning to Full Text Finder), offer e-resource overlap analysis tools based upon a subscribing institution's full-text database and serial holdings. Overlap analysis may be performed for an entire collection or for smaller portions of the collection. An overlap analysis generates absolute and relative indicators of uniqueness and, often, title lists of unique and duplicated titles. Such overlap analysis is based upon an institution's existing collection.

Overlap analysis tools emphasize full-text coverage, but when index/citation coverage must be considered, other solutions may be necessary. Mercer University librarians undertook both full-text and non-full-text analysis of database coverage of journals in 2011 as part of a consolidation and deselection process. Title and coverage spreadsheets were obtained from vendor customer service representatives or vendor websites and were standardized in format. These were then ingested and processed by a Python script and stored in a complexly structured SQL database. A web portal was created to provide access to reports and enabled decision-makers to evaluate databases down to the individual title level. Using this tool, factual data was provided to support strategic deselection decisions. Such a project requires programming expertise, is very time-consuming, and presents a number of challenges. Data must be standardized for ingestion, raw data must be programmatically normalized, journal title variations must be standardized, and unique identifiers utilized or created.[48] The ISSN is the standard identifier for journals, but not all database records have ISSNs for every title, many records have different print and online ISSNs represented, journal titles change and ISSNs sometimes change with them, and in large data sets errors will exist.[49]

Qualitative Data

Qualitative data for the assessment of electronic resources addresses aspects that are often subjective. This data is generated using a variety of methods, such as general surveys; randomly administered point-of-use surveys;[50] exercises including ranking, sorting, and grouping; and evaluative narratives. Qualitative data can be quantified to some extent by the use of instruments such as the Likert scale, in which responses are ranked on a fixed scale (representing levels of perceived importance, agreement, etc.), thereby supporting comparison and some limited quantitative analyses.

Platform and Database Quality

Aside from the full-text content offered by a publisher or aggregator, the platform on which it is searched or accessed can positively or negatively impact a researcher's experience. Intuitive websites are the result of much research and effort, quality search experiences result from the underlying taxonomies, and unique features add value to content.

The quality of indexing of databases helps to distinguish them from each other. Web of Science is built upon a long and illustrious past of helping researchers locate journal articles in quality sources, due to its rigorous selectivity and quality indexing. Zoological Record includes a taxonomic index, while education and medicine databases often include indexing to discipline-specific taxonomies. While the user may not be fully aware of an index's comprehensive underlying infrastructure, its effectiveness is reflected by the ease with which the user can search and discover desired information with precision.

With ever-increasing expectations for personalized web use experiences, platforms have been developed with additional features. Many mainstream database, e-journal, and e-book platforms now offer personal accounts enabling features such as saving search strategies and records, receiving search alerts, customizing search preferences, citation and bibliographic management, and researcher networking. Even though these features are unlikely to be a primary driving force in selection or deselection decisions, a documented awareness of their importance to the research community can help distinguish between two otherwise similar resources.

Coverage of Content

The nature of the information industry assigns monetary value to scholarship. In fields like science, current scholarship commands a premium over older information, whereas in the arts and humanities, information may retain its monetary value more consistently over time. When an institution's subscriptions offer multiple access points for a particular journal, the coverage, or the date range of access, may vary between them. One common frustration for researchers is the presence of embargos on access to current scholarship in aggregated databases, which may range from months to a year or more.

In scientific fields, especially, librarians may subscribe to an e-journal directly with the publisher just to ensure immediate access to published articles, even though potentially full retrospective coverage, except for the embargo period, may exist within one or more aggregated databases already available at the institution. Data about embargoes should be made available in order to ensure that collection management decisions and e-resource use interpretations are made with appropriate contextual awareness. Such data can be obtained directly from database vendors or, perhaps more efficiently, from services such as EBSCO A to Z or Serials Solutions 360 Core.

Completeness of Content

While many e-resources are available in complete form, such as a PDF (Portable Document Format) replica of a printed journal article in its entirety, this is not always the case in some aggregated databases. Electronic content is usually made available as a PDF document, an HTML document, or often in both forms. PDF documents usually provide a complete article, but HTML documents sometimes provide only textual content, omitting images and tables. This may vary within an individual title, between titles on a platform, or may be consistent across all titles on a platform. It is important to note that indications of full-text coverage made within e-journal finder software, such as EBSCO A to Z or Serials Solutions 360 Core, do not distinguish between full textual-only coverage and full text (including all images, tables, figures, etc.) coverage.

For example, a recent investigation into coverage of *Systematic Botany* at the author's institution established that while Serials Solutions 360 Core presented full-text archival coverage as available in JSTOR (an aggregated database), current coverage in IngentaConnect (a direct subscription), and current coverage in Academic OneFile (a GALE CENGAGE Learning aggregated database), there were variations in the completeness of article content. Investigations of randomly selected articles identified that while both the publisher and JSTOR platforms provided complete articles, Academic OneFile provided textual content with no images or figures for the same articles. Similarly, LexisNexis Academic, a premier database aggregating broad coverage of newspaper publications, only provides the textual content from newspaper articles. This serves as a reminder that careful investigation is often necessary, rather than relying purely on metadata for decision-making, and indicators of completeness should be added to metadata about e-resources.

Curriculum Needs

The solicitation of input from teaching faculty at academic institutions is a very important part of collection management. Whether soliciting input for new information resources, checking satisfaction with current holdings, or approaching the faculty with a need to reduce subscriptions due to budget limitations, the importance of faculty members' input cannot be underestimated. Members of the faculty are often leading practitioners in their fields, possessing significant subject-specific knowledge and acting as the primary influence in their students' academic progress.

It is also important to recognize the cyclical aspect of a curriculum. Some members of the faculty teach the same course year after year, while some subjects are taught by one of a pool of professors in turn, over a two-year or more cycle, each potentially teaching with differing tools and emphases. Higher-level courses are not always taught every year, so they may not be in the forefront of consideration during the "off year" of the cycle. These factors may influence the demand for specific resources in a cyclical manner.

Librarians must strive to support the faculty's efforts both in research and in teaching, and can gain valuable insight from their expertise. Regardless of the quality or extensiveness of feedback obtained from the faculty about library subscriptions, holdings, and changes thereto, the diplomatic effectiveness of offering partnership in decision-making can have far-reaching benefits, while the opposite may be true for ineffective or negligent communication. A 2012 study investigated librarian and faculty perceptions of the services provided by subject liaisons to faculty in US university and college libraries. Of thirteen documented services provided by liaisons, three were more highly rated in importance by faculty than by librarians and, notably, included the participation of faculty in collection management decisions.[51]

Feedback from the faculty can be obtained in a variety of ways, and multiple techniques may need to be used to account for differing communication styles and technology preferences. Interviews, online surveys, and spreadsheet-based data/responses are a few options, the responses from which can be synthesized and evaluated as a whole.

Accreditation Needs

An institution may be periodically evaluated by a number of accrediting bodies to maintain its standards of performance. While universities are evaluated broadly, although with great detail, individual academic departments may also be assessed by accrediting bodies specific to their individual disciplines. Accreditation may include an evaluation of library resources and services specific to the discipline. It is prudent, therefore, for subject librarians to maintain awareness of any information resource requirements for the accreditation of their assigned departments as well as the reaccreditation cycle of the department. This data about e-resources and accreditation should be documented so that it does not have to be rediscovered every accreditation cycle, although reconfirmation should be scheduled as appropriate.

STATISTICS

In the context of e-resource metrics, statistics are numerical representations of concepts that cannot be represented by a single raw data item. That is, they consist of two or more data items combined together in logical and meaningful ways to demonstrate proportion, change, and so on. They are also used as a standardized indicator for the purpose of comparison; for example, using the cost-per-use statistic to determine if a subscription or the payment of ILL and copyright fees is the fiscally responsible access method for a journal.

Statistics are an important tool for decision-makers because it is difficult to identify patterns, trends, anomalies, outliers, and so on in masses of raw data. Statistics are best used to draw attention to data that require further investigation to identify if significant changes or events have occurred. Recognizing the limitations of statistics and data is key to avoiding excessive reliance on these indicators. In the case of electronic resource use, statistics reflect the raw data and the raw data reflects events. Neither statistics nor data can explain why a phenomenon was observed. They simply help to identify that it occurred. Consider the following cost-per-use analysis:

> The cost of an e-journal last year was $2,400 and full-text articles were viewed 460 times.
>
> The cost per use last year was $5.22
>
> If the cost per use this year is $6.45, can it be assumed that the journal is of less use or value for money than previously? The cost-per-use statistic cannot explain the change in the data. Any of the following could have caused the change:
>
> $2,967/460 = $6.45 (increase in price, static use)
>
> $2,400/372 = $6.45 (static price, decrease in use)
>
> $2,612/405 = $6.45 (increase in price, decrease in use)
>
> $3,302/512 = $6.45 (increase in price, increase in use)

This example serves to demonstrate that the cost-per-use statistic is useful for alerting managers to a change in the ratio of cost to use, which necessitates a closer look at the raw data.

Each of the data items contributing to cost per use has its own potential nuances and complications. The cost of one e-resource may be determined by subscriptions to other resources. Package deals complicate the identification of the actual cost of an individual journal, especially if it is included free, subject to the ongoing maintenance of other subscriptions. The purchase of back files may cause expenditure in one year to be much higher than in typical years which, if insufficiently documented, might feed into misconceptions about the cost per use. Similarly, the definition of "use" may vary. The word "use" in "cost per use" is often considered to be a full-text download because this offers at least some certainty of derived value.[52] However, this cannot be so with an index/abstract database. Perhaps use might be considered to be a search, or a record view in such a case. This is further complicated by a database with partial full-text content. Can it still not be considered to have been used if the user does not download a full-text document? What if the link resolver is used to access the full text elsewhere? Clearly, use can be represented differently according to context.

Comparing cost per use between e-resources must also be undertaken with contextual awareness. It is reasonable to compare the cost per use of similar products such as Academic Search Complete (EBSCO) and ProQuest Research Library. Each of these databases is broad in subject coverage and is relevant for many areas of research. Similarly, it may be worth comparing cost per use for competing journals within a field. However, to compare the cost per use of an Institute of Physics (IOP) journal package to Academic Search Complete introduces several problems. A scientific product generally falls within a higher price range, by virtue of the information contained therein. Additionally, the user base of IOP journals within, for example, a university may be limited to one or two relatively small academic units while Academic Search Complete is utilized by a broad audience. Lastly, the amount of content contained in the two products may vary substantially, thereby resulting in differing likelihood of use.

Comparison, then, must be undertaken with an awareness of contextual factors that may influence the cost-per-use metric. The challenge of studying metrics for an individual year is that many factors can influence the use of an e-resource. However, studying multiyear changes in data helps to identify trends that can be very informative. This can be accomplished by studying and documenting percentage changes in specific data from a chosen baseline. The University of North Carolina undertook a system-wide study of e-journal use and cost in 2012, paying particular attention to percentage changes occurring between 2009 and 2011 in cost per title, cost per use, and actual expenditures on e-journals. Study was also made of the percentage changes in the number of titles considered to be highly used, within three tiers of designation of "high use."[53]

The possibilities for the generation of statistics are extensive. It is important to remember that synthesizing multiple data items into statistics must be undertaken carefully in order to avoid attributing meaning to inappropriately synthesized data. Additionally, statistics only offer the significance or meaning attributed to them by those who choose to use them. When identifying data to synthesize, it is important to consider the concepts that one wishes to represent, including:

- the size and makeup of the user population, for example, census of counties or full-time equivalent (FTE) count of academic institutions, FTE within specific departments or research fields
- the cost, for example, the cost of subscription/acquisition, processing/maintenance costs
- appropriate measures of use of the e-resource, for example, sessions, searches, record views, streaming, downloads, and so on
- application of output of the e-resource, for example, evidence of outward linking (indexes) or citation (full-text resources)

Statistics are only as reliable as the data from which they are constructed is consistent. Any inaccuracies or inconsistencies in data are automatically reflected in the resulting statistics, unless the statistic is actually designed to mitigate that. For example, if two demographically similar counties of 15,000 and 25,000 residents are provided access to a genealogy database, it would seem reasonable, all other things being equal, to assume that use would be greater in the county with the larger population. The usage data alone is not comparable because it represents use by different-sized populations. Generating a statistic that accounts for the population size differences lends context to the usage data, making comparison more legitimate. Thus, dividing use by population size results in a per-capita use statistic for each county, which can be compared. It should be noted, however, that numerous other demographic factors could also influence use. Some examples of data synthesis to generate statistics include:

- Standardized statistics
  Per capita—standardized (divided) by population count,
    for example, uses per person, cost per person, uses per
    chemistry department FTE (for a chemistry package)
  Per content unit—standardized (divided) by item size, for
    example, cost per journal title (within a database or
    package), cost per article (based upon number of articles
    in a journal in a given year)
  Per use—standardized by use, for example, cost per search,
    cost per download, cost per link out (from an index)
- Ratio statistics—comparing data within a category such as use,
  for example, searches per session, downloads per search
- Time statistics—percentage change in data over a specified time
  range

As previously discussed, no individual data item or statistic can provide sufficient information to make a fully informed decision about an e-resource. Each adds to the understanding of the utility, or value, of an e-resource to the community in light of the investment made to make it available. An attempt was made in recent years to synthesize several data items and statistics programmatically to generate recommendations for the review of serials at a Georgia academic institution. OARS (Ongoing Automated Review System) was developed to provide an experimental and flexible weighting of cost, use, Eigenfactor article influence percentile, and faculty ratings in order to help identify journal titles for potential cancellation.[54] The project served as an introduction to the complexity of synthesizing, weighting, and comparing data and statistics across a whole collection, where cost, use, and journal influence vary by discipline and department size.

ORGANIZING AND REPORTING

Institutional Capacity

The broad array of metrics discussed thus far presents a challenge for e-resource managers. It is not feasible to gather and analyze every conceivable data item and statistic. It is prudent, therefore, to develop an awareness of institutional capacity for organizing and processing metrics and producing reports. Institutional capacity in this context may be considered to be the ability of the institution, or a specific department, to accomplish a task with its current personnel (embodying their individual and collective skill sets and tools), while not neglecting the other responsibilities that must also be satisfied by the same personnel. With many libraries striving to function effectively with less personnel than before the Great Recession that began in 2008, institutional capacity to accomplish a task or project is best established in strategic dialogue with decision-makers. An open discussion of needs and expectations should also consider the costs, challenges, and benefits of producing the information, while agreeing on the select indicators that will best inform decisions.

The University of Mississippi library undertook a 2013 analysis of the cost of gathering cost and usage data, identifying that over $6,000 of staff time was invested in this, which was still considered more cost-effective than outsourcing the process to a third party.[55] Librarians at Texas A&M University-Corpus Christi developed a two-tier approach to evaluation. Searches, sessions, downloads, and link outs comprise the first set of data for analysis in comparison to a baseline derived from multiple e-resources. If further investigation is deemed necessary, other metrics are employed, including overlap analysis data, citations, journal usage, and impact factor.[56] This two-tier approach necessitates limited data for the initial evaluation of all serial titles, and it uses staff time wisely by only requiring additional metrics for titles that warrant further analysis.

In many university libraries, subject liaisons are a logical asset for approaching the library's constituents to undertake qualitative analysis. In other libraries, community representation to the library may exist in the form of a committee or board. Whatever the context, it is important to identify and prepare individuals or teams to undertake the gathering and organizing of qualitative data in a consistent manner.

Storing and Accessing Data

E-resource data reflecting usage, cost, and prestige is often provided in the form of tab-delimited, Comma Separated Value (CSV) or MS Excel files and can be stored in those file formats. CSV and tab-delimited files can easily be converted to, analyzed, and reported in spreadsheet software. However, some electronic resource management (ERM) systems ingest usage data in the COUNTER XML-based format defined by the SUSHI protocol and store the data in SQL-based data structures. Others, like the open-source CORAL ERM system (http:// http://coral-erm.org/), require the ingestion of simple file formats like tab-delimited data before storing them in SQL tables. ERM systems usually provide data reporting interfaces as well as the opportunity to download the data, often in a spreadsheet format.

The creation and use of data bring about an additional responsibility—the preservation and ongoing accessibility of the data. Not only must data be stored in a manner that protects it from inadvertent destruction, but it must also be preserved from software changes by migrating file formats in a timely manner. Large institutions increasingly incorporate data management into workflows, but smaller operations may still rely on initiatives taken at the grassroots level. Data must also be made available for use, subject to any contractual restrictions on access.

Raw data and calculated metrics are best preserved in simple, nonpropri-etary file formats for maximum flexibility, although it would be prudent to store them in multiple file formats. Data in systems that are SQL-based can be exported as files for backup. Similarly, the media on which data are stored should also be current, and preferably of several types. This is because the rate at which hardware and software technologies are evolving, as well as the life expectancy of hardware and storage media, have the potential to render specific formats and media redundant or inaccessible in a relatively short space of time. The migration of data from original file formats and media should be undertaken regularly to ensure ongoing accessibility.

Designing Reports and Recommendations

Reports and recommendations are the culmination of all the effort expended in gathering, synthesizing, and analyzing diverse data and calculating statistics. It is important that reports and recommendations convey the required information for decision-making, while referencing the sources from which the data was obtained in order to facilitate access to the raw data. Having already agreed with administrators upon the indicators to be used for decision-making, reports should clearly communicate the indicators along with any necessary information needed to make accurate contextual interpretations. Recommendations are not always popular, particularly when they are to cancel e-resources. Therefore, the underlying report is important in presenting factual evidence while demonstrating that care and attention were taken in reaching the recommendation.[57]

Data Visualization

Tabular data provides an array of individual data items or statistics, the value of each of which is intended to be read and interpreted. Graphical or visual representation of data, however, enables many viewers to identify trends or accomplish comparison more easily than by looking at data or statistics. Each style of data representation has value for specific purposes. Many types of visualization exist today, ranging from traditional graphs to heat maps, tree maps, and scientific data visualization.

As with other aspects of managing electronic resources, data visualization can be accomplished in a variety of ways. Departments with programming expertise can utilize a programming language, for example Python, and graphing or visualization libraries, such as Matplotlib or Plotly, to generate visual representations of data. Third-party web applications, like Google Charts, enable dynamic generation of visualizations using a web API. Microsoft Excel facilitates the generation of graphs from data contained within workbooks. Some ERM systems provide visual representation of e-resource data, while dedicated visualization software provides many potential variations for the visualization of data.

At Ohio State University's Thompson Library, Tableau Desktop business intelligence software was chosen to present visualizations of data about subject guides and library website use in foreign languages. An advantage of this proprietary software over some of the alternatives mentioned above is the ability to synthesize or juxtapose visualizations of data upon "dashboards" and then manipulate it to exclude, for example, outliers or emphasize subsets of the data. This level of interaction assists library staff with the preparation of data visualizations in a dynamic context in order to create the most useful and meaningful representation of data for reporting.[58]

Whatever the method chosen to create data visualizations, each visual representation of data must be clearly labeled and easy to interpret accurately. As with statistics, any anomalies or fundamental differences in the data used to create visualizations, as well as contextual information necessary to make an accurate interpretation, must be adequately described and communicated.

Because data visualization techniques emphasize particular aspects of data sets and draw the readers' attention to points of comparison or the observance of trends, a successful representation will be accompanied by appropriate narrative in an effective and cohesive report.

CONCLUSION

Extensive potential exists for the analysis of metrics associated with e-resource use, esteem, uniqueness, quality, and significance to the institution. Institutions are encouraged to develop an analytics strategy in order to identify key indicators for the assessment of e-resources, while remaining appropriately scaled to the capacity of the institution to gather, analyze, and report the data for decision-makers. The chosen method for synthesizing data of varying quality and granularity from a variety of sources should include guidance on identifying and reporting data disparities in order to ensure appropriate comparison. A data preservation plan will ensure the availability of metrics into the future. It remains to remind the reader that analytics provides a perspective of the facts about e-resources, yet requires contextual expertise for effective interpretation.

NOTES

1. "Library Budget Predictions for 2016," Publishers Communication Group, www.pcgplus.com/wp-content/uploads/2016/05/Library-Budget-Prediction-2016-Final.pdf.
2. Stephen Bosch and Kittie Henderson, "Fracking the Ecosystem | Periodicals Price Survey 2016," *Library Journal,* last modified April 21, 2016, http://lj.libraryjournal.com/2016/04/publishing/fracking-the-ecosystem-periodicals-price-survey-2016.
3. Narda Tafuri, "Prices of U.S. and Foreign Published Materials," in *Library and Book Trade Almanac 2015,* ed. Dave Bogart (Medford, NJ: Information Today, 2015), 416–52, https://alair.ala.org/bitstream/handle/11213/4934/LMPIArticle2015.pdf?sequence=1&isAllowed=y.
4. Rachael A. Cohen and Angie Thorpe, "Discovering User Behavior: Applying Usage Statistics to Shape Frontline Services," *The Serials Librarian* 69, no. 1 (2015): 29–46, doi:10.1080/0361526X.2015.1040194.
5. Graham Stone and Bryony Ramsden, "Library Impact Data Project: Looking for the Link between Library Usage and Student Attainment," *College & Research Libraries* 74, no. 6 (2013): 546–59, doi:10.5860/cr112–406.
6. Charles R. McClure, Lauren H. Mandel, and Lynnsey K. Weissenberger, "Designing a User and Usage Database to Promote, Market, and Demonstrate the Value of Selected Statewide Databases: The Florida Electronic Library as an Example," *Library Management* 33, no. 6/7 (2012): 365–73, doi:10.1108/01435121211266168.

7. "COUNTER Code of Practice," COUNTER, www.projectcounter.org/wp-content/themes/project-counter-2016/pdfs/COUNTER-code-of-practice.pdf?v=1470847040.
8. "SUSHI for Librarians," National Information Standards Organization, www.niso.org/workrooms/sushi/librarians.
9. "COUNTER Code of Practice," COUNTER, www.projectcounter.org/wp-content/themes/project-counter-2016/pdfs/COUNTER-code-of-practice.pdf?v=1470847040.
10. Deborah D. Blecic, Joan D. Fiscella, and Stephen E. Wiberley Jr., "Measurement of Use of Electronic Resources: Advances in Use Statistics and Innovations in Resource Functionality," *College & Research Libraries* 68, no. 1 (2007): 26–44, doi:10.5860/cr1.68.1.26.
11. Philip M. Davis and Jason S. Price, "E-Journal Interface Can Influence Usage Statistics: Implications for Libraries, Publishers, and Project COUNTER," *Journal of the American Society for Information Science and Technology* 57, no. 9 (2006): 1243–48, doi:10.1002/asi.20405.
12. "Log Format," OCLC, last modified March 2, 2015, www.oclc.org/support/services/ezproxy/documentation/cfg/logformat.en.html.
13. Bosch and Henderson, "Fracking the Ecosystem."
14. Eugene Garfield, "The Agony and the Ecstasy—The History and Meaning of the Journal Impact Factor," presentation, International Congress on Peer Review and Biomedical Publication, Chicago, September 16, 2005, p. 5, http://garfield.library.upenn.edu/papers/jifchicag02005.pdf?utm_source=false&utm_medium=false&utm_campaign=false.
15. Christian Nansen and William Meikle, "Journal Impact Factors and the Influence of Age and Number of Citations," *Molecular Plant Pathology* 15, no. 3 (2014): 223–25, doi:10.1111/mpp.12096.
16. Rebecca Nesbitt, "You're Not Alone in Hating Impact Factors," *Royal Society of Biology Blog*, March 31, 2015, http://blog.rsb.org.uk/youre-not-alone-in-hating-impact-factors.
17. "Journal Ranking," Eigenfactor.org, www.eigenfactor.org/advanced.php.
18. Carl Bergstrom, "Eigenfactor: Measuring the Value and Prestige of Scholarly Journals," *College & Research Libraries News* 68, no. 5 (2007): 315, http://crln.acrl.org/content/68/5/314.full.pdf+html.
19. "About the Eigenfactor Project," Eigenfactor.org, www.eigenfactor.org/about.php.
20. Tibor Braun, Wolfgang Glänzel, and András Schubert, "A Hirsch-Type Index for Journals," *Scientometrics* 69, no. 1 (2006): 169–73, doi:10.1007/s11192–006–0147–4.
21. "About the Eigenfactor Project."
22. Jevin D. West, Theodore Bergstrom, and Carl T. Bergstrom, "Cost Effectiveness of Open Access Publications," *Economic Inquiry* 52, no. 4 (2014): 1315–21, doi:10.1111/ecin.12117.
23. Geoffrey S. Shideler and Rafael J. Araújo, "Measures of Scholarly Journal Quality Are Not Universally Applicable to Determining Value of Advertised Annual Subscription Price," *Scientometrics* 107 (2016): 963–73, doi:10.1007/s11192–016–1943–0.
24. "CiteScore Metrics FAQs," Journal Metrics [Elsevier]: 5, last modified December 2016, https://journalmetrics.scopus.com/downloads/CiteScoreMetrics_FAQ_Scopus_Dec2016_LO.pdf.

25. Ibid., 10.

26. Ibid.

27. Ibid.

28. J. E. Hirsch, "An Index to Quantify an Individual's Scientific Research Output," *Proceedings of the National Academy of Sciences* 102, no. 46 (2005): 16572, doi:10.1073/pnas.0507655102.

29. Braun, Glänzel, and Schubert, "A Hirsch-Type Index for Journals," 170.

30. Pascal Bador and Thierry Lafouge, "Comparative Analysis between Impact Factor and H-Index for Psychiatry Journals," *The Canadian Journal of Information and Library Science* 35, no. 2 (2011): 109–21, doi:10.1353/ils.2011.0009.

31. Anne-Wil Harzing and Ron van der Wal, "A Google Scholar H-Index for Journals: An Alternative Metric to Measure Journal Impact in Economics and Business," *Journal of the Association for Information Science and Technology* 60, no. 1 (2009): 41–46, doi:10.1002/asi.20953.

32. "About Us," SCImago, www.scimagojr.com/aboutus.php.

33. Vicente P. Guerrero-Bote and Félix Moya-Anegón, "A Further Step Forward in Measuring Journals' Scientific Prestige: The SJR2 Indicator," *Journal of Informetrics* 6 (2012): 675, doi:10.1016/j.joi.2012.07.001.

34. Ibid.

35. Henk F. Moed, "Measuring Contextual Citation Impact of Scientific Journals," *Journal of Informetrics* 4 (2010): 266, doi:10.1016/j.joi.2010.01.002.

36. Waltmann Ludo, Nees Jan van Eck, Thed N. van Leeuwen, and Martijn S. Visser, "Some Modifications to the SNIP Journal Impact Indicator," *Journal of Informetrics* 7 (2013): 272–85, doi:10.1016/j.joi.2012.11.011.

37. Wen-Chin Hsu, Chih-Fong Tsai, and Jia-Huan Li, "A Hybrid Indicator for Journal Ranking," *Online Information Review* 39, no. 7 (2015): 858–69, doi:10.1108/OIR-11-2014-0277.

38. Corey J. A. Bradshaw and Barry W. Brook, "How to Rank Journals," *PLoS ONE* 11, no. 3 (2016), doi:10.1371/journal.pone.0149852.

39. Oliver Pesch, "Usage Factor for Journals: A New Measure for Scholarly Impact," *The Serials Librarian* 63, no. 3–4 (2012): 261–68, doi:10.1080/0361526X.2012.722522.

40. "Introduction to Release 1 of the COUNTER Code of Practice for Usage Factors," COUNTER, last modified October 2015, http://beta.projectcounter.org/usage_factor.html.

41. "The COUNTER Code of Practice for Usage Factors for Journals," COUNTER, http://beta.projectcounter.org/documents/Usage%20Factor%20for%20Journals.pdf.

42. Pesch, "Usage Factor for Journals."

43. "The COUNTER Code of Practice for Usage Factors: Release 1," COUNTER, March 2014, http://beta.projectcounter.org/documents/UF_CoP_R1_October_2015.pdf.

44. "Web of Science Release Notes v5.19," Thomson Reuters, 2015, http://wokinfo.com/media/pdf/wos_release_519.pdf.

45. Xianwen Wang, Zhichao Fang, and Xiaoling Sun, "Usage Patterns of Scholarly Articles on Web of Science: A Study on Web of Science Usage Count," *Scientometrics* 109 (2016): 917–26, doi:10.1007/s11192-016-2093-0.

46. "Web of Science Release Notes v5.19."

47. "Altmetric for Scopus," Altmetric.com, last modified June 21, 2016, https://help .altmetric.com/support/solutions/articles/6000062186-altmetric-for-scopus.

48. Jeremy M. Brown and Geoffrey P. Timms, "Striving for Uniqueness: Data-Driven Database Deselection," *Proceedings of the Charleston Library Conference 2012* (West Lafayette, IN: Purdue University Press, 2013), 209–15, doi:10.5703/1288284315104.

49. Ylva Gavel and Lars Iselid, "Web of Science and Scopus: A Journal Title Overlap Study," *Online Information Review* 32, no. 1 (2008): 8–21, doi:10.1108/ 14684520810865958.

50. Martha Kyrillidou, Terry Plum, and Bruce Thompson, "Evaluating Usage and Impact of Networked Electronic Resources through Point-of-Use Surveys: A MINES for Libraries Study," *The Serials Librarian* 59, no. 2 (2010): 159–83, doi:10.1080/ 03615261003674057.

51. Julie Arendt and Megan Lotts, "What Liaisons Say about Themselves and What Faculty Say about Their Liaisons, a U.S. Survey," *Libraries and the Academy* 12, no. 2 (2012): 155–77, doi:10.1353/pla.2012.0015.

52. Michael M. Smith and Jane A. Smith, "What's the Use? A Cost-per-Use Study of Selected Business Databases," *International Information & Library Review* 48, no. 1 (2016): 11–20, doi:10.1080/10572317.2016.1146037.

53. Virginia Bacon and Patrick Carr, "Assessing Value through Cross-Institutional Comparisons: A Discussion of the 2012 University of North Carolina System-Wide E-Journal Survey," *Serials Review* 39, no. 2 (2013): 86–92, doi:10.1016/j.serrev.2013 .04.005.

54. Geoffrey P. Timms and Jonathan H. Harwell, "OARS: Toward Automating the Ongoing Subscription Review," *Proceedings of the Charleston Library Conference 2010* (West Lafayette, IN: Purdue University Press, 2012), 119–23, doi:10.5703/1288284314826.

55. Christina Torbert, "Cost-per-Use versus Hours-per-Report: Usage Reporting and the Value of Staff Time," *The Serials Librarian* 68 (2015): 163–67, doi:10.1080/036152 6X.2015.1017705.

56. Sarah Sutton, "A Model for Electronic Resources Value Assessment," *The Serials Librarian* 64 (2013): 245–53, doi:10.1080/0361526X.2013.760417.

57. Geoffrey P. Timms, "Gathering, Evaluating, and Communicating Statistical Usage Information for Electronic Resources," in *Managing Electronic Resources: A LITA Guide,* ed. Ryan O. Weir (Chicago: American Library Association, 2012), 87–119.

58. Sarah Anne Murphy, "Data Visualization and Rapid Analytics: Applying Tableau Desktop to Support Library Decision-Making," *Journal of Web Librarianship* 7, no. 4 (2013): 465–76, doi:10.1080/19322909.2013.825148.

ABOUT THE CONTRIBUTORS

JENNIFER W. BAZELEY has BM and MM degrees in viola performance from the Eastman School of Music in Rochester, New York, and an MLIS degree from Dominican University in Illinois. She has worked in technical services at the DePaul University Library, the Field Museum Library, and the Cincinnati Art Museum Library. She has worked for the Miami University Libraries (Oxford, Ohio) since 2009 and is currently an associate librarian and coordinator of collection access and acquisitions. Her research interests include the role of libraries in scholarly communication, improving technical services workflows, and analyzing e-resource usage data.

CHRIS BULOCK is the collection coordinator for electronic resource management at California State University Northridge. His research has touched on perpetual access, evaluation of electronic journal packages, and providing access to open access resources within library systems. Chris edits the column "Open Dialog" in *Serials Review*. He is active in NASIG and is currently a member at large on the NASIG Executive Board.

SUNSHINE CARTER is the electronic resources librarian and manager of the E-Resource Management Unit at the University of Minnesota Libraries. Prior to her current role, she held positions as reference and electronic resources librarian at the University of Minnesota Duluth. Carter is interested in the ecosystem of e-resources, from licensing to cancellation. She often presents on the topics of troubleshooting, licensing, and managing e-resources.

LORI DUGGAN is the head of electronic resources acquisitions at Indiana University Libraries (IU). A lifelong Hoosier, Lori received her bachelor of music education degree and her MLS from Indiana University. Duggan is an active member of NASIG and ALCTS, and her research interests include emerging trends in electronic resources management and licensing.

CHRISTINE KORYTNYK DULANEY is the director of technical services at American University Library in Washington, DC, where she is responsible for the management of the Acquisitions, Resource Description, and Electronic Resources units at the Bender Library. She has held positions at the Library of Congress, Catholic University Law Library, and George Washington University Law Library.

JUDITH EMDE is assistant dean for content and access services at the University of Kansas (KU) Libraries. Her previous work at KU included positions in electronic resources and science subject librarianship. She has contributed to the development of e-resource management, content, and discovery in the KU Libraries during her tenure.

RICHARD GUAJARDO is the head of resource discovery systems at the University of Houston Libraries. His responsibilities include electronic resources, discovery tools, and library services platforms. He has presented at many regional and national conferences, including the American Library Association, Electronic Resources & Libraries, NASIG, and the Charleston Library Conference. He earned his master's degree in library and information science from the University of Texas at Austin. Previously he has held positions in library automation and technical services at the University of Houston Law Center.

LEANNA JANTZI is the head of Fraser Library at Simon Fraser University (SFU) located in Metro Vancouver, British Columbia. Prior to that, she was electronic resources, copyright, and liaison librarian at Capilano University, and liaison librarian at Okanagan College, both in British Columbia. Jantzi received her MLIS degree from the University of British Columbia in 2010.

REGINA KOURY is an assistant university librarian for discovery and resource services at the Idaho State University library and oversees cataloging, electronic resources, government documents, and systems. Koury had previously worked at the University of Southern California with experience in electronic resources, print serials, interlibrary loan, and public desk services. She earned her MLIS degree from the University of Pittsburgh and an MEd degree in instructional technology from Idaho State University.

MONICA MOORE has worked with electronic resources management since 2009 and has been an electronic resources librarian at the University of Notre Dame since 2012. She earned her MLIS degree from Syracuse University in 2008.

L. ANGIE OHLER is the director of collection services at the University of Maryland Libraries and has been at Maryland since 2007. She earned her MLS degree at Catholic University in Washington, DC, and holds a master's degree in anthropology from American University. She is currently an editor for the NASIG Conference Proceedings and is a regular contributor to the column "ERM Ideas and Innovations" in the *Journal of Electronic Resources Librarianship*. Ohler's scholarship includes peer-reviewed articles, book chapters, and national conference presentations focusing on electronic resource management, library services platforms and discovery systems, demand-driven collection development, leadership in technical services, and organizational change and change management.

OLIVER PESCH works as chief product strategist for EBSCO Information Services, where he helps set direction for EBSCO's resource management and access products. He is currently cochair of the NISO SUSHI Standing Committee; chair of the COUNTER board of directors; serves on both the COUNTER Executive Committee and Technical Advisory Groups; and chairs the COUNTER Release 5 Technical Working Group.

ANGELA RATHMEL is the head of the acquisitions and resource sharing department at the University of Kansas (KU) Libraries. Formerly she served as electronic resources librarian and interim head of Acquisitions at KU. Her interests include organizational responses to change, particularly with respect to organizational communication, information-seeking, and knowledge management. She is a regular blogger for ACRLog.org and is currently researching how the reference interview, traditionally used by public services, may be applied in technical services and electronic resources troubleshooting.

JENNIFER RICHARD has been an academic librarian at Acadia University in Wolfville, Nova Scotia, Canada, since 1997. Her roles at Acadia have included liaison librarian for the Faculty of Pure and Applied Science, head of research services, and coordinator of electronic resources. She is a former president of the Atlantic Provinces Library Association and the founding editor of *Partnership: The Canadian Journal of Library and Information Practice and Research* (2006–2010). She received her MLIS degree from Dalhousie University (Halifax, Nova Scotia) in 1994.

KARI SCHMIDT is the technical services manager at Montgomery College Libraries in Rockville, Maryland, where she is responsible for management of the acquisitions, cataloging, and electronic resource and discovery services programs within a multi-campus, community college setting. Schmidt previously held positions in electronic resource management at American University Library, Georgetown University Medical Center, and the University of Maryland libraries.

SARAH W. SUTTON is an assistant professor in the School of Library and Information Management at Emporia State University in Kansas. Based on years of experience as an academic electronic resources librarian, her 2011 doctoral dissertation, "Identifying Core Competencies for Electronic Resources Librarians in the Twenty-First Century Library," is the basis for NASIG's "Core Competencies for Electronic Resources Librarians."

GEOFFREY TIMMS is librarian for marine resources at the College of Charleston, where he manages the Marine Resources Library located at the South Carolina Marine Resources Center on James Island. An academic librarian since 2007, his experience includes managing electronic resources and systems; instruction in the use of online research information in the sciences with undergraduate, graduate, and professional researchers; and web application development. His current research interests include analysis of the use of library collections and the information literacy of graduate students.

STACIE A. TRAILL is a metadata analyst at the University of Minnesota Libraries. Prior to her current role, she held positions as cartographic and electronic resources cataloger and special formats cataloging coordinator at the University of Minnesota. Traill has worked extensively with electronic resources metadata and library discovery and management systems over the past decade. She has frequently presented and published on related topics, including e-book metadata quality, bulk metadata management, and troubleshooting.

SANDRA WONG has been electronic resources librarian at Simon Fraser University (SFU) located in Metro Vancouver, British Columbia, since 2010. Prior to that, she was science liaison librarian at SFU for eight years. She has also been science liaison librarian at the University of Calgary and the University of Manitoba. Wong received her MLIS degree from the University of British Columbia in 1998.

INDEX

Novanet, 78. *See also* Primo at Acadia
University within the Novanet
Consortium (case study)

O

oaFindr (1science), 227–228
Ohler, L. Angie, x, 91
OLE (Kuali), 110–111
Ongoing Automated Review System (OARS),
289–290
ongoing development for staff troubleshooting
skills, 246–249
Online Computer Library Center (OCLC),
54–55, 94, 104, 110
open access (OA) publishing. *See also*
management of freely available resources
books, 224
cost containment strategies and, 128–129
evaluation of OA journals, sources for,
129
journals and articles, 222–223
licensing electronic resources and, 7–8
media, difficulty in managing other forms
of, 225
overview, 7
Open Discovery Initiative (ODI) Standing
Committee, 65
open linked-data systems, 113
open systems approach to evolution of library
automation, 98, 101
Orbis Cascade Alliance, 107–108, 123
organizational communication, 137–138. *See
also* communication between public and
technical services departments
organizational models for reorganization
of Acquisitions Department and
Resource Sharing Department into one
department at KU Libraries
format model, 210–211
functional model, 211–212
overview, 208
review and evaluation of, 212
service points model, 209–210
supply chain model, 208–209
organizing and reporting analytics and
assessment of electronic resources
institutional capacity for, 290
reports and recommendations, designing,
291–292

storing and accessing data, 291
visualization of data, 292–293
"Other" worksheet (EBSCO), 62
overlap analysis tools, 282–283

P

PaaS (Platform as a Service), 97
Pace, Andrew, 54
Pastva, Joelen, 185, 186
patron-driven acquisition (PDA), 20,
21, 36, 45–47, 94, 127–128,
203–204
pattern of search prior to web-scale
discovery, 72
pay-per-view (PPV) services, 128
Pedersen, Wayne, 124
Pence Law Library's reorganization of ERM
functions with distributed model,
181–182
per capita statistics used for assessment of
electronic resources, 289
per content unit statistics used for assessment
of electronic resources, 289
per use statistics used for assessment of
electronic resources, 289
"Periodical Prices Survey" (Bosch and
Henderson), 120
personal qualities needed for an e-resources
librarian (core competency for electronic
resources librarianship), 173
Pesch, Oliver, xi, 15, 93, 253
platform and database quality as quantitative
measure of quality or esteem of electronic
resources, 283–284
Plutchak, T. Scott, 119
Pluye, Pierre, 26
Portico, 8
practical and factual information in workshop
on troubleshooting, 240–241
pre- and post-surveys for workshop on
troubleshooting attendees, 243–245
pre-readings for workshop on troubleshooting,
239–240
preservation of electronic resources, 8–9,
27–29
price as quantitative measure of quality or
esteem of electronic resources, 275
price increases in electronic resources,
268–269